Applied UK Macroeconomics

To Robert and Alison

Applied UK Macroeconomics

Roger Backhouse

Basil Blackwell

Copyright © Roger Backhouse 1991

First published 1991

Basil Blackwell Ltd
108 Cowley Road, Oxford, OX4 1JF, UK

Basil Blackwell, Inc.
3 Cambridge Center
Cambridge, Massachusetts 02142, USA

British Library Cataloguing in Publication Data

A CIP catalogue record for this book is available from the British Library.

Library of Congress Cataloging in Publication Data

Backhouse, Roger.
 Applied UK Macroeconomics/Roger Backhouse.
  p.   cm.
 Includes bibliographical references and index.
 ISBN 0-631-17841-4 — ISBN 0-631-17842-2 (pbk.)
 1. Great Britain—Economic conditions—1945- 2. Macroeconomics.
 I. Title.
 HC256.6.B283   1991
 339—dc20   90-23126
                                                                  CIP

Typeset in 10 on 12pt Palatino
by Roger Backhouse
Printed in Great Britain by T J. Press Ltd, Padstow, Cornwall

Contents

Part I Introduction   **1**

1 British economic performance   3
   1.1   The statistical record   3
   1.2   International comparisons   8
   1.3   Politics and economic policy   13
   1.4   Conclusions   19
   Further reading   20

Part II The Demand Side   **21**

2 Consumption and savings   23
   2.1   Introduction   23
   2.2   The 'Keynesian' consumption function   25
   2.3   Permanent income/life-cycle theories   28
   2.4   Modifications to the life-cycle theory   32
   2.5   Explaining the saving ratio   36
   2.6   Conclusions   39
   Further reading   40

3 Investment   41
   3.1   Introduction   41
   3.2   Manufacturing investment   46
   Box 3.1 The accelerator   47
   Box 3.2 Tobin's q 54
   3.3   Investment in housing   56
   3.4   Conclusions   60
   Further reading   60

4 Government spending and fiscal policy   61
   4.1   Government spending   61
   4.2   The government deficit   64
   Box 4.1 The inflation tax   69
   4.3   The government deficit and the national debt   72
   4.4   Conclusions: the stance of fiscal policy   74
   Box 4.2 The dynamics of debt and deficits   76
   Further reading   78

5 International trade   79
   5.1   Introduction   79
   5.2   Export and import functions   89
   5.3   Conclusions   91
   Further reading   93

Part III The Supply Side   **95**

6 Productivity   97
   6.1   Measuring productivity growth   97
   Box 6.1 Total factor productivity   100

6.2	Measuring full-capacity output	107
6.3	The productivity slowdown of the 1970s	111
6.4	UK productivity performance since 1979	115
Further reading		119

7 The labour market, I: real wages, productivity and unemployment 121

7.1	Introduction	121
7.2	Real wages and productivity	122
Box 7.1	Keynesian and classical unemployment	127
7.3	Real wages and unemployment since the 1960s	131
7.4	Conclusions	137
Further reading		137

8 The labour market, II: unemployment, inflation and the NAIRU   139

8.1	Introduction	139
8.2	Unemployment and vacancies	140
8.3	Turnover in the labour market	147
Box 8.1	Unemployment dynamics	150
8.4	Supply-side factors	154
Box 8.2	Benefits and unemployment	156
8.5	Wage determination	163
Box 8.3	The expectations-augmented Phillips curve	166
8.6	The NAIRU	173
Box 8.4	A model of the NAIRU	175
Further reading		180

9 North Sea oil   183

9.1	The UK as an oil producer	183
9.2	Oil and the structure of the UK economy	189
9.3	Conclusions	194
Box 9.1	'Dutch disease' models	195
Further reading		200

Part IV Money and Finance   **201**

10 Money   203

10.1	The money supply	203
10.2	The determination of the money supply	211
Box 10.1	The money multiplier	212
Box 10.2	Portfolio balance theory	218
10.3	Stocks, flows and changes in the money supply	223
10.4	Money and inflation	229
Further reading		230

11 Interest rates and exchange rates   231

11.1	Introduction	231
11.2	Interest rates	231
Box 11.1	Forward markets and expected changes in the exchange rate	238
11.3	Exchange rates	241
11.4	The history of the exchange rate	247
Box 11.2	Exchange rate overshooting	250
11.5	The European monetary system	253

11.6   Conclusions   258
Further reading   258

Part V The Economy as a Whole   **259**

12 Models of the whole economy   261

12.1   Introduction   261
12.2   Comparisons between the models   265
12.3   The usefulness of large-scale macroeconomic models   270
Further reading   273

13 Recent macroeconomic performance and policy   275

13.1   The 1979-1989 business cycle   275
13.2   Macroeconomic policy during the 1980s   281
13.3   The legacy of the 1980s   289
13.4   The 1990s   291
13.5   Conclusions   302
Further reading   303

Appendix: regression equations   304

Index   306

List of Figures and Tables

FIGURES

1.1   Real GDP, 1950-89   4
1.2   GDP per capita, 1950-89   4
1.3   The growth rate of GDP, 1950-89   5
1.4   The labour market, 1950-89   6
1.5   Capacity utilization, 1950-89   7
1.6   Inflation: average earnings and retail prices, 1950-89   8
1.7   Growth rates of GDP, 1960-88   9
1.8   Inflation rates, 1960-89   10
1.9   International living standards, 1960-85   11
1.10   The business cycle, 1950-73   13
1.11   The business cycle, 1973-88   17
2.1   Components of GDP at market prices, 1989   24
2.2   The savings ratio, 1948-89   24
2.3   Income and consumption, 1948-89   25
2.4   Predictions from a simple Keynesian consumption function   27
2.5   Long and short run consumption functions   30
2.6   Predicted errors using the 'random walk' model of consumption   31
2.7   Predicting the 1980s saving ratio   34
2.8   House price inflation and real house prices   34
2.9   The variability of income growth, 1956-89   35
2.10   Predictions of the saving ratio   36
2.11   Inflation, uncertainty and the saving ratio, 1956-89   37
2.12   Real house prices and the saving ratio, 1956-89   38
2.13   Contributions to the saving ratio, 1956-89   38
3.1   Gross fixed investment and GDP   42
3.2   Fixed investment and the change in the capital stock   44
3.3   Stockbuilding as a percentage of GDP   45
3.4   Stock ratios   46

3.5	Capital-output ratios	49
3.6	Actual and predicted investment in manufacturing	50
3.7	Predictions of manufacturing investment using pre-1979 data	51
3.8	The rate of profit on capital and the cost of capital	52
3.9	Gross investment and q	52
3.10	Saving and investment by industrial and commercial companies	56
3.11	Investment in housing	57
3.12	Investment in housing and the price of housing	58
3.13	House price inflation and the GDP deflator	58
4.1	Government spending, 1989	62
4.2	Government spending as a percentage of GDP	62
4.3	The price of government consumption	63
4.4	PSFD and PSBR, 1963-88	66
4.5	Inflation and cyclical adjustments	70
4.6	PSFD adjusted for inflation and the cycle	71
4.7	Alternative inflation adjustments	73
4.8	Real and nominal interest payments, 1963-88	74
4.9	National debt as a proportion of GDP	75
4.B2.1	Debt and GDP	77
5.1	The balance of payments, 1950-89	81
5.2	The balance of payments as a percentage of GNP, 1950-89	81
5.3	Exports and imports at constant (1985) prices, 1948-88	83
5.4	The terms of trade, 1948-88	83
5.5	The terms of trade and real income, 1967-88	85
5.6	GNP and real national disposable income, 1967-89	85
5.7	Measures of international competitiveness, 1963-89	88
6.1	Output per head, 1961-89	98
6.2	Productivity growth rates, 1961-89	102
6.3	Output per head in manufacturing, 1961-89	107
6.4	Estimates of full-capacity GDP, 1961-89	108
6.5	Estimates of the output gap, 1961-89	109
6.6	Output, employment and capital in manufacturing, 1961-89	116
6.7	Gross value added per person hour, 1950-88	117
7.1	The ratio of export prices to the GDP deflator, 1963-88	123
7.2	The real wage rate (whole economy), 1963-88	123
7.3	The real wage rate (manufacturing), 1963-88	124
7.4	Real wages and productivity, 1963-88	126
7.B1.1	The demand for labour	128
7.B1.2	Keynesian and classical unemployment	129
7.5	The share of wages in national income, 1960-88	133
7.6	Output and productivity, 1960-88	134
7.7	Actual and full-capacity output per worker, 1963-88	135
7.8	The real wage gap, 1963-88	136
7.9	Real wages and full-capacity output per worker, 1963-88	136
8.1	Unemployment and vacancies	141
8.2	The U-V curve	142
8.3	Regional shares of unemployment and vacancies, 1988	143
8.4	Percentage shares of manufacturing in unemployment and vacancies	144
8.5	Measures of mismatch	145

8.6	Percentage of firms expecting labour shortages to limit output	146
8.7	A measure of mismatch, 1956-88	147
8.8	Inflows, outflows and unemployment	148
8.9	The duration of unemployment	149
8.B1.1	Unemployment dynamics	151
8.10	Inflow, outflow and unemployment rates, I	152
8.11	Inflow, outflow and unemployment rates, II	152
8.12	The replacement ratio	155
8.13	Union power	159
8.14	Real house prices	161
8.15	Real company profits per employee	162
8.16	The Phillips curve	165
8.B3.1	The Phillips curve	167
8.B4.1	The determination of the NAIRU	177
9.1	The nominal price of oil, 1961-89	184
9.2	The real price of oil, 1961-89	185
9.3	Investment in oil and gas extraction, 1973-88	185
9.4	UK oil production, 1970-89	186
9.5	The trade deficit in oil, 1973-88	186
9.6	Oil and the balance of payments, 1973-88	188
9.7	The sectoral composition of output, 1973-87	190
9.8	Output in manufacturing and oil extraction, 1960-89	190
9.B1.1	The labour market	196
9.B1.2	The goods markets	197
9.B1.3	The overall effect of an oil discovery	198
10.1	UK monetary aggregates	206
10.2	Growth rates of M1, M4 and M5, 1964-89	208
10.3	Growth rates of M2, M3 and M4, 1964-89	208
10.4	The velocity of circulation, 1965-89	210
10.5	Money multipliers for M1, M4 and M5, 1970-89	214
10.6	Growth rates of money multipliers, 1970-89	214
10.7	The growth rate of M4, 1970-89	215
10.8	The supply of high-powered money	217
10.B2.1	The determination of the money supply	219
10.B2.2	An increase in the supply of high-powered money	220
10.B2.3	A rise in the demand for money	221
10.9	Counterparts to changes in M4, 1965-89	227
10.10	Domestic counterparts to growth of M4, 1965-89	228
10.11	PSBR and the growth of M4, 1965-89	228
10.12	Inflation and the growth rate of M4, 1965-89	230
11.1	Nominal interest rates, 1960-89	232
11.2	The yield curve	233
11.3	Interest rates and inflation, 1960-89	235
11.4	Real interest rates I, 1960-89	235
11.5	Real interest rates II, 1981-90	236
11.6	Interest rates and the forward premium, 1965-89	240
11.7	Covered interest rate parity, 1965-89	240
11.8	Exchange rates, 1960-89	242
11.9	Measures of the real exchange rate, 1962-89	243
11.B2.1	Exchange rate overshooting	251

11.10	Currency weights within the ECU since September 1989	254
11.11	Currencies in relation to the ECU, 1980-9	257
12.1	The effects of a £2 billion rise in government spending	267
12.2	The effects of a 1 per cent cut in short term interest rates	269
12.3	The effects of a 10 m. t. reduction in North Sea oil production	271
13.1	Real GDP, 1979-89	276
13.2	Unemployment, 1979-89	279
13.3	Inflation, 1979-89	280
13.4	The current account balance as a percentage of GDP, 1979-89	280
13.5	Investment in stocks, 1979-89	282
13.6	The exchange rate, 1979-89	282
13.7	Interest rates	286
13.8	The government deficit as percentage of GDP, 1979-89	287
13.9	The growth of demand, 1979-89	289
13.10	Consumption and income, 1979-89	291
13.11	Forecasts made in February/March 1990	292
13.12	The effects of a $6 oil price rise (HMT model), I	296
13.13	The effects of a $6 oil price rise (three models)	297
13.14	The effects of a $20 oil price rise (LBS model)	298
13.15	The effects of a $6 oil price rise (HMT model), II	299

TABLES

1.1	UK Governments since 1945	12
4.1	The public sector deficit, 1989	64
4.2	PSFD and PSBR in 1989	65
5.1	The balance of payments, 1988	80
6.1	Productivity growth — period averages	102
6.2	Productivity growth in manufacturing, 1960-89	106
6.3	International productivity growth rates	111
6.4	Energy prices and energy-output ratios	113
7.1	Product wage and productivity growth rates, 1963-88	130
7.2	Wages and productivity in Europe and the US	130
8.1	Benefits and unemployment	157
8.2	Unemployment incidence by replacement ratio	158
8.3	Estimates of the NAIRU, I	169
8.4	Estimates of the NAIRU, II	178
8.5	Causes of the rise in the NAIRU	179
8.6	Causes of the rise in unemployment	179
9.1	Capital, labour and output by sector, 1988	189
9.2	The UK economy in 1976	192
9.3	The effects of North Sea oil: stage I	193
9.4	The effects of North Sea oil: stage II	194
10.1	A simplified Banking Sector Balance Sheet	225
11.1	PPPs and comparative dollar price levels in 1985	245
11.2	The composition of the ECU	254
11.3	EMS divergence indicators	255
12.1	Government expenditure multipliers	265
13.1	Performance indicators	277
13.2	International productivity growth rates, 1979-88	278
13.3	The Medium Term Financial Strategy, March 1980	284
13.4	Successive targets for PSBR	285

Preface and Acknowledgements

This book is intended for students who have already taken an introductory course in macroeconomics in that it takes for granted an understanding of national income accounting and some elementary macroeconomic theories.

Readers familiar with *Macroeconomics and the British Economy*, published eight years ago, may ask what relationship the two books bear to one another. The answer is that though they are addressed to the same audience the approach adopted here is completely different. *Macroeconomics and the British Economy*, though containing an unusually high empirical content, was in many ways a conventional textbook, in which macroeconomic theory was central. In this book, on the other hand, it is the applied material that comes first, with theory being kept in a subordinate role. Most of the macroeconomic theory that is usually found in intermediate macroeconomics textbooks is left out, and where theory has to be discussed, either because (as in the case of the accelerator) the discussion of applied issues could not be understood without it, or because (as with Tobin's q) it is covered inadequately or not at all in most conventional textbooks, it is confined to clearly defined boxes.

This book can be used in two ways. One is as a supplement to a more orthodox intermediate macroeconomics or macroeconomic theory textbook. The other is on its own as the basis for a purely applied macro course. Suggestions for further reading are included at the end of each chapter to make it easier to use in this way.

The entire contents of this book was prepared on IBM-compatible PCs. The text was written using Protext. The data were processed using Micro TSP and then turned into graphs using GEM Graph. GEM Draw was used to prepare the remaining diagrams and to get the figures produced by GEM Graph into the correct format. The diagrams and text were then put together using DESK*press*, which produced postscript files containing descriptions of the final pages.

Preparing the book in this way has made it possible to add material at a comparatively late stage in the production process. However, the appearance of new statistics and new material is a never-ending process, and so a line has to be drawn somewhere. The rule I have adopted is that all tables and graphs have been revised to take account of information available in July 1990. In addition, I have modified parts of the text to take account of developments in the period up to the end of October 1990. Thus I have discussed the recent rise in oil prices and British entry into the exchange rate mechanism of the EMS, and I have taken account of some new evidence on productivity growth, but I have not systematically revised all tables and figures to include all new statistics published in the last three months. Such a task would have taken up more time than was available, and in most cases would not have made much difference to the arguments.

Except where something different is indicated, all constant-price variables are measured using 1985 prices. Where no units are specified, variables are measured as index numbers with 1985 = 100.

I should like to thank those colleagues who have read and commented on parts of the book, and who have provided me with ideas, data, and encouragement, particularly Gianna Boero, Simon Burgess, Peter Burridge, Paul Kong, Ben Knight and Robin Marris. Garry MacDonald and David Turner supplied their Ready Reckoner program, on which virtually all of chapter 12 is based. Needless to say, none of them can be held responsible for the use I have made of their ideas. Because this is a textbook, references to sources have been kept at a minimum. The main sources on which I based this book are listed in the suggestions for further reading.

DESK*press* is a trademark of GST Holdings Ltd.
GEM Draw and GEM Graph are trademarks of Digital Research Inc.
IBM and IBM PC are registered trademarks of International Business
  Machines Corp.
Micro TSP is a trademark of Quantitative Micro Software.
Protext is a trademark of Arnor Ltd.

R. E. B.
November 1990

I

Introduction

British economic performance

1.1 THE STATISTICAL RECORD

Output and employment

The measure of output that we shall use is Gross Domestic Product (GDP) in 1985 prices. Figures 1.1 to 1.3 show what has happened to GDP and GDP per head since 1950. We can learn a number of things from these figures: the existence of a fairly regular cycle prior to 1973; the exceptional nature of the 1970s; and the sustained recovery of the 1980s.

❑ In the period leading up to 1973 we can see a marked cyclical pattern with GDP growing at over 4 per cent per annum in 1953-5, 1960, 1964, 1968 and 1973 with slower growth in the intervening years. This stands out most clearly in figure 1.3, but can also be seen from figure 1.1. After 1973 a cyclical pattern is much harder to distinguish: apart from the two major recessions discussed below, the growth rate has been between about 2 per cent and 4 per cent all the time.

❑ The 1970s and early 1980s were clearly exceptional: in the 1973 boom the growth rate was much faster than in any of the previous booms; and the recessions of 1974-5 and 1980-1 were much deeper than any other post-war recessions. These were the only years in the whole period when GDP and GDP per head fell substantially.

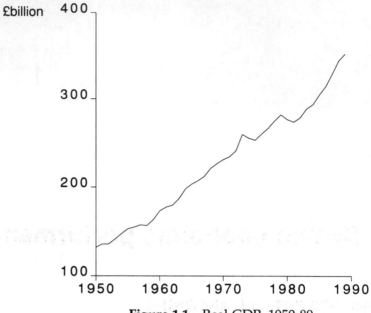

Figure 1.1   Real GDP, 1950-89

Source: Economic Trends.

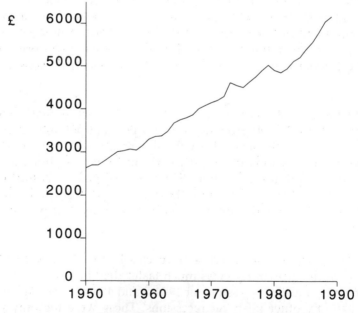

Figure 1.2   GDP per capita, 1950-89

Source: Economic Trends.

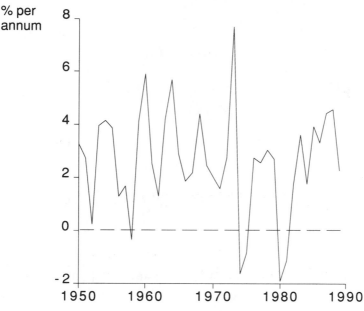

Figure 1.3 the growth rate of GDP, 1950-89

Source: Economic Trends.

Previous post-war recessions had seen low growth rates but, with the exception of 1958 when it fell *very* slightly, GDP had not actually fallen.

❑ After 1981 the boom was sustained longer than in any previous business cycle, the downturn not coming until 1989.

Though the average growth rate (not shown explicitly) is clearly different, similar remarks could be made concerning GDP per capita. The reason is that population growth is comparatively steady.

Statistics on employment and unemployment, shown in figure 1.4, paint a similar though far from identical, picture (for a discussion of this, and other, definitions of unemployment, see chapter 8). The unemployment rate fluctuated, though remaining fairly low, until the early 1970s; during the mid-1970s and early 1980s it rose dramatically; and it began to fall in the late 1980s.

Figure 1.4   The labour market, 1950-89

Source: Economic Trends.

❏ Up to about 1967 the unemployment rate fluctuated around 1.5-2 per cent of the labour force. Unemployment then grew steadily from 2.3 per cent in 1967 to 3.7 per cent in 1972. In the boom year of 1973 it fell sharply to 2.6 per cent, though this was still higher than at any time during the 1960s.

❏ The recessions of 1974-5 and 1980-1 both produced large rises in unemployment, the unemployment rate rising to 5.8 per cent in 1977 and to 10.6 per cent in 1981.

❏ From 1981 to 1986 unemployment remained relatively constant at over 10 per cent, until it started to fall in 1987. By 1989 it had fallen to just over 6 per cent.

One of the most important questions in UK macroeconomics is whether or not the economy is operating below full capacity. If unemployment is high because aggregate demand is insufficient for the economy to operate at full capacity one set of policies is appropriate, whereas if the problem is low productive capacity a different set of policies is more

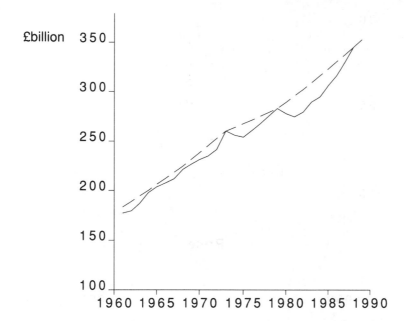

Figure 1.5 Capacity utilization, 1950-89

Source: Figure 1.1 and author's calculations discussed in chapter 6.

likely to be required. One estimate of full capacity output is shown in figure 1.5. If we believe this estimate (some of the problems involved in estimating full capacity output are discussed in chapter 6) it confirms the conclusions we drew from the GDP figures. Prior to 1973 the UK experienced a series of cycles, reaching full-capacity in most of the booms; after 1973 the cycles were much deeper and longer-lasting.

Inflation

The second major question relates to inflation. Figure 1.6 shows the behaviour of wages and prices (the retail price index) since 1949. Once again the period can be divided into two, though the dividing line would appear to be the late 1960s rather than 1973. Apart from 1951-2 when the Korean War produced a sharp rise in the inflation rate, inflation remained below 5 per cent for the 1950s and most of the 1960s. From the late 1960s inflation increased steadily, reaching over 20 per cent per annum in 1975. It then fell sharply to under 10 per cent in 1977, rising to a new peak in 1980. Since then it has fallen to around 5 per cent per annum and risen to over 10 per cent per annum.

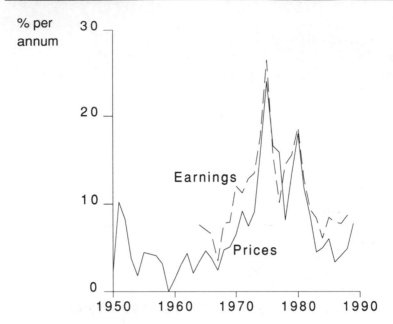

Figure 1.6   Inflation: average earnings and retail prices, 1950-89

Source: Economic Trends.

Also shown is the rate of growth of average earnings. The series only goes back to 1963 because of difficulties in obtaining comparable data; as it is, the earnings data shown in figure 1.6 are obtained by merging together one series for 1963-76 and another for 1976-89. They show that, with the exception of 1977, earnings rose faster than prices throughout the period. This means that real wages rose continuously, the only exceptions being 1976-7, when they fell, and 1980-1, when they barely changed.

1.2 INTERNATIONAL COMPARISONS

Fluctuations

Figures 1.7 and 1.8 compare British inflation and growth rates with those of the United States, France, Germany and Italy. In these graphs the solid line denotes the country indicated, with the dotted line showing comparable figures for the UK. Figure 1.8 shows that during the 1970s British inflation rates fluctuated much more than those in any country except Italy. The pattern was the same but the UK peaks of around 25 per cent and 20 per cent were much higher. The fall in

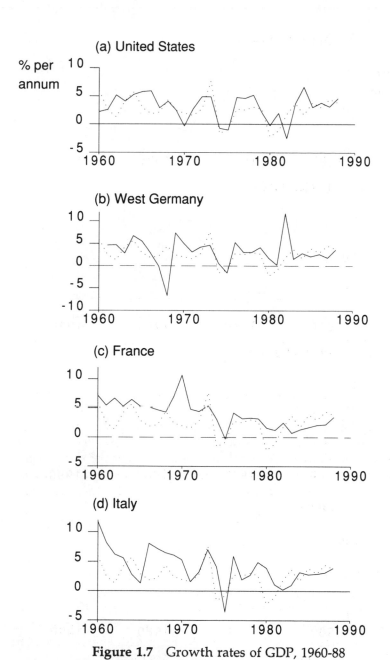

Figure 1.7 Growth rates of GDP, 1960-88

Source: International Financial Statistics Yearbook, updated from Datastream.

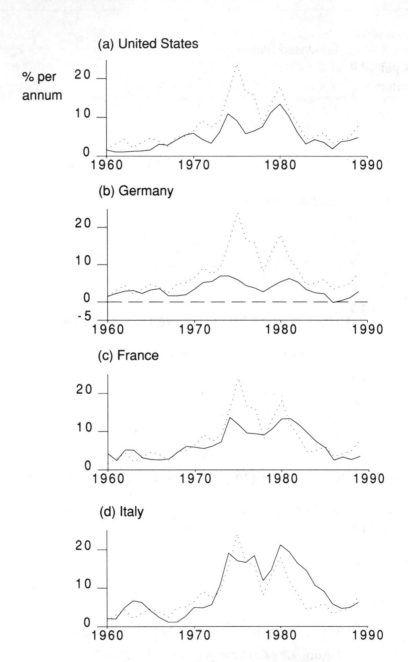

Figure 1.8 Inflation rates, 1960-89

Source: International Financial Statistics Yearbook, updated from *Datastream.*

inflation which has taken place since 1980 has been common to all the countries shown here. From figure 1.7 we can see that the UK experienced a cycle similar to that of most of the other countries shown, with major recessions in 1974-5 and 1980-81. The 1980-1 recession was, however, much more severe in Britain than in any of the other countries shown here.

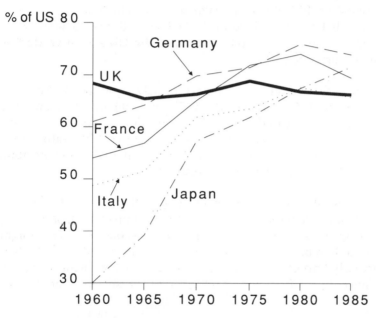

Figure 1.9   International living standards, 1960-85

Source: OECD National Accounts, supplement on purchasing power parities.

Growth

Since the end of the nineteenth century Britain has been growing more slowly than its main European rivals, notably France, Germany and Italy. In the nineteenth century British living standards were on average much higher than those in continental Europe, but more recently the position has been reversed. It is, however, difficult to compare national income and living standards across countries when different countries use different currencies. One way is to convert incomes into a common currency using market exchange rates. Such comparisons are misleading because exchange rates do not reflect relative prices in different countries: exchange rates fluctuate, sometimes by large amounts, without there being any corresponding change in living standards (prices do not fluctuate by the same amount). To get round this problem it is better to use *purchasing power parities*. The purchasing power parity (PPP) between two currencies is the exchange rate at which prices of goods are the same in both countries (see chapter 11 for a more detailed discussion).

Figure 1.9 provides a comparison of GDP per head in several countries based on PPP data. The two main conclusions to be drawn from this are that between 1966 and 1980 the UK was overtaken by West Germany, France and Japan, and that the UK's relative decline slowed down during the 1970s.

❏ The UK was overtaken, in terms of GDP per head, by West Germany in 1966, France in 1972 and Japan in 1980. The equivalent dates based on earlier, non-PPP comparisons were 1959, 1965 and 1972 respectively. The use of of PPPs rather than exchange rates to make the comparisons makes Britain's position look better compared with other countries.

❏ Britain's relative decline slowed down during the 1970s. The greatest improvement was relative to the European Community, because of the slowdown of the European economies. This might be for a number of reasons: the discovery of oil, which was particularly important during the 1974-9 upswing; rising productivity since 1979 (discussed in chapter 6); or simply that the UK

Table 1.1 UK Governments since 1945

	Party	Prime Minister(s)
1945-51	Labour	Atlee
1951-64	Conservative	Churchill/Eden/Macmillan/Home
1964-70	Labour	Wilson
1970-74	Conservative	Heath
1974-79	Labour	Wilson/Callaghan
1979-	Conservative	Thatcher/Major

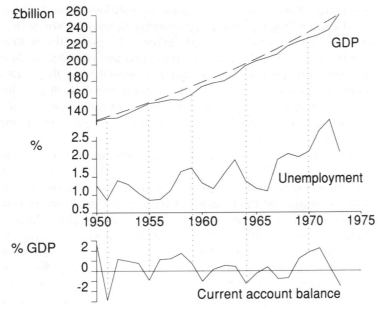

Figure 1.10   The business cycle, 1950-73

Source: Economic Trends.

performs relatively well in recessions, and poorly in times of rapid growth. A world recovery or a British recession might make the picture look much worse.

1.3 POLITICS AND ECONOMIC POLICY

Introduction

The natural way to divide up the period is according to the political party in power, which gives us the periods shown in table 1.1. Our starting point will be the period from 1951 to 1964. The period of the previous Labour government was dominated by problems of reconstruction after the war with the result that, though there are certainly interesting things to say about the macroeconomic policies pursued then, there are so many special problems that we will neglect it.

1951-1964: the period of 'stop-go'

This period was dominated by Keynesian ideas, in particular the use of fiscal policy to achieve a high level of demand, low unemployment and a high growth rate. Policy would be used to stabilize the economy, expanding and contracting the economy in order to smooth out booms and slumps. Very little importance was attached to monetary policy, though controls on credit (in particular hire-purchase regulations and quantitative restrictions on the amount banks were allowed to lend to different types of customer) were used to help regulate consumer demand. Little interest was shown in the 'money supply' and figures for it were not even constructed. The exchange rate was fixed throughout the period under the Bretton Woods system, at a rate of $2.80 to £1. Governments were committed to maintaining this exchange rate.

The main problem facing policy-makers was the balance of payments: if the economy grew too fast the balance of payments would deteriorate and put pressure on the exchange rate. The Bank of England's gold and foreign currency reserves would fall. In order to put such a situation right there would have to be deflation, reducing imports and freeing resources for exports. What actually happened, therefore, was not continuous high employment and rapid growth, but a period of 'stop-go', the timing of which was, arguably, linked to general elections. In the run up to an election the economy would be expanded, using mainly fiscal policy plus a relaxation of credit controls. After the election a balance of payments crisis would emerge, leading to the imposition of a contractionary fiscal policy and a tightening of credit controls. When the balance of payments had turned round the economy would be expanded again, prior to the next general election.

Some of the evidence for this is shown in figure 1.10. The exception to the pattern is 1959, for the peak of the boom did not come till after the election. But then this was the election that everyone expected Labour (under Gaitskell) to win. Three comments are worth making.

❑ Causation could run both ways: to or from politics. It could be that governments called elections when the economy was doing well, or that they ran the economy with a view to the election.

❑ It has been disputed whether policy succeeded in stabilizing the economy. It has been argued that the timing of policy was frequently wrong and that this made fluctuations worse.

❑ Inflation was seen as part of the balance of payments problem, various types of price and wage policies being introduced in order to maintain competitiveness. Remember that, although economists argued that excess demand could cause inflation, policy was not thought of in terms of a trade-off between inflation and unemployment. With the exception of the Korean war years, the inflation rate was always low by modern standards.

1964-1970: the balance of payments and the failure of planning

In many ways this period was similar to the previous one, but with balance of payments problems being much more dominant.

❏ There was an attempt to introduce a 'National Plan', the idea underlying this being to plan for a higher rate of growth in the hope that firms would do the same and a higher growth rate would result. This was not a new idea, for the Conservatives had attempted to introduce some elements of planning a few years earlier, but it was on a much larger scale. Planning came to nothing because the government found itself having to introduce restrictive policies, inconsistent with the plan's targets. There were other problems, such as an over-optimistic target for productivity growth.

❏ The government inherited a balance of payments deficit from its predecessor, but this time it seemed to be larger and more persistent than after previous booms. According to the Pink Book for 1967, the current account deficit was £102m. in 1964, £110m. in 1965 and £59m. in 1966. Restrictive measures were taken to improve the current account and support sterling. Later figures, incidentally, showed that the deficit was much smaller: the problem was on the capital account.

❏ There was a greater emphasis on controlling prices in order to restore competitiveness. The National Board for Prices and Incomes was used to control prices and wages. There was a complete wage freeze in the second half of 1966. Unemployment rose and inflation fell.

❏ Despite these measures devaluation came in November 1967, sterling falling from $2.80 to $2.40. This was followed by a further period of deflationary policy to provide resources for exports, and to ensure that inflation did not erode the competitive advantage given by devaluation. The policy worked: growth remained low and unemployment remained high, but exports grew rapidly and the current account went into surplus at the beginning of 1969.

1970-1974: U-turn and dash for growth

The period was one of rising inflation (see figure 1.6). The causes of this are too complicated to go into here, but note that this was a worldwide phenomenon which started in the late 1960s (though inflation did rise more in Britain than in most similar economies). Policy falls into two phases.

❏ A period of *laissez-faire*. The government came into office committed to a policy of *laissez-faire* and stimulating enterprise. Fiscal policy was neutral, and there was an attempt to reduce government intervention in industry. There was a slight change in policy in 1971 when expansionary fiscal policy was introduced to deal with rising unemployment, and attempts were made to keep prices down (an agreement with the CBI).

❏ Early in 1972 unemployment rose to nearly a million (4 per cent), prompting a change in policy. The aim became to expand output at 5 per cent a year in order to reduce unemployment to 500,000 by the end of 1973. Inflation was to be kept down first by TUC/CBI negotiations and later by statutory incomes policy. The output and unemployment targets were met (nearly enough).

One significant aspect of this policy was the exchange rate. Previous booms had come to an end because of balance of payments problems, so this time the government decided that if balance of payments problems occurred the exchange rate would be allowed to fall: they announced this policy as part of their attempt to persuade people that growth would be sustained.

The policy's main problems concerned inflation.

❏ Inflation was never controlled, partly because of the world commodity price boom from 1972-3 and partly because by 1973 the economy was operating at full capacity, growing at an unsustainably high rate. Many western economies were expanding rapidly and US spending in Vietnam was high.

❏ War between Israel and Egypt in 1973 reduced oil supplies to the west.

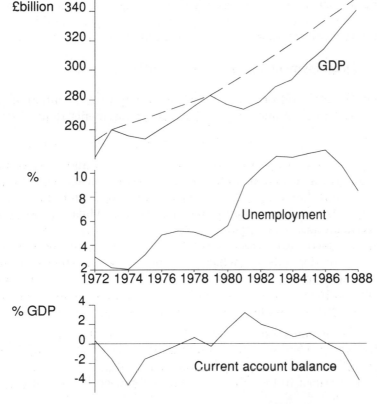

Figure 1.11   The business cycle, 1973-88

Source: Economic Trends.

❏ OPEC raised the price of oil by 66 per cent in October 1973 and a further 100 per cent in January 1974.

❏ There was a series of strikes with unions refusing to accept the statutory incomes policy. Particularly important was the miners' strike at the end of 1973. This together with the oil shortage led to the imposition of a 3-day working week to save energy. This was when speed limits were introduced on motorways.

The boom came to a very abrupt end.

1974-1979: responding to the oil crisis

The government elected in 1974 faced a number of severe problems that needed to be resolved:

❏ the miners' strike;

❏ high and rising inflation;

❏ rising unemployment;

❏ the effects of the oil price rise. These included a rise in inflation, a fall in real income and a large balance of payments deficit (see figure 1.11).

The main problem was that the rise in unemployment and the rise in inflation called for different policies: the supply shock was both 'deflationary' and 'inflationary'. Contractionary fiscal and monetary policy would have made unemployment worse, whilst expansion would have made inflation worse.

Inflation increased during 1974-5, reaching 25-30 per cent per annum (the exact figure depends on what price index and what period is taken). Unemployment rose and output fell, this leading to an improvement in the balance of payments. The real adjustment to the oil shock came in 1976-7, especially following the sterling crisis of 1976.

❏ A severe incomes policy (year 2 of the 'social contract', the agreement between the government and the TUC) led to reduced wage inflation and a *fall* in real wages (see figure 1.6). This was needed to adjust to the fall in real income caused by the oil price rise.

❏ Restrictive fiscal and monetary policies were imposed, with targets for both the public sector borrowing requirement (PSBR) and the growth rate of the money supply.

These measures were largely successful: inflation fell; the balance of payments increased; and sterling appreciated in 1977.

From 1978 to 1979 wages and output rose, output reaching a new peak in 1979. The incomes policy had broken down, causing rising consumer spending, and controls on public spending were no longer so tight.

This episode is important, because it shows that 'monetarist' policies did not come in with Mrs Thatcher. The Labour government introduced monetary targets and managed greater reductions in government spending than the Conservatives were able to achieve. They were a response of the Labour government, in common with many other western governments of the period, to a new and unfamiliar set of economic problems.

1979-1990: the 'Thatcher experiment'

Whereas the Labour government turned to 'monetarist' ideas as a response to a specific policy problem, the Conservative government elected in 1979 committed itself to such ideas much more whole-heartedly, offering what it called a 'Medium term financial strategy.' This was a 5-year plan involving targets for the growth of the money supply and the PSBR. The idea was gradually to reduce monetary growth, and hence the rate of inflation over the period. The results were rather different, for although inflation was gradually reduced, the result was an exceptionally severe recession. Though the policy was gradually modified right through the 1980s, 1990 is taken as marking the end of this period, on the grounds that entry into the exchange rate mechanism of the EMS marked a decisive change in the rules.This period of economic policy is discussed in greater detail in later chapters, in particular chapters 11 and 13.

1.4 CONCLUSIONS

❑ There was a clear break in the problems faced in the early 1970s.

❑ The main features of UK economic performance were shared by other countries: the rise in inflation in 1973-5, the recession of 1974-5, the inflation of 1979, the recession of 1980 and the subsequent recovery, and the fall in inflation during the 1980s.

❑ British performance differed from that of similar economies in a number of ways: (a) the recession of 1974-5 was longer lasting; (b) inflation was much higher in the UK than in most similar economies; (c) the recession of 1980-1 was much more severe than elsewhere, because of the behaviour of sterling in 1979-80; (d) the recovery since 1981 has been relatively fast, but it is not clear how far this is simply because of the depth of the recession.

❑ The links between politics, economic policy and economic perfor-mance are not clear-cut. There was a change in ideology after 1979, but the movement towards monetarism came earlier and was a response to urgent economic problems. It is not clear that policy has always had the effects claimed for it: either that

Keynesian stabilization policies were the cause of high employment in the 1950s and early 60s, or that monetarist policies were
the cause of the fall in inflation during the 1980s.

FURTHER READING

One of the best introductions to UK macroeconomics is Christopher
Johnson *Measuring the Economy: A Guide to Understanding Official
Statistics* (London: Penguin Books, 1988), which provides a very
thorough discussion of how the main macroeconomic statistics are
constructed and what they mean. The most useful statistical source is
probably *Economic Trends* (London: Central Statistical Office, monthly)
and *Economic Trends Annual Supplement* (usually published between
January and March).

A short survey of post-war macroeconomic policy is contained in the
chapter on the UK, by M. J. C. Surrey, in *The European Economy: Growth
and Crisis* (Oxford: Oxford University Press, 1982). More detailed
discussions of specific periods can be found in: J. C. R. Dow *The
Management of the British Economy, 1945-60* (Cambridge: Cambridge
University Press, 1964); F. T. Blackaby (ed.) *British Economic Policy,
1960-74* (Cambridge: Cambridge University Press, 1978); R. E. Caves *et
al. Britain's Economic Performance* (Washington DC: Brookings Institution); and Rudiger Dornbusch and Richard Layard (eds.) *The Performance of the British Economy* (Oxford: Oxford University Press, 1987). A
very clear account of the major policy issues as seen from around 1980
is found in R. C. O. Matthews and J. R. Sargent (eds.) *Contemporary
Problems of Economic Policy* (London: Methuen, 1983) which contains
reprints of articles published in the *Midland Bank Review* between 1977
and 1982. More detailed references on recent policy can be found at the
end of chapter 13. Regular analysis of macroeconomic policy and
current events in the UK and the world economy is contained in *OECD
Economic Surveys: United Kingdom* (annual); in the *National Institute
Economic Review* (quarterly); and the *Bank of England Quarterly Bulletin*.
Chapter 13 contains more detailed references on the 1980s.

An accessible discussion of long-run economic performance in the UK
is provided in *Oxford Review of Economic Policy* 4(1), 1988, in which
general surveys of economic growth are provided by Nick Crafts,
Geoffrey Meen and Charles Feinstein, with other articles discussing
more specialized problems.

II

The Demand Side

Consumption and savings

2.1 INTRODUCTION

Consumption is important for three main reasons: it is the largest category of spending; the multiplier depends on the marginal propensity to consume; and in recent years the savings ratio has been very unstable.

❏ Consumption is the largest category of spending. As shown in figure 2.1, consumption amounted to 66 per cent of GDP in 1989, the next largest category being exports, at 29 per cent. It is thus important to forecasters to be able to predict consumption correctly, for even a small percentage error may involve a large absolute error. For example, suppose that forecasters make an error of 1 per cent in predicting consumption (what might be thought a very small error). This will amount to an error of 0.6 per cent of GDP. This may not seem very much, but it is the difference between a growth rate of, say, 2 per cent (which would be considered low) and 2.6 per cent (a much more reasonable growth rate).

❏ The marginal propensity to consume is one of the factors determining the size of the multiplier, which is important for determining the effects of changes in investment and government spending.

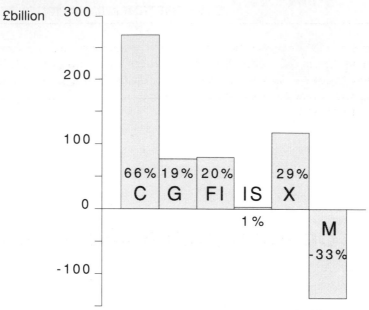

Figure 2.1 Components of GDP at market prices, 1989
Source: Economic Trends. Percentages are shares of GDP.

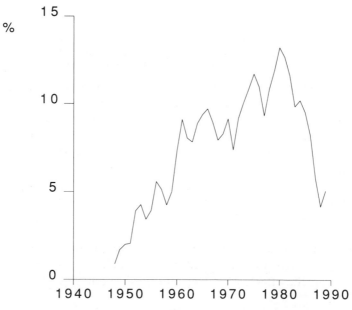

Figure 2.2 The savings ratio, 1948-89
Source: Economic Trends.

❏ Changes in the savings ratio (the average propensity to save) are shown in figure 2.2. Since 1948 the savings ratio has fluctuated between 1 and 14 per cent, some of the changes being very rapid. During the 1980s, for example, the savings ratio fell from 14 per cent to 4 per cent.

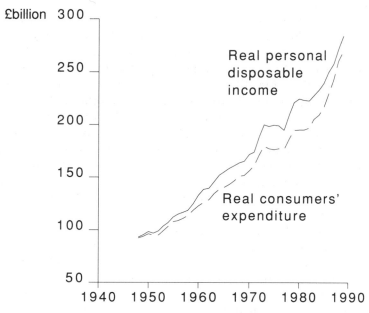

Figure 2.3 Income and consumption, 1948-89

Source: Economic Trends.

Figure 2.3 shows the behaviour of real personal disposable income and real consumers' expenditure. The increase in the saving ratio in the 1970s appears as a widening gap between income and consumption.

2.2 THE 'KEYNESIAN' CONSUMPTION FUNCTION

A simple 'Keynesian' consumption function

The simplest one we could use is a Keynesian consumption function such as:

$$C = A + \beta Y$$

where C is consumption, A is autonomous consumption, Y is income and β is the marginal propensity to consume. If we fit this equation to the data we obtain the following equation:

$$C = 3.65 + 0.89Y.$$

The marginal propensity to consume is 0.89 and autonomous consumption is (just) positive.

Before we can start assuming that the MPC is in fact 0.89, however, we need to decide whether this equation is an acceptable description of what has happened to consumption. There are two ways in which this can be done. One is to use a number of statistical tests to decide whether the equation fits the data properly (some statistics are provided, without discussion, in the appendix). The other is to look at how well the equation predicts consumption. This is done in figure 2.4, where the lines labelled $C = \alpha + \beta Y$ give the values of consumption and the saving ratio predicted by this equation (ignore the lines marked $c = \alpha + \beta y$ for the moment). Figure 2.4(b) suggests that the equation does quite well in predicting consumption but when we turn to the savings ratio in figure 2.4(a) we find that, though it captures the long term rise in the savings ratio it completely fails to explain the fluctuations which took place during the 1970s and 1980s: it predicts neither the sharp rise during the 1970s nor the fall during the 1980s. This is hardly surprising, because with this equation the only thing that can cause the savings ratio to change is changes in income, and for virtually the whole period income was rising. We need to consider other factors if we are to explain the behaviour of the savings ratio.

Before going on to consider other consumption functions, we will make one small change to this simple Keynesian consumption function. This is to use logarithms of consumption and income and to estimate a consumption function of the form

$$c = \alpha + \beta y,$$

where $c = \log(C)$ and $y = \log(Y)$. This implies that the relationship between C and Y is of the form

$$C = AY^\beta$$

where $\alpha = \log(A)$. Note that with this log-linear consumption function, β is not the marginal propensity to consume, but the *elasticity* of consumption with respect to income. Though such a consumption function may look less familiar it often makes more sense to assume that it is elasticities rather than ratios of quantities that are constant. Estimating this consumption function we obtain

$$c = 0.19 + 0.95y.$$

The savings ratio obtained from this consumption function is shown in figure 2.4(a). It is very similar to the one obtained from the linear consumption function. The level of consumption predicted by this equation is not shown, because it would be so similar to the other one that it would merely clutter up the diagram.

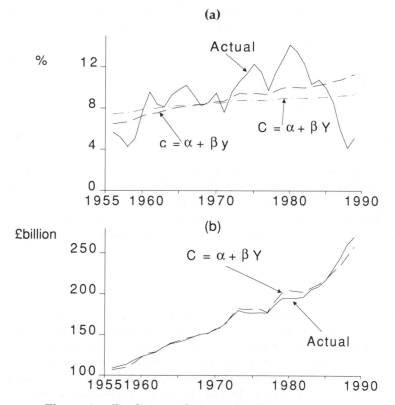

Figure 2.4 Predictions from a simple Keynesian consumption function

Source: see text.

2.3 PERMANENT INCOME/LIFE CYCLE THEORIES

The most commonly-used theory of the consumption function is the permanent income/life cycle theory (we use these two terms interchangeably as the two theories differ only in small details). This states that consumers base their consumption on expected lifetime income, saving and dis-saving so as to smooth out short-term fluctuations in income. Permanent income is defined as the constant income stream which has the same present value as an individual's expected lifetime income, and can thus be taken as a simple measure of lifetime income. It gives rise to a consumption function of the form $C = kY^p$, where Y^p is permanent income, and $k < 1$ (k is the average propensity to consume). Using logarithms of C and Y, this gives $c = \alpha + \beta y^p$, where $\alpha = \log(k) < 0$ and $\beta = 1$.

The problem, of course, is how to measure permanent income, for it depends on consumers' expectations. We consider the two main solutions to this problem: the assumption that permanent income responds with a lag to actual income; and the assumption of rational expectations.

Permanent income as lagged income

The conventional way to measure permanent income (and implicitly expected lifetime income) is to take a weighted average of past incomes. The rationale for such a measure is that transitory fluctuations in income will be random, and that if we take an average over several periods, these fluctuations will cancel each other out.

The simplest formula for y^p is one such as $y^p = (y_t + y_{t-1} + y_{t-2})/3$ (the choice of three here is not significant). Using this definition of y^p we obtain

$$c_t = 0.27 + 0.94 y^p{}_t.$$

This may look very similar to the consumption function estimated in the previous section, with an elasticity of consumption with respect to permanent income of 0.94 (compared with 0.95 when y_t was used). In the short run, however, there isa big difference between the two consumption functions. To see this, consider the effect of raising current income by 10 per cent. In the first period, permanent income rises by 3.3 per cent, and consumption rises by 3.1 (= 0.94 × 3.3) per cent. In the second period permanent income rises by a *further* 3.3 per cent, with the result that consumption rises by a *further* 3.1 per cent.

The full effect on consumption is not seen until the third period, by which time permanent income has risen by a full 10 per cent, with the result that consumption has risen 9.4 per cent above its original level. In other words, with this consumption function the long-run (3 year) elasticity of consumption with respect to income is 0.94, but the short-run (one year) elasticity is only 0.31. We thus have different short and long-run consumption functions.

A more common approach to modelling permanent income is to use a more complicated lag structure which turns out to give a much simpler consumption function. This is to assume that permanent income is a weighted average of *all* past incomes, with geometrically declining weights:

$$y^p_t = (1-\lambda)y_t + (1-\lambda)\lambda y_{t-1} + (1-\lambda)\lambda^2 y_{t-2} \ldots$$

where $1 > \lambda < 0$. This can be rearranged to give

$$y^p_t = (1-\lambda)y_t + \lambda[(1-\lambda)y_{t-1} + (1-\lambda)\lambda y_{t-2} + (1-\lambda)\lambda^2 y_{t-3} \ldots]$$

$$= (1-\lambda)y_t + \lambda y^p_{t-1}.$$

If $c = ky^p$ we then have

$$c_t = k(1-\lambda)y_t + \lambda c_{t-1}.$$

This means that we can model permanent income by including lagged consumption in the consumption function. Estimating such a consumption function we obtain

$$c_t = 0.26y_t + 0.73c_{t-1} + 0.05.$$

Like the previous equation gives different short and long run consumption functions. In the short run, the elasticity of consumption with respect to income is 0.26, whereas in the long run (defined as a period sufficiently long for consumption to be constant) it is $0.26/(1 - 0.73) = 0.96$. The constant is nearly zero (further details of all these equations are given in the appendix). In figure 2.5 the long-run consumption function and two short-run consumption functions (corresponding to two different values of c_{t-1}) generated by this equation are plotted. They have the usual properties.

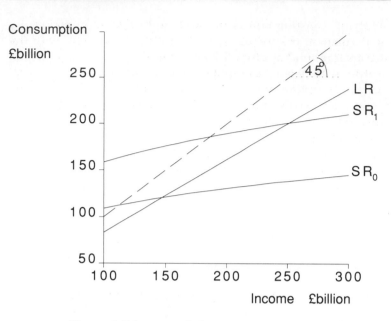

Figure 2.5 Long and short run consumption functions

Source: as described in the text.

Permanent income as determined by rational expectations

The most elegant answer to the question of how to model consumers' expectations of future income is to assume rational expectations: to assume that consumers predict income as accurately as it is possible for them to predict it, given the information available to them. This means that consumption in period t, C_t, will reflect all the information that is available up to time t. This information can be divided into two parts: information that was already known at time t-1, and new information that has become available since time t-1. Of these, information known in period t-1 will be reflected in C_{t-1}. Rational expectations imply that any new information since time t-1 must be uncorrelated with any information available at time t-1. Given that, under the life-cycle theory, consumers will be planning to smooth out their lifetime consumption, this means that the consumption function should have the form

$$c_t = \beta c_{t-1} + \varepsilon_t,$$

where ε_t is 'white noise' — a random variable with zero mean and uncorrelated with any information (including past values of ε_t) available at time t-1. Note that there is *no* constant term in this equation. If $\beta = 1$ this is a *random walk*: in any period, consumption is equally likely to rise or to fall. In practice, however, β is likely to be greater than one, for several reasons. The most important one is probably that consumption is being undertaken not by an unchanging population but by a population in which per capita incomes are rising over time. This means that each generation is wealthier than the previous generation and will plan to achieve a higher level of consumption.

Estimating such a consumption function, we obtain

$$c_t = 1.006c_{t-1} + \varepsilon_t.$$

Although an error term is implicit in all the consumption functions we discuss in this chapter, we have specified this one because the way we have to test this theory is by looking at the error term. If it is correlated with previous values of variables known in period t-1, such as consumption, income, or itself, the theory cannot be correct. The

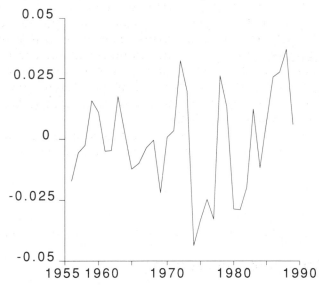

Figure 2.6 Predicted errors using the 'random walk' model of consumption

Source: as described in the text.

simplest way to test this is to look at the behaviour of ε_t, shown in figure 2.6. This appears to show a cyclical pattern, implying that each value of ε is correlated with its predecessor (the relationship can be shown to be $\varepsilon_t = 0.36\varepsilon_{t-1} + \eta_t$, where η is 'white noise'). Though this is hardly a thorough test, it does suggest that this hypothesis about consumption is not correct. More thorough testing has suggested the same conclusion.

2.4 MODIFICATIONS TO THE LIFE-CYCLE THEORY

Inflation

The consumption functions discussed in the previous section are clearly much better than the simple Keynesian consumption functions discussed in section 2.2, but they are still very bad at predicting the saving ratio, especially during the 1970s and 1980s. Additional factors clearly need to be taken into account. The first one we will consider is inflation. Inflation should affect consumption and the saving ratio because it reduces the real value of any debts denominated in money. As the value of debts is reduced, debtors gain (they receive a real capital gain) and creditors lose (they have a real capital loss). The government and the corporate sector are large net debtors, and so gain from inflation, but the personal sector is a large net creditor, so inflation reduces its real income. This reduction in real income is often referred to as *the inflation tax* on the grounds that inflation is acting as if it were a tax on holding money (or any asset the value of which is fixed in money terms). Because this tax is not taken into account in calculations of personal disposable income, we need to bring inflation into the consumption function.

We could easily add inflation to the life-cycle consumption function used in the previous section to obtain an equation such as

$$c_t = k(1-\lambda)y_t + \lambda c_{t-1} + \gamma \pi_\tau,$$

where π is the inflation rate. Rather than see how such a consumption function performs, however, we will introduce another modification.

Error correction mechanisms

One problem with consumption functions of this type is that standard consumer theory suggests that in the long run permanent income will be proportional to actual income, and hence consumption should be proportional to income (i.e. we should have $c = \alpha + y$). In the short run, however, we would not expect consumption to be strictly proportional to income. This has led economists to use what are known as *error correction mechanisms*. This involves building a consumption function from two components.

❏ In the long run we assume that there is some target level of consumption that is proportional to income.

❏ In the short run consumption will not equal the desired proportion of income (because mistakes and unexpected shocks will always be occurring). In the short run, therefore, we assume that consumers adjust their consumption towards their target level, this adjustment being spread out over time.

If we adopt such an error correction mechanism, we obtain a consumption function such as

$$\Delta c_t = \alpha + \beta \Delta y_t + \gamma s_{t-1} + \delta \pi_\tau,$$

where s is the savings ratio (because the variables are in logarithms this is equal to $y_{t-1} - c_{t-1}$).

Consumption functions incorporating inflation and error correction mechanisms were widely used around 1980, and were successful in predicting consumption and savings. However, these consumption functions failed to predict the fall in saving that took place during the 1980s. The extent of this failure is shown by estimating a version of this last consumption function on data for the period from 1956 to 1980, and using it to predict the savings ratio during the 1980s (on the assumption that income is predicted correctly — i.e. actual income is used). The equation is

$$\Delta c_t = -0.001 + 0.63 \Delta y_t + 0.19 s_{t-1} - 0.13 \pi_\tau.$$

The predictions from this equation are shown in figure 2.7. The equation performs very well up to 1980, but completely fails to predict the decline in the savings ratio after 1980.

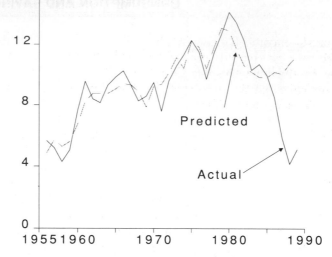

Figure 2.7 Predicting the 1980s saving ratio

Source: as described in the text.

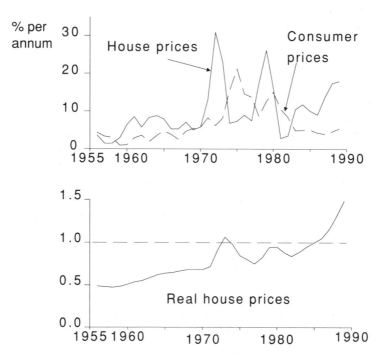

Figure 2.8 House price inflation and real house prices

Source: Nationwide Anglia index of house prices from *Datastream;* consumer price index from *Economic Trends.* Real house prices are the ratio of house prices to consumer price index.

House prices and uncertainty

A variety of explanations has been put forward to explain why consumption should have risen more rapidly than is predicted by such equations. We will consider two of these: credit liberalization and rising house prices, and reduced uncertainty about the growth rate of income.

❑ The main one concerns the joint effects of credit liberalization, which made it much easier for households to borrow than was the case in the 1960s and 1970s, and rising house prices. During the 1980s house prices rose much more rapidly than other prices, as is shown in figure 2.8, producing a very large rise in real house prices, and hence in the personal sector's wealth. This increased wealth could be used to finance higher consumption either through people selling houses (for example, ones that have been inherited) or through households borrowing more, using housing as a security. Consumption will thus have risen because households were wealthier and because fewer households faced a constraint on the amount that they were allowed to borrow.

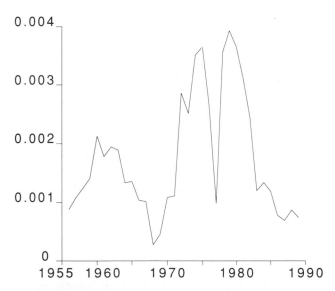

Figure 2.9 The variability of income growth, 1956-89

Source: growth rate of real personal disposable income (from *Economic Trends*), and its four-period standard deviation.

❏ The second argument is that households save more when there is greater uncertainty about income levels. In the 1980s personal disposable income grew much more steadily than in the 1970s, with the result that households faced less uncertainty. This will have caused precautionary saving to decline. Figure 2.9 shows the standard deviation (over the previous four years) of the growth rate of real personal disposable income, (σ). This shows that there was a marked reduction in uncertainty during the 1980s compared with the 1970s.

If we include real house prices (*RHP*) and uncertainty (σ) in our consumption function, we obtain

$$\Delta c_t = -0.009 + 0.73\Delta y_t + 0.19s_{t-1} - 0.09\pi + 0.018RHP - 0.51\sigma.$$

The saving ratio predicted by this equation is shown in figure 2.10. This shows clearly that the equation now fits the data much better. In particular, the equation captures the decline in the savings ratio during the 1980s.

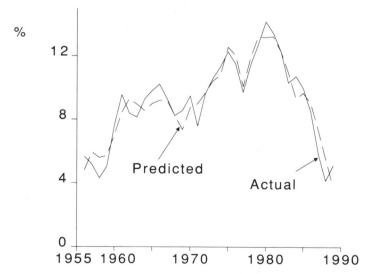

Figure 2.10 Predictions of the saving ratio

Source: as described in the text.

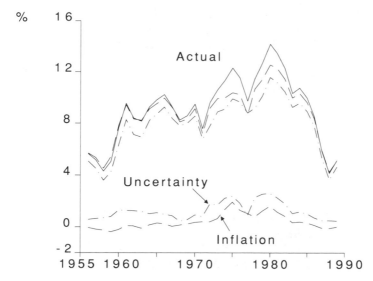

Figure 2.11 Inflation, uncertainty and the saving ratio, 1956-89
Source: as described in the text.

2.5 EXPLAINING THE SAVING RATIO

Having derived a consumption function we can use it to explain movements in the saving ratio. Using the coefficients in the last equation in the previous section we can calculate the contributions of inflation, real house prices and uncertainty about the growth rate of income to the savings ratio. The contribution of inflation to consumption in any one year is defined as $0.09(\pi - \pi^*)$, where. π^* is the mean value of π. If we subtract this from c we obtain what (the logarithm of) consumption would have been if inflation had been equal to its mean value, of 6.7 per cent per annum. We can then calculate what the saving ratio would have been with inflation equal to its mean value. Similarly, the contribution of income uncertainty to (the logarithm of) consumption is -0.51σ. Figure 2.11 shows these contributions together with the adjusted saving ratios. The main feature in figure 2.11 is that during the 1970s increased inflation and increased uncertainty about income growth between them raised the saving ratio by about two to three percentage points compared with what it would have been had they remained at the same level as in the 1960s.

Figure 2.12 shows the contribution of real house prices to the saving ratio, evaluated in a similar way as $0.18(RHP - RHP^*)$ where RHP^* is

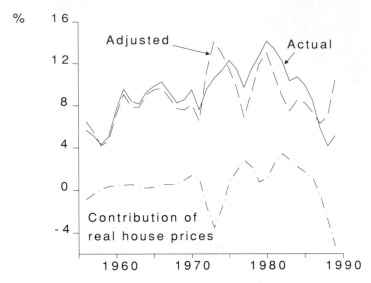

Figure 2.12 Real house prices and the saving ratio, 1956-89
Source: as described in the text.

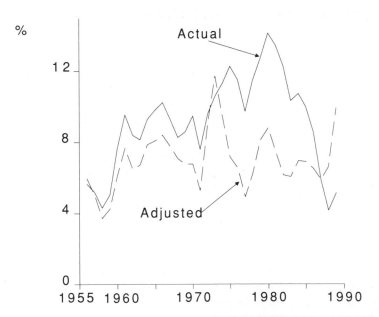

Figure 2.13 Contributions to the saving ratio, 1956-89
Source: as described in the text.

the trend value of real house prices (as shown in figure 2.8, real house prices rose steadily throughout the period). This shows that rising real house prices served sharply to reduce savings in 1972-3 and in the late 1980s. Between 1980 and 1988 the saving ratio fell from just over 14 per cent to just over 4 per cent. If we accept the estimates shown in figure 2.12, rising real house prices contributed 5 percentage points towards this fall.

The effect of adjusting for all three variables is shown in figure 2.13. If the consumption function has been estimated correctly, the adjusted saving ratio (the remainder after deducting the effects of inflation, real house prices and uncertainty) shows fluctuations in the saving ratio that arise from random disturbances and the dynamic adjustment processes implied by the consumption function. It is important, however, to note that our consumption function, elaborate as it is, is most unlikely to provide a complete account of the factors affecting consumption and the saving ratio. For example, we have assumed that real house prices had the same impact on consumption throughout the period, whereas the arguments used earlier in this chapter suggested that, because of credit liberalization, they should have had a greater impact during the 1980s than before.

2.6 CONCLUSIONS

In this chapter we started with the simple Keynesian consumption function, introducing a number of additional factors that should influence consumption. The result is a consumption function that is recognisably similar to some of the consumption functions used in serious applied work, notably that associated with Hendry and Muellbauer, cited in the suggestions for further reading. It remains, however, oversimplified in a number of respects.

❑ The lag structure is still relatively simple.

❑ The equation applies to total consumers' expenditure, whereas separate equations would normally be estimated for durable and non-durable expenditure. The reason for this is that the factors determining these two types of consumption can be very different, consumer durables being, in some respects, more like investment goods than non-durable consumption goods.

❑ There are further factors that should be taken into account — such as demographic changes and changes in income distribution.

For all these reasons, therefore, even the best of the consumption functions discussed in this chapter must be used with care. Understanding them, however, will make it easier to understand more complicated consumption functions.

FURTHER READING

A good introduction is Christopher Johnson *Measuring the Economy* (London: Penguin, 1988), chapter 2, 'Personal income and saving'. The article in which error correction mechanisms were introduced is J. Davidson, D. F. Hendry, F. Srba and S. Yeo 'Econometric modelling of the aggregate time-series relationship between consumers' expenditure and income in the United Kingdom', *Economic Journal* 88(4), 1978, pp. 661-92. One of the most recent investigations of UK savings behaviour in the 1980s, on which our final equation is based, is J. Muellbauer and A. Murphy 'Why has UK personal saving collapsed?' (Credit Suisse First Boston, July 1989). This contains much technical material, but it is almost the only discussion of the role of the housing market in determining saving behaviour. Similar arguments are contained in J. Muellbauer and A. Murphy 'Is the UK balance of payments sustainable?', *Economic Policy* 11, 1990, pp. 347-96.An international perspective is provied in Andrew Dean *et al.* 'Saving trends and behaviour in OECD countries', *OECD Economic Studies* 14, Spring 1990, pp. 7-58; and Lawrence Summers and Chris Carroll 'Why is US national saving so low?' *Brookings Papers on Economic Activity* 1987 (2), pp. 607-35. Inflation-adjusted savings ratios, and discussion of the 'inflation tax' are published in the *Bank of England Quarterly Bulletin* in May of each year. See also E. P. Davis 'The consumption function in macroeconomic models: a comparative study', *Applied Economics*, 1984.

3

Investment

3.1 INTRODUCTION

Investment expenditure includes spending on a large variety of assets. The main distinction is between fixed investment, or fixed capital formation (the purchase of durable capital goods) and investment in stocks (inventories). These two categories of investment are in turn divided into three. Fixed investment comprises plant and machinery, buildings and vehicles; investment in stocks includes work in progress, raw materials and finished goods. For much of the time, however, it will be enough to look simply at the two categories of fixed investment and investment in stocks.

Fixed investment

The simplest definition of fixed investment is *gross* fixed investment, or gross domestic fixed capital formation (GDFCF) which is simply the sum of all spending on new investment goods. The behaviour of gross investment since 1948 is shown in figure 3.1. Three main conclusions can be drawn from these graphs.

❑ Investment clearly fluctuates together with output, but it fluctuates more.

❑ During the 1970s there was a progressive decline in the proportion of real GDP being devoted to investment.

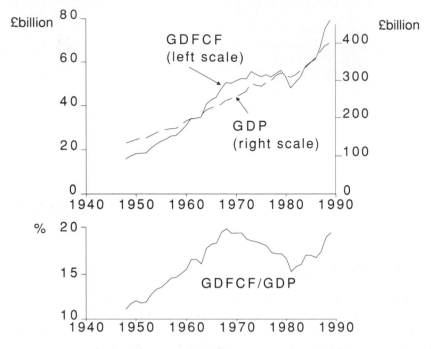

Figure 3.1 Gross fixed investment and GDP

Source: Economic Trends. Measured in constant (1985) prices.

❑ From 1979 to 1981 there was a sharp fall in investment, followed by a recovery since 1981.

One reason for being interested in investment is that we are interested in the capital stock. To calculate the capital stock, however, it is not enough to know the level of gross investment (the quantity of new capital being created) — we also need to know how much capital is being 'lost' from the capital stock each year. There are two ways this can be measured: depreciation and scrapping.

❑ *Depreciation* (or *capital consumption*) is the loss of value of the existing capital stock due to machinery wearing out, becoming obsolete, and so on.

❑ *Scrapping* is the amount of capital that is scrapped and withdrawn from the capital stock.

These are similar, but are not the same. A machine will depreciate continuously in that its value declines all the time it is in use. Scrapping, on the other hand, occurs only once. Consider an example. A machine costs £100 to purchase, and it wears out gradually over 10 years, after which it is scrapped. Depreciation is £10 per annum. At the end of 10 years it is scrapped. Scrapping is thus zero for the first nine years, and £100 in the tenth year.

Using these two concepts we obtain two different measures of the capital stock.

❏ *Gross capital stock* includes the value (at replacement cost) of all capital goods that have not been scrapped. A machine thus remains in the gross capital stock valued at its full replacement cost until it is scrapped. Gross capital stock is estimated using the formula:

$$GK(t) = GK(t-1) + GI(t) - S(t),$$

where GK(t) is the gross capital stock at the end of period t, GI(t) is gross investment during period t and S(t) is scrapping in period t.

❏ *Net capital stock* includes the value of all capital goods net of depreciation. A machine that is part of the capital stock is valued at a smaller and smaller price as it depreciates. It is calculated according to the formula:

$$NK(t) = NK(t-1) + GI(t) - D(t),$$

where NK denotes net capital stock and D denotes depreciation.

Which measure of capital should we use? The answer depends on what we want to use it for. If we are interested in finance, then net capital stock, which measures the *value* of the capital stock, is the right one. If, on the other hand, we are interested in productive capacity, then the gross capital stock is more appropriate. Consider, for example, a car. If we are concerned with the financial aspects of investment, we should value a used car at its value on the second-hand market (i.e. allowing for depreciation): a 2-year old car may thus be worth only half a new car. This is what would appear in the net capital stock. On the other hand, the 'productive capacity' of a 2-year old car is the same as that of a new car. The car should be valued at replacement cost (the price of a new car) until it is scrapped. This is what happens with gross capital stock.

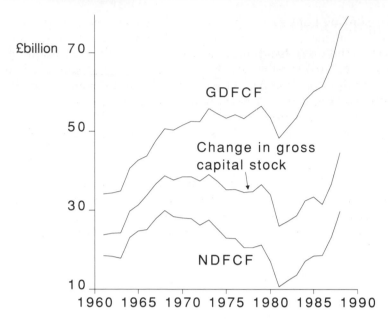

Figure 3.2 Fixed investment and the change in the capital stock

Source: United Kingdom National Accounts. Measured in constant (1985) prices.

The relationship between investment and the capital stock depends on which measure of capital we use. Net investment (gross investment minus depreciation) is the change in the net capital stock. The change in the gross capital stock is gross investment minus scrapping. Figures for these two measures of the change in the capital stock are shown in figure 3.2.

The main pattern revealed by figure 3.2 is that investment, according to all three definitions, rose substantially for most of the 1960s, but that after about 1968 net investment fell. From 1968 to 1978 the slight rise in gross investment was insufficient to keep pace with either scrapping or depreciation, both of which obviously increase with the size of the capital stock. The period from 1979 to 1981 was dominated by the fall in gross investment, since when there has been a limited recovery. Note, however, that whereas gross investment is now at its highest ever, net investment still remains low compared with the early 1970s. The implications of this low rate of investment and the resulting fall in the growth rate of the capital stock are considered in chapter 6.

Investment in stocks

When considering investment in stocks it is important to distinguish
between changes in the value of stocks that are the result of inflation
(stock appreciation) and the physical change in stocks, for it is only the
latter that constitute investment in stocks, or stockbuilding. As shown
in figure 3.3, stockbuilding is a fairly small component of GDP.
However, it fluctuates far more dramatically than any other category of
spending: unlike other categories of spending it is sometimes negative.
In the 1974-5 and 1980 recessions, for example, the change in the level
of stockbuilding accounted for all of the change in GDP: from 1973 to
1975 GDP fell by £6.3b., with stockbuilding falling by £10.3b.; from 1979
to 1981 GDP fell by £9.3b. with stockbuilding falling by £6.5b. (all these
are in 1985 prices).

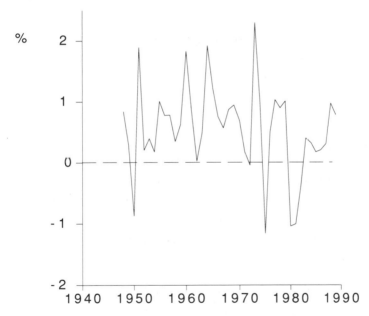

Figure 3.3 Stockbuilding as a percentage of GDP

Source: Economic Trends.

Demand for stocks is clearly related to current output. Figure 3.4
shows the ratio of stocks to output for manufacturing and for the
economy as a whole. Before 1979 there was little evidence of any trend,
suggesting that firms kept the ratio of stocks to output fairly steady,

though both ratios fluctuated with the cycle. Since 1979, on the other hand, there has been a steady fall in stock ratios, suggesting that after about 1981, when we would have expected stock ratios to increase as the economy recovered from recession, firms changed their behaviour. Though the figures are not sufficient to prove this, they are consistent with firms having become more efficient after 1979, economizing on their holdings of stocks.

Figure 3.4 Stock ratios

Source: Stock levels calculated from stockbuilding figures in *Economic Trends.*

3.2 MANUFACTURING INVESTMENT

Investment and output

The level of aggregate demand is clearly an important factor underlying firms' investment decisions. To illustrate how this problem can be tackled we consider the case of manufacturing investment. The theory we will use to explain manufacturing investment is the flexible accelerator (see box 3.1), according to which,

$$\Delta K = \alpha v Y - \alpha K.$$

BOX 3.1 THE ACCELERATOR

The most widely used version of the accelerator is based on two assumptions:

❏ The capital stock adjustment mechanism. Firms have a desired capital stock, K^* (which will be explained below) which is not necessarily the same as the capital stock they have actually got, K. If there is a gap between the desired capital stock and the actual capital stock, firms will plan to get rid of a certain fraction α of this gap each period. This gives the following equation to determine the change in the capital stock, ΔK:

$$\Delta K = \alpha(K^* - K).$$

❏ The capital-output ratio (v). To produce any given level of output there will be an optimal (cost minimizing) level of capital that is required. The optimal ratio of capital to output, which we will call v, will in general depend on the relative price of labour and capital, but to keep things simple it is often assumed that it is constant. We thus have

$$K^* = vY.$$

Note that the use of actual output, Y, is another simplification, for we should really use expected output, something we cannot observe.

Putting these two equations together, we have

$$\Delta K = \alpha vY - \alpha K.$$

This is known as the *flexible accelerator*.

The version we will use is the following:

$$\Delta GK_t = \alpha v Y_{t-1} - \alpha GK_{t-1},$$

where GK is the gross capital stock (discussed above). To obtain total (gross) investment we have to add on replacement investment. In this equation investment in period t is assumed to depend on Y and GK in the previous period. The reason for including GK_{t-1} is that capital stock statistics refer to the stock at the *end* of the period concerned. The reason for using Y_{t-1} is that when firms decide how much to invest in period t they will not know what Y_t is going to be. They will have to base their decisions on previous levels of output, and the simplest assumption to make is that investment depends on Y_{t-1}.

If we estimate this equation we get the following:

$$\Delta GK_t = 0.30 Y_{t-1} - 0.076 GK_{t-1}.$$

This suggests that α is 0.076 and that v is about 4 (0.3 divided by 0.076). This is consistent with the observed capital output ratio shown in figure 3.5 and implies that if output rises by £100, firms want their capital stock to rise by approximately £400.

If we assume that firms have a desired ratio of stocks to output the flexible accelerator could also be applied to stockbuilding. Such an equation for manufacturing is

$$\Delta S_t = 0.22 Y_t - 0.36 S_{t-1}$$

where S denotes stocks and ΔS stockbuilding (the value of the physical change in stocks). Notice that we have used current output, not last period's output, on the grounds that firms can vary stock levels relatively quickly in response to changes in demand. Two points are worth noting about this equation:

❑ The value of α is 0.36, which is much higher than its value for fixed investment. This is what we would expect: that firms respond much more quickly to differences between desired and actual stock levels than they do to differences between desired and actual levels of fixed capital.

❑ The equation suggests that firms wish to hold stocks equal in value to about 85 per cent (0.22 divided by 0.36) of current output. This is higher than the observed ratio of stocks to output (see figure 3.4).

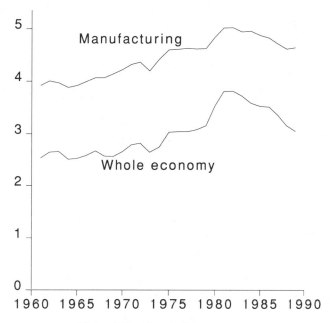

Figure 3.5 Capital-output ratios

Source: Ratios of gross capital stock to output at factor cost (constant prices), from *United Kingdom National Accounts*.

To see how well these equations explain variations in investment in manufacturing, consider figure 3.6, which shows investment and stockbuilding compared with the values predicted by these equations. It is clear that our accelerator model fits the data for fixed investment much better than for stockbuilding. This is what we would expect: stockbuilding is volatile and depends on many other factors.

❑ Many changes in stocks will be unplanned: if firms find that they cannot sell their output the result will be a rise in stocks.

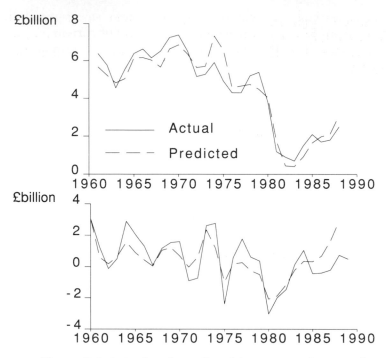

Figure 3.6 Actual and predicted investment in manufacturing

Source: Calculated from equations discussed in the text.

❏ Because stockbuilding is a short-term decision, easy to change, it ought to be sensitive to fluctuations in costs and expectations about the future. Being a longer-term decision, fixed investment ought to be more stable.

One of the main features of the behaviour of fixed investment is the dramatic fall which took place from 1979 to 1981. Our simple accelerator model captures this fall quite well. The question which arises is whether the equation predicted this fall so well simply because this fall was part of the sample period over which the equation was estimated. To show that this was not the case, consider the version of the equation estimated over the period 1961-79 (i.e. leaving out all data on the 1979-81 fall in investment and the subsequent recovery). The equation we obtain is,

$$\Delta GK_t = 0.31 Y_{t-1} - 0.082 GK_{t-1}.$$

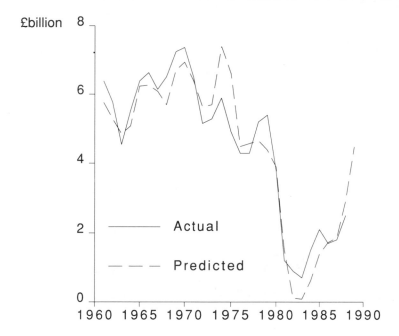

Figure 3.7 Predictions of manufacturing investment using pre-1979 data

Source: Calculated from equation discussed in the text.

The coefficients are, not surprisingly, slightly different from those obtained when estimating the equation over the period 1961-88. The equation, however, still predicts the collapse in investment from 1979 to 1981 successfully, together with the subsequent recovery, as is shown in figure 3.7.

Investment and profitability

Investment should also depend on profitability. There are two reasons for this. The first is that firms are assumed to maximize profits, and high profitability provides an incentive to invest. The second is that high profits provide firms with the funds they need to carry out investment projects.

The incentive to invest depends on two factors: the profits that firms expect to obtain on new investment, and the cost of obtaining finance. The relationship between these is best described by what is usually known as 'Tobin's q', or just 'q' (see box 3.2). Estimates of the cost of

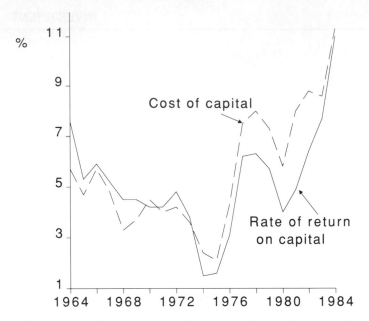

Figure 3.8 The rate of profit on capital and the cost of capital

Source: James H. Chan-Lee 'Pure profits and Tobin's *q* in nine OECD countries,' *OECD Economic Studies* 7, 1986, pp. 205-32.

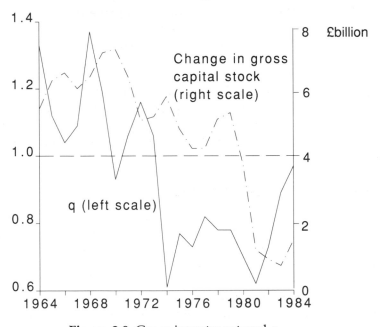

Figure 3.9 Gross investment and *q*

Source: as figure 3.8 and *United Kingdom National Accounts*.

capital, the rate of return on capital, and the value of q that results from them are shown in figures 3.8 and 3.9. In figure 3.8 there is a clear relationship between the rate of profit and the cost of capital. On average they move together, but q has nonetheless changed substantially over the period. The most noticeable change was the decline in q in the mid-1970s, followed by a partial recovery in the 1980s.

The evidence from figure 3.9 does not suggest a particularly close relationship between q and investment (measured here by the excess of gross fixed investment over scrapping). These statistics are, however, subject to a number of particularly severe measurement problems. In times of rapid change, such as the 1970s, it becomes particularly difficult to measure the capital stock, because the rates of depreciation and scrapping are liable to increase. Measures of depreciation and scrapping based on conventional lifetimes for different types of capital equipment will thus understate the true extent of depreciation and scrapping. It is thus likely that the capital stock was rising less rapidly than these figures suggest: there may thus have been more of a fall in investment during the mid-1970s than figure 3.9 suggests. In addition, if depreciation is under-estimated, the capital stock will be over-estimated. The result will be that q will be under-estimated (see box 3.2 for the alternative definition of q). It is thus possible that figure 3.9 overstates the fall in q in the mid-1970s. For these reasons, therefore, it is hard to use evidence such as that contained in figure 3.9 to say whether or not investment is or is not related to q.

Profits and the availability of finance

The other way to link profits to investment is to argue that high profits provide the funds that firms need to finance investment. This is an argument that makes sense only if the capital market is imperfect: in a perfect capital market the opportunity cost of finance would be exactly the same whether a project were financed by borrowing or from internal funds. Imperfections may arise in a number of ways: borrowing and lending rates may be different; transaction costs may be associated with borrowing and lending (new share issues, for example, are very expensive); new issues may dilute control of the company; and issuing debt may be regarded by the market as making a company too risky (the problem of gearing). Given problems such as these there may be a preference for financing investment projects out of retained profits rather than from external finance. Historically this has been the case, most investment in the UK being financed out of retained profits (the same is not true in other countries).

BOX 3.2 TOBIN'S *q*

'*q*', often called Tobin's *q* after the economist who developed the concept, can be defined in two ways.

❏ The ratio of the rate of return on capital (*R*) to the cost of capital (r_K). The rate of return on capital gives the amount of profit that the firm will make from investing £100 in capital goods. The cost of capital is the percentage return that has to be paid to the people who supply finance to the firm. The cost of capital includes not only interest on debt but also the return to equity shareholders. We thus have $q = R/r_K$.

❏ The second definition is the ratio of the market value of a firm (the value of its equity plus net debt), *V*, to the value of its capital stock at replacement cost, *PK* (because we have defined *K* as the physical stock of capital we have to multiply it by the price level, *P*, to obtain its value in current prices): $q = V/PK$.

We can easily show that these two definitions are equivalent. The cost of capital is defined by $r_K = $ profits$/V$. The reason for this is that profits ultimately accrue to the suppliers of finance: if profits are not paid out as interest on loans they are either paid as dividends to ordinary shareholders or are retained in the firm, in which case the shareholders should get a return in the form of capital gains. The price of shares, and hence *V*, will be determined in the market so that, given the firm's profits, profits$/V$, the return to investing in the firm, equals r_K, the rate of interest at which investors are willing to supply finance to the firm. If profits$/V$ is too low, for example, people will be unwilling to hold the firm's shares and so *V* will fall.

We can similarly define the rate of profit on capital as $R = $ profits$/PK$. This rate of return is determined by the productivity of capital (in perfect competition, the marginal product of capital). It follows that

$$q = R/r_K = (\text{profits}/PK)/(\text{profits}/V) = V/PK$$

These two definitions of q are equivalent.

The value of q is that it provides a measure of the incentive to invest. In a simple world with no taxation there will be an incentive to invest in new capital goods if q is greater than 1: if q is greater than 1 then investing £100 in new capital equipment will increase the value of the firm by more than £100. The difference between q and 1 measures the profit to be made over and above the cost of capital. Similarly, if q is less than 1 there will be a disincentive to invest.

In the absence of taxation the equilibrium valuation ratio is 1: if $q = 1$ firms have no incentive either to increase or to decrease the capital stock. If we allow for taxation, however, the equilibrium valuation ratio may not be equal to 1. Consider the firm's decision about whether to give £1 to shareholders as dividends or to retain it to invest in new capital goods. If firms are run so as to maximize the returns to their shareholders the return to shareholders from an additional £1 invested should be the same as the return from an additional £1 in dividends. If this were not the case then firms would wish to change their dividend policy so as to make shareholders better off. The return to shareholders of an additional £1 in dividends is £$(1-t)$ where t is the marginal rate of income tax. The return from an additional investment of £1 is £$(1-z)q$, where z is the marginal rate of capital gains tax. The reason is that £1 worth of new capital raises the value of the firm by £v and that this gain is subject to capital gains tax. If the firm's dividend policy is to be optimal, therefore, we must have $1-t = (1-z)q$, or $q = (1-t)/(1-z)$. If income and capital gains tax rates are different, therefore, the equilibrium valuation ratio will be different from 1.

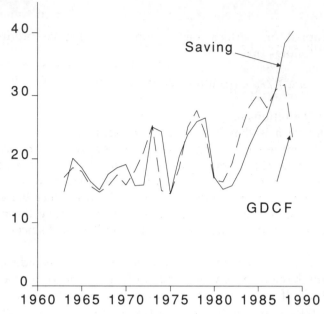

Figure 3.10 Saving and investment by industrial and commercial companies

Source: Economic Trends.

Evidence on this is given in figure 3.10 which shows saving by industrial and commercial companies (roughly retained profits) together with investment. It is clear that there is a close connection between the two. Causation, however, could run in either direction. It could be that the availability of finance influences investment. Alternatively, it is possible that the need to finance investment determines the level of profits that companies choose to retain.

3.3 INVESTMENT IN HOUSING

Investment in housing is shown in figure 3.11. Total investment in housing is divided between private and public-sector investment. Before 1968 these were both increasing, but since then public-sector investment in housing has been falling, whist private-sector investment has been rising. Because changes in public-sector housebuilding are determined by government policy, dominated in this period by pressure to reduce government spending, the rest of this section will be concerned only with private-sector investment in housing.

Private-sector investment in housing can be explained using a theory very similar to Tobin's q. The theory is that the market price of housing depends on supply and demand for the *stock* of housing, with demand depending on factors such as household incomes and the cost of mortgages. Because second-hand houses are bought and sold so frequently the market price of housing is easily observed. The level of investment in housing (the number of new houses built) depends on the price of housing relative to the cost of building new housing: if this ratio is high, there will be a great incentive to build houses, and if it is low few houses will be built. Eventually new housing will increase the stock of housing and thus affect price, but because the existing stock is

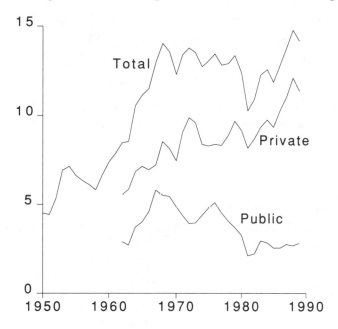

Figure 3.11 Investment in housing

Source: Economic Trends.

so large relative to the amount of new housing this process will take a long time. Although the gap between the price of housing and its replacement cost measures the incentive to build, however, we would not expect the two to be equal. The reason is that building new housing requires land, and the supply of land, combined with planning restrictions, limits the amount of new construction that can take place.

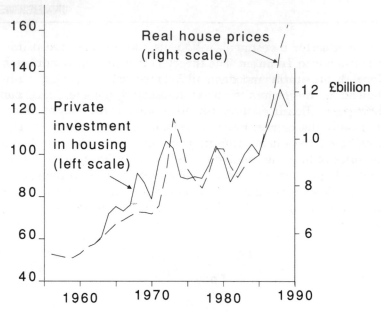

Figure 3.12 Investment in housing and the price of housing

Source: Economic Trends, Housing and Construction Statistics, Datastream.

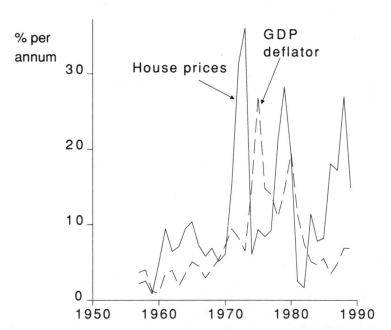

Figure 3.13 House price inflation and the GDP deflator

Source: as figure 3.12.

In practice, however, it is difficult to find a measure of the cost of housing which is different from the price at which houses are sold. There is the further problem that houses are not all the same: new housing is physically different from older housing and thus commands a different price. In figure 3.12, therefore, we use a measure of the real price of housing calculated by dividing the average price of new housing by the GDP deflator. The GDP deflator is used as a broad measure of costs: a measure of replacement cost (comprising labour, materials and normal profits) would be preferable, but is not available.

Figure 3.13 shows changes in the two variables that make up the real price of housing. Since the 1970s there have been three periods when house prices were rising rapidly: 1972-3, 1979-80 and 1983-7. In all three periods house prices rose much faster than the general price level and the real price of housing rose. The real price of housing fell during 1974-5 and 1980, when house prices failed to keep pace with the general price level.

Figure 3.12 strongly suggests that there is a close connection between the real price of housing and investment in housing by the private sector (we would expect public-sector investment to be less responsive to prices). The real price of housing and private-sector investment both move with the business cycle: there was a housing boom, associated with high prices, in 1973, followed by falls in both in 1974-5. There was a further boom in 1978-9, followed by a sharp recession in 1980 since when there has been another boom. There is, of course the possibility that there is no direct link, both being determined by some common cause, but a causal link from the real price of housing to the level of private- sector investment seems likely.

The price of housing depends on demand (in the short run the stock of housing changes little) and demand should depend on income and interest rates. Figure 3.13 also shows real personal disposable income alongside the real price of housing. The relationship is much what we would expect. In the boom of 1978-9 the rise in the price of housing was associated with rising real incomes and a low real interest rate. The sharp fall in the price of housing relative to costs in 1980-1 was the result of a fall in real income and a sharp rise in the real interest rate. The boom since 1981 has been caused primarily by rising real incomes, for real interest rates have, by the standards of the 1970s, remained very high.

3.4 CONCLUSIONS

Investment is one of the most difficult components of aggregate demand to explain, for it depends, to an even greater extent than do other categories of demand, on expectations. Many investment projects yield returns over long periods of time, so firms may have to form expectations concerning events even 20 or 30 years away. Such long-term expectations are unlikely to be directly related to current conditions, and to the variables economists can observe. With investment in stocks, the problems are different, for stockbuilding will reflect not only the planned changes in firms' inventories, but also unplanned changes. Such mistakes are, by their nature, hard to predict.

Notwithstanding these problems, the theories of investment discussed in this chapter appear to have some value as explanations of investment: the simple accelerator model performs better than might be expected in predicting manufacturing investment. Real house prices seem very closely connected to private investment in housing. Investment is thus not completely unpredictable.

FURTHER READING

K. F. Wallis *et al.* 'Econometric analysis of models of investment and stockbuilding', in *Models of the UK Economy: a Fourth Review by the ESRC Macroeconomic Modelling Bureau* (Oxford: Oxford University Press, 1987) provides a short, clear account of the theory of investment and an appraisal of the investment functions used in the main macroeconomic forecasting models. Colin Mayer 'The assessment: financial systems and corporate investment', *Oxford Review of Economic Policy*, 3(4), pp. i-xvi, examines the way UK investment is financed and discusses the implications of financial market liberalization for investment. The housing market is investigated in John Ermisch (ed.) *Housing and the National Economy* (Aldershot and Brookfield, VT: Avebury, 1990), a book which covers much more than simply investment in housing. Investment is discussed in the context of capital accumulation and changing productive capacity in chapter 6.

Government spending and fiscal policy

4.1 GOVERNMENT SPENDING

The scale of government spending

Government spending is divided into the five categories shown in figure 4.1, where the different items are shown both in £billion and as percentages of GDP at market prices (£509 billion in 1989). At first sight the figure of £195.8 billion for total government spending, amounting to just over 38.5 per cent of GDP seems enormous. However, most of this comprises transfer payments which do not form a part of GDP. The only items that enter GDP are government consumption and investment, the sum of these being government spending on goods and services, amounting to only 21 per cent of GDP. Current grants and subsidies comprise primarily social security payments and unemployment benefits. Capital transfers are grants made to businesses, whilst debt interest is received as income by individuals or institutions.

When assessing the quantity of resources that the government 'uses up' we usually focus on the ratio of government consumption to GDP. It is important to be careful here because, perhaps surprisingly, the results are very different depending on whether we use current or constant prices. These two measures are shown in figure 4.2, where the series labelled 'real' is the ratio of real government consumption to real GDP and the series labelled 'nominal' is the ratio of nominal government consumption to nominal GDP. When measured using

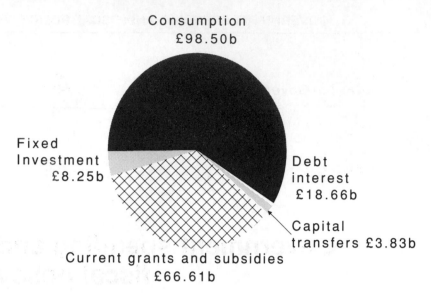

Figure 4.1 Government spending, 1989

Source: Economic Trends.

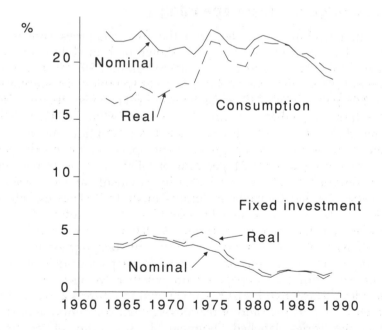

Figure 4.2 Government spending as a percentage of GDP

Source: Economic Trends.

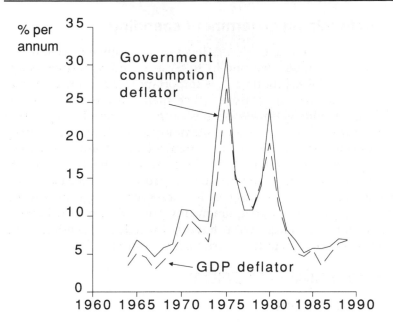

Figure 4.3 The price of government consumption

Source: Calculated from data in *Economic Trends.*

current price data, the ratio rose from around 17 per cent in 1965 to nearly 22 per cent in 1975, since when it has fluctuated between 20 and 22 per cent. When measured using constant price data, on the other hand, the ratio fluctuated between 21 and 23 per cent throughout the 1960s and 1970s, falling steadily during the 1980s to around 19 per cent.

The explanation for this contrast is that the price of government consumption has risen faster than the GDP deflator. The two inflation rates are shown in figure 4.3. With the exception of 1977-8, the price of government consumption was rising faster than the GDP deflator. One reason is that because most government services are not marketed, it is either difficult or impossible to measure improvements in the quality of government services. Much government spending is measured by the adding up the resources used, which means that the figures fail to reflect productivity growth.

Also shown in figure 4.2 is government fixed investment. The main feature here is that government fixed investment roughly halved during the 1970s, remaining very low since then. Compared with government current expenditure (consumption) government investment is very small.

Factors determining government spending

In many macroeconomic models the level of government spending is taken as exogenous, often constant. In so far as spending reflects policy decisions this may be appropriate. It is important to note, however, that spending also changes for reasons other than changes in economic policy. Education and health service spending, for example, depend on the age structure of the population; unemployment and social security payments depend on the level of unemployment, the level of income and the distribution of income. Whilst we are not directly concerned with such issues here, they are important because it is a mistake to see government policy as underlying every observed change in government spending. The fall in government investment happened because the government was faced with having to reduce spending, and investment was easier to cut than current expenditure.

4.2 THE GOVERNMENT DEFICIT

Measuring the deficit

In macroeconomic theory the meaning of the term government deficit is simple: it means total government spending (including transfer payments) minus taxation. In practice, however, the problem is slightly more complicated. We have to decide whether to include just central government, all government or the whole public sector. In addition there is the problem of what items to include as income and expenditure. If we focus on the public sector as a whole the nearest to

Table 4.1 The public sector deficit, 1989

	£billion
Government expenditure	
Total (see figure 4.1)	195.9
Government income	
Taxes and social security contributions	188.0
Trading income, rent etc.	14.5
Total	202.5
Government financial deficit (expenditure - income)	-6.6
Public corporations financial deficit	-1.0
Public sector financial deficit	-7.6

Source: Economic Trends.

this measure of the deficit is probably the *public sector financial deficit*. The term *public sector financial balance* is often used instead, the only difference being that the sign is reversed. The origins of the PSFD for 1989 are shown in table 4.1. It is made up of government spending minus income, plus the deficit of public corporations (such as the Post Office, British Coal and so on) which are part of the public sector but are not included within the government. In 1989 revenues exceeded current and capital expenditure, so that there was a negative deficit (a surplus).

The most widely cited measure of the government deficit, however, is the *public sector borrowing requirement* (PSBR) or, when this is negative, the *public sector debt repayment* (PSDR). PSDR is just the negative of PSBR. The relationship of this to the PSFD is shown in table 4.2. The difference between the two is the item labelled 'net lending to the private sector and overseas.' This included net purchases of company securities, which explains why it is so large and negative, for it includes the proceeds of privatizing public corporations. When the government privatizes a public corporation it is selling securities in the new company to the public. The revenue raised enters here. If the

Table 4.2 PSFD and PSBR in 1989

	£billion
Public sector financial deficit	-7.6
Net lending to private sector and overseas	-3.1
Public sector borrowing requirement	-9.1

Source: Economic Trends. Note that the item 'Net lending etc.' also includes 'Other financial transactions.'

government raises finance through selling shares in newly-privatized companies it reduces the amount it has to borrow, and hence the PSBR.

The behaviour of PSFD and PSBR, both in £billion and as a percentage of GDP, are shown in figure 4.4. Several features of this graph are worth picking out: the low level of the deficit in the 1960s; the sharp rise in the deficit in the early 1970s; and the fall during the 1980s.

❑ For most of the 1960s the deficit, by either measure, was fairly small. A surplus was achieved in 1969-70 because of the Labour government's restrictive policies.

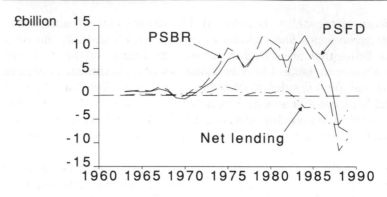

Figure 4.4 PSFD and PSBR, 1963-88

Source: Economic Trends. GDP is at market prices.

❑ The deficit rose enormously between 1970 and 1974, and from then until the mid-1980s it fluctuated about a much higher level. This rise in the deficit is something to which we will return later on.

❑ Since about 1983 both PSBR and PSFD have fallen greatly. The increasing gap between them was caused by the massive rise in privatization proceeds, causing net lending to become large and negative.

Faced with these two measures of the government deficit, which should we choose? To answer this we need to think about why the deficit matters. The usual answer is that, assuming the government is not going to finance it by increasing the money supply (this question will be considered later, in chapter 10), it must be financed by borrowing. Large scale borrowing, is is argued, will push up interest rates: the increased supply of government bonds will lower their price. Keeping government borrowing low enables the government to keep interest rates lower, encouraging private sector activity. If we accept this argument (some other factors influencing interest rates are discussed in chapter 12) the question of how we should measure the deficit becomes one of how far the public considers shares in newly privatized companies to be a substitute for government bonds. The easiest way to see this is to consider two extreme cases.

Case (a): Suppose that people regard equities as more risky than government bonds and as a result require a given risk premium if they are to hold shares rather than bonds. Given this risk premium people do not care whether they hold bonds or equities. In this situation increasing the supply of equities will have exactly the same effect as increasing the supply of government bonds, for the public is concerned only with the overall quantity of bonds-plus-equities that it has. A government deficit financed by selling equities in public corporations will raise interest rates just as much as will one financed by selling bonds: the interest rate on bonds and the yield on equities will rise and fall together so as to keep the risk premium constant. In this case the PSFD is clearly the best measure of the government deficit.

Case (b): The other extreme is the one where the public considers equities to be so different from other financial assets that there is no relationship between its holdings of equities and its demand for bonds. In this case issuing equity will have no effect at all on the price of bonds and hence on interest rates. It may thus be appropriate to focus on the PSBR, not the PSFD. The problem with this is that although, in this case, the sale of privatized companies will not affect interest rates, it should affect the price of equities and hence Tobin's q. The government should, therefore, be just as concerned about raising money through privatization as through bond issues. On the other hand, if privatization creates new investors who before either did not save or held simply cash, then it may be a way of raising finance without any adverse effects on interest rates or the price of equities, and so all the government needs to be concerned about is the PSBR.

Adjusting for inflation and the cycle

If we are to use the government deficit as a measure of the stance of fiscal policy, there are two factors which need to be taken into account: the 'inflation tax' and the tendency of the budget deficit to change automatically over the business cycle. The same arguments apply whichever measure of the deficit (PSBR or PSFD) we use.

The case for adjusting the deficit to allow for the inflation tax can be expressed in two ways.

❑ The inflation tax transfers resources from the private sector to the government and should, therefore, be included alongside other forms of taxation.

❑ When calculating the cost of interest payments we should include only the real cost of interest payments: interest should be calculated using the real rate of interest. Given that the PSFB includes nominal interest payments we need to deduct the inflation tax to get the real interest payments.

These are discussed in more detail in box 4.1.

The business cycle is relevant to the problem of assessing the government deficit because even without any change in government policy the deficit would vary over the cycle. When unemployment is high and incomes are low the government will be faced with a large bill for unemployment and social security benefits and its tax revenues will be comparatively low. In a time of prosperity, on the other hand, benefits will be lower and tax revenues higher. These effects mean that, even if the government does not change its policy (by which we mean that its spending programmes, rates of unemployment benefit, income tax schedules and so on are unchanged) the deficit will change over the cycle: there will be a larger deficit in recessions than in booms. To allow for these effects it is possible to calculate a *cyclical adjustment*, the resulting deficit being the *cyclically corrected deficit*. This is sometimes called the *structural balance* or *full-employment deficit* (this is the term commonly used in the US). This is the deficit which would occur, given current policies, if there were full employment together with the lower benefit payments and higher tax revenues that go with this.

Figures 4.5 and 4.6 show the effects of adjusting the PSFD for the cycle and inflation. Everything is expressed as a percentage of GDP. Note that although we have used the PSFD, the adjustments could equally well have been applied to the PSBR. The cyclical correction shown in figure 4.5 is one derived by economists at the OECD using methods we will not go into here. It is easy to see that it follows the same pattern as GDP or unemployment, with 1973 and 1979 being taken as years of full employment (1973 is in fact taken as having over-full employment). The cyclical adjustment increased dramatically in 1980. The inflation tax, on the other hand, peaked in the mid-1970s. Since 1975 it has fallen, with the fall in inflation, to only about 2 per cent of GDP.

Applying these two adjustments to the PSFD makes an enormous difference to the trends we observe over the 1970s and 1980s. There was a surplus (a negative PSFD) in 1969-70, after which the deficit rose to nearly 8 per cent of GDP by 1974. This deficit remained substantial right through to the mid-1980s. The inflation-adjusted deficit, on the other hand, shows a different story. Far from there being a deficit during the 1970s, there was a surplus. It was only during the 1980s that a deficit emerged, the reason being the sharp fall in inflation, which reduced the inflation tax to a small fraction of what it had been during the 1970s. Much of this deficit, however, was caused by the large rise in unemployment and the associated fall in output. This is shown by

BOX 4.1 THE INFLATION TAX

Inflation reduces the real value of all debts denominated in money. If there is 5 per cent inflation a debt of £100 will be worth approximately £95 at the end of a year. Inflation, therefore, makes debtors better off and creditors worse off: it redistributes wealth from those who have lent money to those who have borrowed it.

In most countries the government is the largest net debtor, its debts being far larger than its holdings of financial assets. This means that the government benefits from inflation. Another sector to benefit in this way is the corporate sector. The sector to lose most is the personal sector which is a large net creditor.

The inflation tax is closely linked to interest rates. If the inflation rate is π the inflation tax will be $\pi.NML$, where NML is the government's net monetary liabilities (the value of debts denominated in money less any assets). Define r as the average nominal interest rate on government debt, so that nominal interest payments are $r.NML$. Real interest payments are found by multiplying NML by the real interest rate, $r-\pi$. It follows that,

$$(r-\pi).NML = r.NML - \pi.NML,$$

or,

real interest payments =

nominal interest payments - inflation tax.

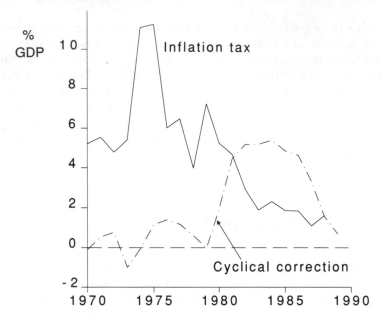

Figure 4.5 Inflation and cyclical adjustments

Source: Inflation tax from *Bank of England Quarterly Bulletin*, May 1990 and earlier issues.

comparing the inflation-adjusted deficit with the deficit corrected for the cycle as well as for inflation (the 'inflation-adjusted structural PSFD'). This suggests that despite the rise in the inflation-adjusted deficit, policy was very contractionary in 1980. Had it not been for the rise in unemployment, there would have been a large increase in the surplus. If we discount 1974-5 (for reasons that are explained below), the full- employment surplus was much larger in 1980 than at any time since 1970.

The inflation tax is calculated by multiplying the market value of the government's net monetary liabilities by an appropriate inflation rate. In the figures used above the inflation rate used was the consumers' expenditure deflator. This is the usual inflation rate to use, the argument being that the inflation tax is important because it affects consumers' spending decisions (see chapter 2). The issue is, however, more complicated than this. Here we have a problem. The reason is that over the past 20 years the inflation rate has fluctuated enormously from year to year. This means that when we calculate the inflation tax using the actual inflation rate we find that it varies greatly from year to year. In particular we have the inflation tax rising to around 11 per cent

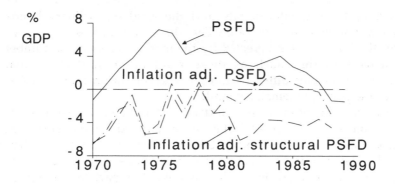

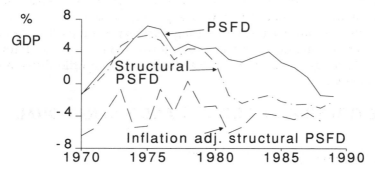

Figure 4.6 PSFD adjusted for inflation and the cycle

Source: Calculated from data used in figures 4.4 and 4.5.

of GDP in 1974-5. If private sector decisions depend on income flows over a longer period this measure of the inflation tax will not measure the impact that inflation is having on the behaviour of the private sector. We should instead use an inflation tax based on a longer term, expected inflation rate.

Further evidence that this is appropriate is found in interest rates. For several years (notably 1974-5) real interest rates were negative. If investors had not regarded such negative rates of interest as temporary, the price of index-linked debt would have risen without limit! It did not. This suggests that the private sector was to a certain extent disregarding negative real interest rates and a high inflation tax as transitory phenomena. It can thus be argued that in addition to the inflation tax based on actual *ex post* interest rates, it may be appropriate to calculate an *ex ante* inflation tax, based on expected interest rates. The way such an expected interest rate can be calculated is through the yield on index-linked bonds. The yield on index-linked bonds gives us a measure of the real interest rate and the yield on ordinary bonds gives us a nominal interest rate. The difference between the two measures the inflation rate expected by the market. There are a number of problems with this (such as those resulting from the fact that different investors pay different rates of tax on income and capital gains) but the principle remains sound.

The difference between *ex ante* and *ex post* inflation adjustments is shown in figure 4.7. Expected inflation, as implied by the yields on index-linked and non-index-linked debt, has fluctuated much less than the actual inflation rate (the retail price index is used because it is to this that the value of index-linked debt is linked). In particular the large rise in actual inflation in 1980 hardly shows up in the series for expected inflation: presumably it was expected to be short-lived and did not have a significant impact on long term expectations. The result is that the *ex ante* inflation tax was much lower than the *ex post* figure around 1980, though since around 1983 there has been little difference between the two.

4.3 THE GOVERNMENT DEFICIT AND THE NATIONAL DEBT

Interest payments

It is argued that government deficits impose a burden on the economy through raising interest payments. Figure 4.8 shows interest payments as a percentage of GDP. They were roughly constant during the 1960s, and increased during the 1970s. Overall interest payments amounted to about 4 per cent of GDP. Here again, however, the inflation tax is important. The reason is that it is the *real* interest rate that measures the cost of debt. To obtain the cost of debt when the real interest rate rather than the nominal rate is used we have simply to deduct the inflation tax from total interest payments. Figure 4.8 shows that real interest payments were negative throughout the 1970s, but that after 1980 they became positive. The real burden of interest payments on the national debt has increased much more sharply since 1980 than figures for nominal interest payments suggest.

Government debt

Instead of focusing on interest payments we may also be interested in the effect of the government deficit on the level of government debt. Here there are three issues to take account of: the inflation tax; growth in GDP; and the dynamic behaviour of government debt.

Figure 4.7 Alternative inflation adjustments

Source: Bank of England Quarterly Bulletin.

❏ The first is the inflation tax. If inflation is reducing the real value of the government debt, it is possible to run a deficit without the real value of the debt increasing: real debt will increase only if the inflation-adjusted balance is negative. Here it is the *ex post* inflation rate that matters.

❏ If GDP is growing at *g* per cent per annum the government can run a deficit equal to *g* per cent of the national debt each year without the ratio of debt to GDP rising. Given a constant real interest rate this means that the ratio of real interest payments to GDP, arguably the best measure of the burden of debt, will not rise.

❏ The third issue is more complicated and involves the dynamic behaviour of government debt. The argument is that provided the growth rate of GDP exceeds the real interest rate, a condition that is likely to be satisfied on average over a reasonably long period of time, the ratio of government debt to GDP will converge to a stable long run equilibrium value. A high government deficit does not lead to an ever-increasing debt/GDP ratio. This is discussed in more detail in box 4.2.

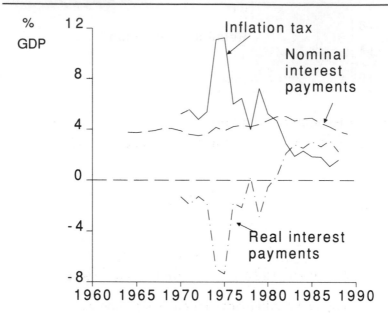

Figure 4.8 Real and nominal interest payments, 1963-88

Source: Economic Trends and figure 4.5.

These arguments are consistent with the behaviour of the national debt in relation to GDP, shown in figure 4.9. During the 1960s the national debt fell from about 100 per cent of GDP to about 50 per cent, since when it has been approximately constant. Note that figure 4.9 gives the nominal value (i.e. face value) of the national debt, not its market value. This means that the fall in the ratio of debt to GDP cannot be attributed to rising interest rates pushing bond prices down.

4.4 CONCLUSIONS: THE STANCE OF FISCAL POLICY

It would be very useful if it were possible to have a simple measure of the stance of fiscal policy: if this measure rose policy would be more expansionary (inflationary); if it went down policy would be more deflationary. The government deficit is a tempting choice for such a measure, for it reflects taxation as well as government expenditure. The larger the deficit, the more money is being injected into the economy. The distorting effects of inflation tax and cyclical factors can be eliminated by using the inflation-adjusted structural deficit as our measure of fiscal stance. The inflation-adjusted structural deficit would thus seem to be a suitable measure of the stance of the fiscal policy.

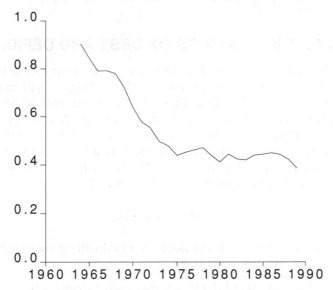

Figure 4.9 National debt as a proportion of GDP

Source: Economic Trends and Financial Statistics.

The situation is, however, more complicated than this, for several reasons.

❏ The level of government spending and taxation affects the level of aggregate demand independently of the size of the deficit, as is shown by the balanced budget multiplier theorem.

❏ Different types of spending or taxation may have different effects on aggregate demand. The marginal propensity to consume, and hence the multiplier, is not the same for all types of income. This means that different types of spending will have different multiplier effects.

❏ The way in which a deficit is financed may affect the level of aggregate demand. This is not simply a question of whether a deficit is financed by increasing the money supply or by increasing the quantity of government debt (which we might regard as an aspect of monetary policy, not fiscal policy): it also involves the type of debt the government issues, and how the private sector regards this debt in relation to other assets it holds. This is illustrated by the choice (discussed earlier in this chapter) between financing a deficit by selling equity in privatized companies or by selling government bonds.

BOX 4.2 THE DYNAMICS OF DEBT AND DEFICITS

Our aim here is to show that the ratio of government debt to GDP is, given certain assumptions, self-limiting. It will not go on rising for ever. To show this we divide the real (inflation-adjusted) deficit into two parts: the 'primary' deficit (government spending on goods and services less taxation) and real interest payments. We assume that the primary deficit is a given fraction, γ, of GDP. The change in the real value of the debt is equal to the inflation-adjusted deficit, which is

$$\gamma \, \text{GDP} + (r\text{-}\pi)\text{Debt}.$$

If we divide through by the debt we obtain the growth rate of the government debt.

$$
\begin{aligned}
\text{Growth rate of debt} \;&=\; \text{Increase in debt/Debt} \\[4pt]
&=\; [\gamma \, \text{GDP} + (r\text{-}\pi)\text{Debt}]/\text{Debt} \\[4pt]
&=\; \gamma \, (\text{GDP/Debt}) + (r\text{-}\pi).
\end{aligned}
$$

From this it follows that as the ratio of debt to GDP rises the growth rate of the debt falls. This is shown in figure 4.B2.1. Also shown is the growth rate of GDP, which we assume is greater than the real interest rate.

The ratio of debt to GDP will be constant if debt and GDP grow at the same rate. Where the growth rate of GDP equals the growth rate of government debt the ratio of debt to GDP will be constant. This is the equilibrium marked on figure 4.B2.1. It is easy to check that if the ratio of debt to GDP is higher than this equilibrium level GDP will be growing faster than debt and the ratio of debt to GDP will fall. Similarly if it is lower debt will be growing faster than GDP and the ratio of debt to GDP will rise. The debt/GDP ratio will thus always move towards the equilibrium shown in figure 4.B2.1.

In this equilibrium, the growth rate of government debt equals the growth rate of output, g.

$$\gamma \, (\text{GDP/Debt}) + (r\text{-}\pi) \;=\; g$$

From this it follows that

$$\text{Debt/GDP} \;=\; \gamma/[g\text{-}(r\text{-}\pi)]$$

A rise in the ratio of the primary deficit to GDP will lead to a rise in the debt/GDP ratio, but the debt/GDP ratio will not rise indefinitely.

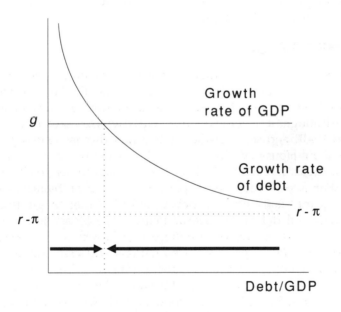

Figure 4.B2.1 Debt and GDP

It is for reasons such as these that there is, in general, no simple measure of fiscal stance. Any measure of fiscal stance has to be specific to a specific model of the economy. The inflation-adjusted structural deficit, for example, can serve as a measure of the stance of policy only if an extra £1 million spent on road-building has the same effects on aggregate demand as an additional £1 million in supplementary benefits, or a £1 million reduction in income tax. For a specific economy it may be possible to find a measure of fiscal stance which balances the effects of different fiscal actions against each other, but we should not expect such a measure to be simple, nor should we expect it to work in other situations. This is not to say that measures such as the inflation-adjusted structural deficit are useless; *ceteris paribus*, they do tell us about fiscal stance. It is important, however, not to neglect the other factors, which may be different.

It is important to note that in this chapter we have completely ignored the link between the government deficit and the money supply. The reason for this is simply a desire to tackle issues one-at-a-time. Money is considered in chapter 10.

FURTHER READING

A clear account of the main issues in fiscal policy can be found in D. Begg 'Fiscal policy,' in R. Dornbusch and R. Layard (eds.) *The Performance of the British Economy* (Oxford: Oxford University Press, 1987). Although it is now a little old, the concept of an inflation-adjusted PSBR and some of the other issues discussed here are clearly explained in House of Commons Select Committee *Monetary Policy, volume I: Report* (HC163-I, 1980-1), chapter 6 and annex to chapter 6 (pp. xcix-c). For a very thorough exploration of the problems involved in measuring the stance of fiscal policy, see W. Buiter 'A guide to public sector debt and deficits,' *Economic Policy* 1, 1985, pp. 14-79. M. Miller 'Measuring the stance of fiscal policy,' *Oxford Review of Economic Policy* 1(1), 1985, pp. 44-57, provides explanations and estimates of different inflation and cyclical adjustments, building on the earlier empirical work of P. Mueller and R. Price 'Structural budget indicators and the interpretation of fiscal policy stance in OECD economies,' *OECD Economic Studies*, 1984. Links between fiscal policy and the balance of payments are explored in José Vinals 'Fiscal policy and the current account', *Economic Policy* 3, 1986, pp. 711-44. An international perspective on the rise in government deficits in the 1970s, and the fall during the 1980s, is provided by Nouriel Roubini and Jeffrey Sachs 'Government spending and government deficits in the industrial countries', *Economic Policy* 8, 1989, pp. 99-132.

5

International trade

5.1 INTRODUCTION

The balance of payments

In this chapter we are concerned with the remaining two items that enter GDP: exports and imports. The difference between exports and imports, which is what enters GDP, is the *trade balance*. This should be distinguished from both the *current account balance* and the *balance of payments* (the balance for official financing through changes in foreign exchange reserves). The differences between these various concepts are illustrated in table 5.1 which gives figures for 1988. In table 5.1 exports and imports of goods and services are entered separately: trade in goods is defined as 'visible' and trade in services as 'invisible'. The balance of trade which enters into national income is the sum of the invisible and visible balances. It is important to note that the commonly used term 'invisibles' covers both trade in services and current account transfers (such as dividends, rents, interest, gifts and so on). When these transfers are added to the trade balance we have the current account balance.

The behaviour of the current account since 1950 is shown in figure 5.1. Two things stand out from this: the importance of the trade balance in determining the current account balance; and the seemingly unprecedented increase in both the trade deficit and the current account deficit in the late 1980s — in 1989 they stood at £23.1 billion and £20.8 billion respectively. The apparently unprecedented size of these deficits is, however, partly illusory, being the result of high

Table 5.1 The balance of payments, 1988

	£billion	
Exports of goods	80.6	
Imports of goods	101.4	
Visible trade balance		**-20.8**
Exports of services	27.9	
Imports of services	23.8	
Invisible trade balance		**4.1**
Balance of trade		**-16.7**
Interest, dividends, profits and transfers	2.1	
Current account balance		**-14.6**
Capital account transactions		
UK Private sector	4.5	
Public corporations	-0.4	
Government (excluding official reserves)	0.9	
Total, capital account		**5.0**
Balancing item		**12.3**
Overall balance (increase in official reserves)		**2.7**

Source: United Kingdom Balance of Payments.

inflation since the mid-1970s, the last time when there was a substantial deficit. The scale of the balance of payments problem is better seen from figure 5.2, which gives these balances as a percentage of GNP. This shows a deficit comparable with that of the mid-1970s. There is an important difference between these two situations, however: that is that in the mid-1970s the deficit was caused by a sudden rise in the price of energy, of which the UK was a net importer, whereas the deficit of the late 1980s has arisen despite the UK being a net exporter of oil (see chapter 9). The non-oil, visible trade deficit is *far* larger than at any time during the 1970s.

Also shown in figure 5.2(b) are the two invisible items. Between them, invisible trade and transfer payments have been in surplus throughout this period.

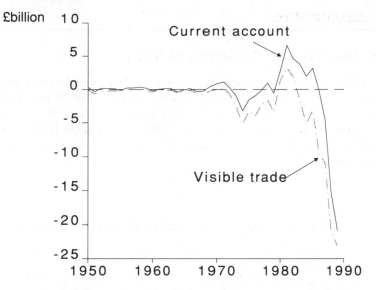

Figure 5.1 The balance of payments, 1950-89

Source: Economic Trends.

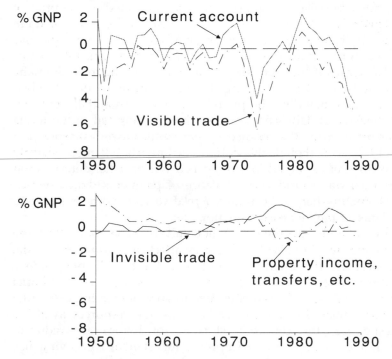

Figure 5.2 The balance of payments as a percentage of GNP, 1950-89

Source: Economic Trends.

Exports, imports and the terms of trade

In figure 5.3 we show exports and imports at 1985 prices. Exports and imports are defined as in the national income accounts, including both visible and invisible items. The gap between these two, however, is not the same as the trade balance (except for 1985). The reason is that the trade balance is the difference between the *value* of exports and the *value* of imports:

$$P_X X - P_X M.$$

If we divide through by a price index such as the price of imports we obtain

$$P_M[(P_X/P_M)X - M].$$

The balance of trade depends not only on the physical quantities of exports and imports, X and Y (exports and imports measured in constant prices), but also on the price of exports divided by the price of imports. This ratio is known as the *terms of trade*. If the terms of trade fall, for example, exports become cheaper relative to imports and exports have to rise relative to imports to maintain a constant balance of trade. The terms of trade are shown in figure 5.4. The most dramatic change in the terms of trade during this period came in 1973-4, when commodity prices including the price of oil rose substantially with no corresponding rise in UK export prices. The resulting fall in the terms of trade explains why the balance of payments moved sharply into deficit in 1974, even though the volume of imports fell more sharply than the volume of exports. What happened was that the deterioration in the terms of trade produced a balance of payments deficit, which meant that imports had to be reduced relative to exports in order to restore balance of payments equilibrium.

The terms of trade are important not only because they affect the balance of payments, but also because they affect the real income of the country concerned. If the terms of trade deteriorate (fall) more goods and services have to be exported to pay for a given volume of imports: to prevent the balance of payments deteriorating either imports must fall or exports must rise. Whichever happens, the resources available for domestic use (the country's standard of living) are reduced. Similarly, if the terms of trade improve, the standard of living has risen.

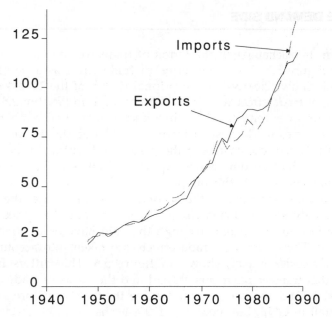

Figure 5.3 Exports and imports at constant (1985) prices, 1948-88

Source: Economic Trends.

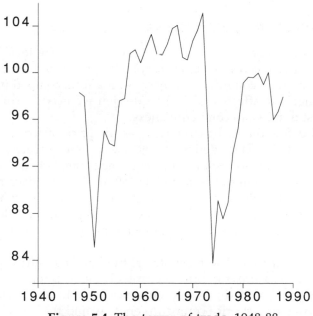

Figure 5.4 The terms of trade, 1948-88

Source: Export price divided by import price, calculated from national accounts data in *Economic Trends Annual Supplement*. Note that it refers to all trade, not just visible trade.

The effects of changes in the terms of trade are shown in figures 5.5 and 5.6. Figure 5.5 shows the terms of trade effect as a percentage of GNP. This shows clearly the exceptional nature of the 1973-4 oil crisis: the terms of trade effect was equivalent to a fall in GNP of 2.5 per cent in 1973 and 3 per cent in 1974. This effect was gradually reversed over the next few years. The loss of income in 1986 of about 1 per cent can also be attributed to a change in the price of oil, but this time a fall. By 1986 the UK had become a net exporter of oil (see chapter 9) which meant that changes in the oil price had the opposite effect from in 1973-4. In 1979, the time of the second OPEC price rise, the UK was approximately self- sufficient in oil, which meant that price changes had no effect on real income (though they did have other effects — see chapter 8). These terms of trade effects are taken into account in *real national disposable income*, shown in figure 5.6. This differs from real GNP in that transfer payments abroad and the terms of trade effect are deducted. 1974-5, the two years following the first OPEC price rise, saw a sharp fall in GNP, but, because of the terms of trade effect, an even larger fall in RNDI. After the 1979 oil price rise real GNP fell sharply, but because there was no significant terms of trade effect, RNDI fell only by a similar amount.

Measures of competitiveness

In addition to income the main factor determining the level of exports and imports is the competitiveness of UK producers compared with producers in other countries. It is because it affects competitiveness that the exchange rate affects trade. The question we need to consider now is how best to measure competitiveness.

We will define the exchange rate, e, as the price of foreign currency: e.g. $1 = £0.50. This definition is used here because it is the conventional way to define the exchange rate in the economics literature (the economics literature has followed US practice rather than British), even though in the UK we often define it the other way round (e.g. £1 = $2). Note that defining the exchange rate as the price of foreign currency means that a devaluation *raises e* and if sterling appreciates *e falls*.

Price competitiveness. The most straightforward measures of competitiveness are measures of price competitiveness. Suppose the world price of a good is P^* (in foreign currency) and the UK price is P (in sterling). An index of price competitiveness would then be

$$P/eP^*$$

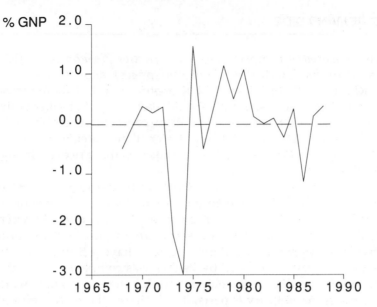

Figure 5.5 The terms of trade and real income, 1967-88

Source: Economic Trends Annual Supplement.

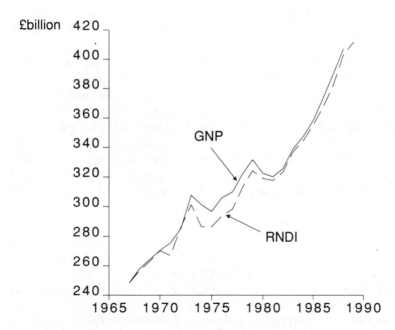

Figure 5.6 GNP and real national disposable income, 1967-89

Source: as figure 5.5.

Two such measures of competitiveness are *relative producer prices* (RPP — the ratio of foreign to UK wholesale prices) and *relative export prices* — REP the ratio of foreign to UK export prices). If these indices *rise* this indicates that UK producers are becoming *less* competitive relative to foreign producers. Such a fall in competitiveness can arise either because UK prices are rising faster than foreign prices, or because sterling is appreciating (i.e. because e, the price of foreign currency, is falling).

The problem with such measures, whether we use export prices or domestic prices, is that they give no indication of what is happening to profitability. If UK firms are forced by foreign competition to accept lower profit margins this will not show up in measures of price competitiveness. Suppose, for example, that we have a British industry which faces rising costs not faced by its overseas competitors, and that the market for its product is so competitive that there is a single world price. As long as the industry exports, it will charge the world price for its product and when costs have risen sufficiently high it will stop producing. At no time in this process will measures of price competitiveness change: whilst goods are being produced prices are unchanged, and when they stop being produced they are no longer considered. Measures of price competitiveness give no indication of the situation facing potential producers or potential exporters.

Profitability. An alternative approach is the index of the *relative profitability of exporting* (RPE). This is the ratio of export prices to domestic prices. The index of domestic prices that is commonly used is the wholesale price index. If the index rises we can deduce that exporting is becoming more profitable compared with producing for the home market, which means that firms should have a greater incentive to export. Note that changes in the exchange rate should affect this measure of competitiveness: if the foreign currency price of exports is determined by overseas demand conditions a change in the exchange rate will change the sterling export price and hence the ratio of export prices to domestic wholesale prices.

The relative profitability of exporting has two major weaknesses. The first is that, like measures of price-competitiveness, it gives no indication of the situation facing potential exporters. The second is that it takes no account of the level of profitability in exporting firms. High profits, whether earned through exports or through domestic sales, may be important in determining exporters' competitiveness: profits at home may enable exporters to subsidize exports, or they may cover the investment needed to sustain exports. A rise in domestic prices and profits will in practice improve export competitiveness, but the relative profitability of exporting will be reduced, suggesting a reduced incentive to export.

Cost competitiveness. The final measure to consider is *relative unit labour costs* (RULC). Unit labour costs (i.e. labour costs per unit of output) in the UK are given by

$$ULC = WL/Y = W/y,$$

where W is the wage rate (in sterling), L is labour employed, Y is output and y is output per unit of labour input (Y/L). Similarly, overseas unit labour costs are

$$ULC^* = eW^*L^*/Y^* = eW^*/y^*$$

where the asterisks indicate the rest of the world. The rest of the world's wage rate, W^*, is of course in foreign currency, which means we have to multiply by the exchange rate to convert to sterling. If we take the ratio of UK to foreign unit labour costs we obtain relative unit labour costs (RULC):

$$RULC = ULC/ULC^* = (1/e)(W/W^*)(y/y^*).$$

RULC thus depends on three things: the exchange rate, relative wage rates and relative productivity levels.

Two measures of RULC are usually calculated. The first is calculated exactly as described so far. The second, referred to as *normalized* RULC — RULC(N), takes account of cyclical variations in productivity. The reason for this is that output per head varies over the business cycle, not because of any fundamental change in productivity, but simply because the degree of capacity utilization changes as output changes (see chapter 6). The argument for taking account of this in measuring RULC is that international competitiveness depends on the underlying productivity trend, not on short-term productivity levels.

RULC has the important advantage over other measures of competitiveness that it measures what is happening to costs, something that the other measures of competitiveness discussed above do not do. Its major disadvantage is that it ignores non-labour costs. A change in the price of imported raw materials, for example, could affect competitiveness without having any effect on RULC.

The main measures of UK international competitiveness are shown in figure 5.7. Several conclusions can be drawn from this figure.

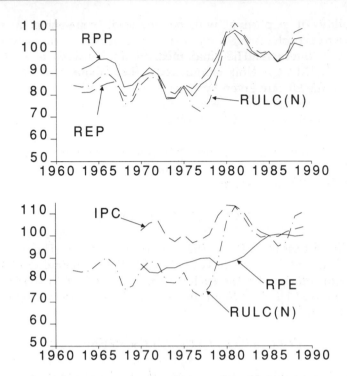

Figure 5.7 Measures of international competitiveness, 1963-89

Source: Economic Trends.

❏ From 1963 to 1967, competitiveness, whichever measure we take, was falling (relative costs and prices rising): inflation was higher in the UK than elsewhere. The government was attempting to prevent this decline in competitiveness by using incomes policy to reduce the rates of wage and price inflation. Devaluation, in November 1967, when sterling fell from $2.80 to $2.40, produced a sudden improvement in competitiveness, which was then gradually eroded over the next few years.

❏ From 1972 to 1977, the fall in the value of sterling improved competitiveness, except in 1975 when UK inflation was very high relative to world inflation.

❏ We then have the main feature of the graph: the *enormous* rise in all three indices, especially RULC, between 1977 and 1981, the rise being particularly steep in 1979-80. In the space of 2 years RULC rose by 50 per cent. This loss of competitiveness was the result of sterling appreciating very fast at a time when wages were rising much faster in the UK than in the rest of the world.

❑ Since 1981 there has been an improvement in competitiveness, again because of a falling exchange rate (wage inflation has remained higher than in most industrial economies).

In this section we have focused on exchange rates and relative inflation rates, because these have fluctuated far more than have productivity growth rates. Productivity growth rates are discussed in chapter 6.

5.2 EXPORT AND IMPORT FUNCTIONS

Exports

The theory underlying both export and import functions is very simple: it is that demand should depend on the purchasing country's income and on the exporting country's competitiveness. Exports are purchased by the rest of the world, so we need a variable to measure world demand. Rather than use world GDP, however, it is common to use world trade: total world exports. There are two main reasons for this. The first is that data on world trade are easier to obtain. The second is that world trade is likely to be more closely linked to world demand than a variable such as world GDP. Because data were easily accessible, the equation below uses total OECD exports. Competitiveness could be measured by any of the measures discussed above. The one used here is RULC (normalized to eliminate fluctuations due solely to changes in capacity utilization — see section 5.1 above). If we estimate a simple export equation we obtain the following,

$$X_t = 0.05WX_{t-1} - 0.29RULC_{t-1} + 40.2$$

where X and WX are exports and world exports (world exports are measured at 1980 prices as data in 1985 prices were not available). As expected, exports increase with world trade and they decline when relative unit labour costs rise (when competitiveness declines).

This is a very simple equation. Not only is it mathematically simple, but it is also simple in the sense that we have a single equation to determine exports as a whole, rather than separate equations for goods and services. In most econometric models exports are disaggregated into manufactures, oil, services, etc. In addition, much more complicated lags are used in order to find an equation that fits the data even better. The income and price elasticities in this equation are, however, consistent with those in more complicated models.

❏ It implies that the 'world trade' elasticity of demand for exports is 0.84: that a 1 per cent increase in world trade is associated with a rise of less than 1 per cent in UK exports. This is consistent with the UK's share of world exports having fallen progressively over time as world trade has expanded.

❏ It suggests a low 'price' elasticity of demand, of around 0.35. This is probably the result of our having lumped all exports together. The National Institute model, for example, has a much higher elasticity of demand for manufactures, and a zero elasticity of demand for non-manufactured goods (excluding oil).

Imports

The main variable we will use to determine imports is total final expenditure (*TFE*):

$$TFE = C + I + G + X,$$

where *C*, *I*, *G* and *X* are consumption, investment, government expenditure and exports respectively — total spending on goods and services before deducting imports. If we deduct imports we have GDP. As a cost variable, normalized relative unit labour costs will be used. In addition we use a measure of excess capacity. The justification for this is that when the economy is being run at a relatively high level of demand businesses will turn to imports because the goods they want are unavailable at home. For example, at the moment many construction firms are importing bricks and cement even though they would not normally do so: the reason is that demand is so high that domestic producers are quoting delivery dates of several months.

If we estimate a simple import function we obtain the following.

$$M_t = 0.34TFE_{t-1} + 0.39RULC_{t-2} - 0.55XSC_t - 78.7$$

Here *M* is imports and *XSC* is the measure of excess capacity shown in figure 1.5. It is zero in 1973 and 1979. It has been modified to give full capacity in about 1989, on the grounds that, despite high unemployment, the UK is exhibiting many of the symptoms associated with full capacity, notably rising imports and rising inflation.

The coefficients in this equation are much what we would expect. The marginal propensity to import is about 1/3, implying an income elasticity of demand of about 1.5 Imports appear to be less responsive to relative unit labour costs than are exports. The elasticity of demand is slightly higher (0.48 compared with 0.35). On the other hand, a change in RULC takes 2 years to affect imports, but only one year to affect exports. This conclusion that imports respond more slowly to relative costs than do exports is supported by more complicated models: the National Institute model, for example, has a similar difference. Finally, we get the result that if excess capacity falls by £1 billion, imports rise by £0.55 billion. This means that if output rises without any rise in capacity the effective marginal propensity to import is much higher than 0.34.

An alternative way of specifying this equation is to have the marginal propensity to import depending on competitiveness. If we estimate such an equation we obtain:

$$M_t = \alpha TFE_{t-1} - 0.57 XSC_t - 43.9$$

where

$$\alpha = 0.25 + 0.0010 RULC_{t-2}$$

This is the type of import function used in some macroeconomic models (e.g. the National Institute model). It is easy to check that it gives income and price elasticities that are very similar to those given by the simpler import function described above.

5.3 CONCLUSIONS

The evidence from these equations concerning income elasticities can be summed up in terms of a number of 'stylized facts' about UK trade.

❏ UK imports have grown more quickly than UK demand (the high income elasticity).

❏ UK exports have grown more slowly than world trade (the low income elasticity).

These two stylized facts, which we can describe in terms of income elasticities, have been used to provide a very pessimistic diagnosis of Britain's perennial balance of payments problems. One of the main problems confronting the UK economy since the war has been the high level of imports: booms have frequently ended because of a balance of payments crisis caused by high imports. It has been suggested that the reason for this can be found in the income elasticities contained in the export and import functions we have just considered. The argument is that if the income elasticity of demand for imports is high and the income elasticity of demand for exports is low, then if the UK grows at the same rate as the rest of the world imports will grow faster than exports. This argument has very pessimistic implications for it suggests that if the UK is to avoid balance of payments problems it must grow more slowly than the rest of the world in order to prevent imports from rising faster than exports.

There is also, however, a third stylized fact about UK trade:

❑ UK exports have grown more quickly than UK output (the same is true of world trade and world output).

It is possible that exports rise more quickly than output simply because of increasing specialization. If the trade balance is to remain constant on average a high growth of exports must lead to a high growth of imports. In this case a high level of import penetration (a high ratio of imports to GDP) may be nothing to be concerned about. This argument may not be enough to explain the UK's apparently poor export performance but it should serve as a warning against seemingly persuasive, over-simple explanations such as the one discussed above.

The evidence also suggests that competitiveness has a significant effect on both exports and imports, with exports responding more quickly and more strongly. Given the importance of exports and imports in the UK economy (in 1988 exports were 28 per cent and imports 32 per cent of GDP) together with significant price elasticities of demand it can be argued that the exchange rate, which affects competitiveness, is a key variable in regulating the level of aggregate demand. This effect may be more important than the effect, stressed in elementary macroeconomics textbooks, of interest rates on investment.

FURTHER READING

One of the best discussions of international competitiveness is contained in the House of Commons Select Committee *Monetary Policy, Volume I: Report* (HC163-I, 1980-1), chapter 7; or the memorandum 'Competitiveness', by W. Buiter in Volume II (HC163-II, 1980-1), pp. 102-20. The issue is also discussed in 'Measures of competitiveness', *Bank of England Quarterly Bulletin* 22, 1982, pp. 369-75. The links between exchange rates, productivity and competitiveness are explored in V. Rossi *et al* 'Exchange rates, productivity and international competitiveness,' *Oxford Review of Economic Policy* 1(3), 1986, pp. 56-73. To see an example of the trade equations that appear in large forecasting models, see S. Brooks 'Exports and imports,' in A. Britton (ed.) *Employment, Output and Inflation: the National Institute Model of the British Economy* (London: Heinemann, 1983).

The focus of this chapter has been fairly narrow. Readers wanting a wider discussion of trade policy and protection could consult: V. Rossi and M. Clements 'The world economy: analysis and prospects,' *Oxford Review of Economic Policy* 1(1), 1985; A. Boltho and C. Allsopp 'The assessment: trade and trade policy,' *Oxford Review of Economic Policy* 3(1), 1987; S. Page 'The rise of protection since 1974,' *Oxford Review of Economic Policy* 3(1), 1987; F. Cripps and W. Godley 'Control of imports as a means to full employment and expansion of world trade,' *Cambridge Journal of Economics* 1978, pp. 327-34; Anthony Venables and Alasdair Smith 'Trade and industrial policy under imperfect competition,' *Economic Policy* 3, 1986, pp. 621-72.

The Supply Side

Productivity

6.1 MEASURING PRODUCTIVITY GROWTH

Output per head

The simplest, and most frequently used, measure of productivity is output per head, shown in figure 6.1. This gives data for both the whole economy and for manufacturing. Manufacturing is picked out for two main reasons. The first is that, for reasons discussed below, it is easier to measure productivity in manufacturing than in some other sectors of the economy. The second is that manufacturing is important for foreign trade and manufacturing productivity is a crucial influence on international competitiveness, which means that more concern is often paid to manufacturing productivity than to productivity in other sectors of the economy.

Four points are worth making about figure 6.1: the strong cyclical behaviour of productivity; the difference between economy-wide and manufacturing productivity growth rates; the poor productivity performance of the mid to late 1970s; and the recovery after 1980.

❏ Productivity growth exhibits a strong cyclical pattern. Productivity rises fast in booms and falls or rises more slowly in recessions. This can be accounted for simply by variations in utilization rates: in booms factors, both capital and labour, are more fully utilized, so output per head and total factor productivity rise. In recessions the reverse occurs. This 'hoarding' of capital and labour during recessions is usually explained in terms of adjustment costs. It is

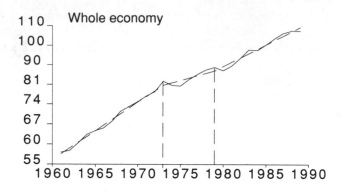

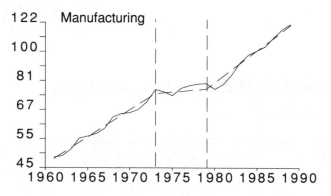

Figure 6.1 Output per head, 1961-89

Source: Economic Trends. Broken lines give trends.

expensive for firms to change both their capital stock and their labour force. There are costs attached to hiring and firing workers and, in addition, if firms were to reduce employment too far during a recession they might find that they were unable to recruit suitable replacements when the boom came.

❑ Productivity has risen faster in manufacturing than in the economy as a whole. This may reflect more rapid technical change in manufacturing, but it probably also reflects measurement problems. Most manufacturing output is directly measurable which means it is fairly easy to observe productivity growth, despite the inevitable index-number problems. In contrast, many services have to be valued at the cost of the inputs used, the reason being that output cannot directly be measured. Education and public administration, for example, may be becoming more efficient without this being reflected in measures of output.

❏ The growth rate of productivity fell sharply during the 1970s. In the recessions of 1974-5 and 1980 productivity *fell* and in the intervening years (1976-9) it rose very slowly. This poor productivity performance during the 1970s is part of a worldwide phenomenon, usually referred to as the productivity slowdown of the 1970s.

❏ Finally we have a period of improved performance since 1980.

The reasons for these last two phenomena are considered in the next section.

Total factor productivity

For many purposes it is enough to use output per head as a measure of productivity. When it comes to productivity growth, however, it is important to develop a better measure, for output per head may rise for several reasons. (1) Firms may be using more capital-intensive methods. (2) Capital and labour may be being more fully utilized. (3) There may be systematic measurement errors causing measured output per head to rise even though there has been no 'real' change. (4) Resources may be being used more efficiently. When we talk about productivity growth we are usually concerned simply with the last of these. To measure this, therefore, we have to find a way to separate this from the other three effects.

The way economists most often attempt to disentangle the effects of productivity growth from the other factors which cause output per head to change is to calculate what is usually referred to as the growth of either *total factor productivity* or *multi-factor productivity*. To calculate this we start with output per unit of labour input and then deduct the effects of any change in capital per worker (for more detail see box 6.1). This is done using the formula

$$g_{TFP} = g_{Y/L} - 0.33 g_{K/L}.$$

where g_{TFP} is the growth rate of total factor productivity, $g_{Y/L}$ is the growth rate of output per worker and $g_{K/L}$ is the growth rate of capital per worker. The share of profits in output is assumed to be as near 1/3

BOX 6.1 TOTAL FACTOR PRODUCTIVITY

Assume that we have a production function, relating output to inputs of capital (K) and labour (L). Output also rises with time (t) as productivity increases.

$$Y = F(K, L, t)$$

From this it follows that,

$$\Delta Y = MPK.\Delta K + MPL.\Delta L + MPT.\Delta t$$

where MPK and MPL are the marginal products of capital and labour. MPT is what might be described as the 'marginal product of time': the amount by which output would increase over time if inputs of capital and labour were constant. Dividing by Δt we obtain

$$\Delta Y/\Delta t \;=\; MPK(\Delta K/\Delta t) + MPL(\Delta L/\Delta t) + MPT$$

If we divide both sides by Y and rearrange the terms we can obtain

$$g_Y \;=\; MPK(K/Y)g_K + MPL(L/Y)g_L + MPT/Y$$

where g_Y, g_K and g_L are the proportional growth rates of output, capital and labour respectively, these being defined by $g_Y = (1/Y)(\Delta Y/\Delta t)$, $g_K = (1/K)(\Delta K/\Delta t)$ and $g_L = (1/L)(\Delta L/\Delta t)$.

If there is perfect competition, the wage rate (w) will equal the marginal product of labour, and the rate of profit (r) will equal the marginal product of capital. Our equation can thus be re-written as

$$g_Y = (rK/Y)g_K + (wL/Y)g_L + z,$$

where $z = MPT/Y$ is the rate by which output will grow if capital and labour are constant. This variable, z, is the growth rate of *total factor productivity* or *multi-factor productivity*. This equation provides an easy way to measure z, because rk/Y and wL/Y are the shares of profits and wages in output. If we assume that the shares of profits and wages in national income are constant at one third and two thirds respectively (this is a good enough approximation, as small changes would make very little difference to the results), z can be calculated using the formula

$$z = g_Y - 0.33g_K - 0.67g_L.$$

We can also derive the relationship between the growth rate of total factor productivity and the growth rate of output per head.

$$z = g_Y - g_L - 0.33(g_K - g_L) = g_{Y/L} - 0.33g_{K/L}.$$

If we are concerned to estimate trend growth rates of multi-factor productivity, a slight variation in this method is appropriate. It can be shown that, assuming that there is perfect competition, the shares of profits and wages in national income will be constant if and only if the production function has the special form,

$$Y = Ae^{nt}K^\alpha L^{1-\alpha},$$

where the parameter α is the share of profits in income, with $1-\alpha$ being the share of wages. Taking logarithms of both sides, this becomes

$$\log(Y) = \log(A) + nt + \alpha\log(K) + (1-\alpha)\log(L).$$

Given data on Y, K and L we can obtain estimates of A, n and α.

This method has the advantage that, once we have worked out these parameters, we can calculate 'full-employment' output by replacing the labour that is actually employed, L, with the size of the labour force, N:

Using this, we can work out full-employment output, Y^f by replacing actual employment, L, with N the total labour force, to obtain:

$$Y^f = Ae^{nt}K^\alpha N^{1-\alpha}.$$

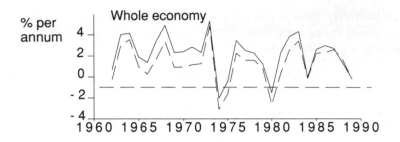

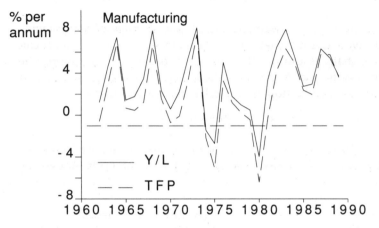

Figure 6.2 Productivity growth rates, 1961-89

Source: see appendix.

Table 6.1 Productivity growth — period averages

	Economy		Manufacturing	
	Y/L	TFP	Y/L	TFP
1961-73	2.9	1.6	3.8	2.4
1973-79	1.3	0.3	0.5	-1.2
1979-88	2.2	1.6	4.4	3.1

Source: as for figure 6.2.

as makes no difference. The results are shown in figure 6.2. The main trends are summarized in table 6.1.

The estimates of total factor productivity growth shown in figure 6.2 and table 6.1 show that the productivity slowdown of the 1970s cannot be explained by the fall in the rate of capital accumulation which took place then. The decline in total factor productivity growth was just as great as the decline in the growth rate of output per worker: the two series move very closely together.

The importance of allowing for changes in the rate of growth of the capital stock is shown by looking at the figures for the productivity growth in the whole economy. Since 1979 output per head has been growing more slowly than before 1973, suggesting that productivity growth, though it has certainly recovered compared with the 1970s, has not even regained its former level. On the other hand, total factor productivity has grown faster since 1979 than before 1973. The explanation is that investment has been low since 1979 and capital per head has been growing more slowly.

Measurement errors

All the estimates of productivity growth discussed so far ignore the problem of variations in capacity utilization and the possibility of systematic measurement errors. If the average growth rates calculated in table 6.1 were for very long periods we might be able to assume that the effects of measurement errors and changes in capacity utilization would be averaged out. For the fairly short periods we are considering this cannot be assumed.

There are several reasons why we might expect there to be systematic errors in the measurement of output per head and total factor productivity during the 1970s. Consider first some of the reasons why there may have been systematic biases in the measurement of output during the 1970s. The Central Statistical Office (CSO), the organization responsible for constructing estimates of the UK capital stock, starts with data on the money value of gross output produced by a large number of firms. To get from this to a measure of output (real value added) it is necessary to do three things: (1) to aggregate data on individual firms to obtain measures for the economy (or sector) as a whole; (2) to convert data on gross output into estimates of value added; and (3) to use price indices to convert values into estimates of real output. During the 1970s there were enormous fluctuations in prices, exchanges rates and output, which caused a number of problems with the last two of these stages.

❏ It has been argued that when energy and raw material prices rise, as happened during the 1970s, firms will economize on energy and raw materials, raising the ratio of value added to gross output. If the CSO uses the same weights as in previous periods, therefore, rising energy and raw material prices will lead to the growth in value added being under-estimated. The CSO's estimates of productivity will be too low.

❏ There are problems in obtaining the correct prices with which to convert values into measures of real output. As no suitable deflators exist for export prices, domestic prices are used instead. When exchange rates are changing, export prices are likely to be changing relative to domestic prices, the result being incorrect estimates of output. If the change in export prices is over-estimated, for example, the volume (value divided by price) will be under-estimated. Changes in the exchange rate and the inflation rate also cause problems because of divergences between list prices and the prices at which transactions actually take place. If sterling appreciates, for example, exporters will have to reduce their sterling prices to maintain their competitiveness in terms of foreign currency. List prices will take time to adjust. If it is list prices that are reported, there will be an upward bias in the price index, and downward bias in measuring output. Finally, problems are caused by price controls, which were important between 1973 and 1977. Because firms were subject to price controls they will have had an incentive to keep reported prices low.

For various reasons, therefore, the growth of output during the 1970s may be under-estimated by the official statistics.

A potentially even more serious problem arises with the measurement of the capital stock. Capital stock is estimated by starting with an initial stock, adding new investment and subtracting the capital which is thought to have been scrapped during the year (this gives the gross capital stock; to obtain the net capital stock we subtract depreciation instead of scrapping). To do this we need an estimate of the lifetime of capital equipment so that we can calculate how much scrapping is taking place. The major problem here is that the lifetime of capital equipment is not fixed, but depends on economic factors: capital is scrapped not when it no longer works but when it becomes uneconomic to continue to use it. In a time of rapid economic change the statisticians' estimates of capital goods' lifetimes are liable to become out of date, with the result that scrapping will be wrongly estimated. This is thought to have been a particular problem during the 1970s: for example, sharply rising energy prices made much capital uneconomic earlier than would otherwise have been the case.

Improved estimates of productivity growth

To improve on the estimates of total factor productivity given above we need to adjust for both variations in capacity utilization and possible measurement errors. This is not the impossible task it might seem, for although neither utilization rates nor measurement errors can be directly observed, they are both likely to be correlated with other variables which can be measured.

❑ Utilization rates will be linked to overtime hours worked. If overtime hours are being worked we can assume that the labour force is fully utilized. If no overtime is being worked then we do not know whether or not labour is working to capacity. Using information on overtime hours, therefore, it is possible to work out a measure of 'effective hours' worked and to use this in place of actual hours as the measure of labour input.

❑ Biases in measuring output can be allowed for by assuming that they varied depended on changes in competitiveness, raw material prices relative to output prices and the intensity of price controls. These variables can therefore be included in a regression equation so as to capture the effects of measurement errors.

Estimates of total factor productivity growth estimated using these methods are shown in table 6.2. The columns give the growth rates of output per head and total factor productivity calculated in the same way as the estimates discussed earlier in this chapter. The only difference is that here the 1979-80 recession is separated from the later period. The data from which these estimates are derived are shown in figure 6.3.

Given the large fall in productivity during 1979-80, the average growth rates for 1980-88 are clearly much higher than those for 1979-88 given in table 6.1. Both sets of figures (i.e. with and without a break in trend in 1980) are provided because it is not clear which is best. If we are concerned with long run productivity trends we should try to avoid changes in productivity which are simply the result of the business cycle. It makes sense, therefore, to go from one cyclical peak to another (i.e. 1979-88). If our trend runs from a depression year to a boom year (i.e. 1980-8) it will include the productivity growth caused by the

Table 6.2 Productivity growth in manufacturing, 1960-89

	Y/L	TFP1	TFP2	TFP3	TFP4
1960-73	3.7	2.3	2.3		
1973-79	1.3	0.0	0.6	0.8**	0.95
1979-80	-3.8	-8.5	-1.9	-1.5	-1.07
1980-88	5.0	4.1	2.76*	3.5***	

*1980-85; **1970-79; ***1980-87.

Source: Y/L — growth rate of output per head. TFP1 — TFP growth rates calculated as $g_{Y/L} - 0.33 g_{K/L}$. TFP2 — TFP growth rates allowing for utilization as described in the text, from J. Muellbauer, *Oxford Review of Economic Policy*, 2(3), pp. i-xxv. TFP3 — TFP growth rates allowing for utilization from *Bank of England Quarterly Bulletin* 29(1), pp. 23-6. TFP4 — TFP2 adjusted for capital measurement errors.

upswing of the business cycle and will be an over-estimate of the long term trend (compare figures 6.1 and 6.3). On the other hand, if we believe that the 1979-80 recession was unusual and that there was a change in productivity performance after 1980, then we do need to distinguish these two periods. The only satisfactory solution, therefore, is to provide both sets of figures (i.e. tables 6.1 and 6.2).

Column 3 of table 6.2 contains estimates, labelled TFP2, of total factor productivity growth made by Muellbauer. The regression equations from which these were obtained included overtime hours and various inflation and exchange rate terms, designed to eliminate the effects of measurement errors and variations in capacity utilization. Column 4, labelled TFP3, contains more recent estimates prepared by the Bank of England using the same methods as Muellbauer. These have the advantage of being based on more up-to-date data than Muellbauer's estimates. The disadvantage is that they do not go back to the 1960s and the break is taken in 1970, not 1973.

For the 1960s it makes little difference which method is used to estimate total factor productivity growth. This is not surprising. Comparison of TFP1 with TFP2 suggests that some of the apparent slowdown after 1973 was the result of measurement errors and a fall in utilization rates: when these are taken into account total factor productivity grew at 0.6 per cent per annum, whereas the 'unadjusted' measure shows no growth at all. The main contrast, however, comes during the 1979-80 recession when the 'unadjusted' measure, TFP1,

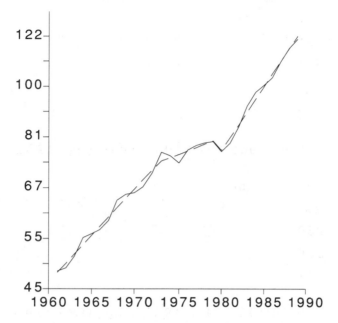

Figure 6.3 Output per head in manufacturing, 1961-89

Source: Economic Trends.

shows an 8.1 per cent per annum fall in productivity. Comparison with either of the other two measures suggests that, though the fall in total factor productivity (either 1.5 per cent or 1.9 per cent) was still substantial, most of this 8.1 per cent was the result of a fall in capacity utilization (measurement errors may have been present but are hardly likely to have been substantial compared with the fall in utilization). For the period since 1980 there is, once again, little difference between the two methods. TFP1 is slightly higher than either of the other measures but this could easily be because the other measures are for earlier periods (ending in 1985 and 1987).

6.2 MEASURING FULL-CAPACITY OUTPUT

In figure 6.4 are three different estimates of full-capacity output. The reason three different estimates are given is to illustrate some of the problems involved in such a seemingly simple concept. The first estimate, shown in figure 6.4(a), is the simplest. It is based on the assumption that full-capacity GDP can be obtained from actual GDP using the unemployment rate: by dividing actual GDP by the level of

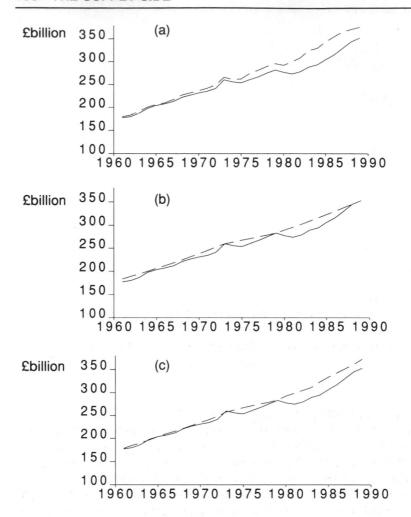

Figure 6.4 Estimates of full-capacity GDP, 1961-89

Source: see appendix. Solid lines give actual output

employment and multiplying by the labour force. There are, however, enormous problems with this method: it assumes that the number of additional people who could be employed is the same as the number of those registered as unemployed and that each of them would produce the same output, on average, as those already employed. We would not expect either of these to be true. There is also the problem that potential output may be limited by the available capital stock (by physical productive capacity). If this is the case, 'full-employment output', in the

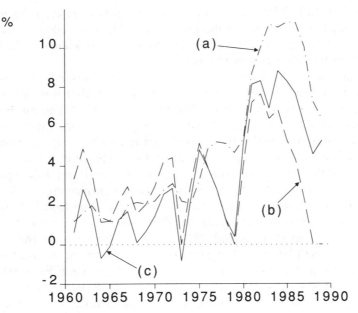

%

Figure 6.5 Estimates of the output gap, 1961-89

Source: Percentage differences between measures of full-capacity output and actual output shown in figure 6.4.

sense of the output that would be produced if the labour force were utilized as fully as possible given existing resources, may be very different from the level shown in figure 6.4(a).

A second way of estimating full-capacity output is to pick out certain years in which the economy is known to have been operating at roughly full capacity and to assume that full capacity output grew at a constant rate between this years. This is the basis for the estimates of full-capacity output given in figure 6.4(b). In calculating this the years 1950, 1955, 1964-5, 1973, 1979 and 1989 were taken to be years of full-capacity output. In such years firms complain of labour shortages, prices rise more rapidly and so on. For the years before 1973 such a method presents few problems, for the evidence is consistent with the hypothesis that full-capacity output grew at a constant rate from the early 1950s to 1973: a single trend links all these years of full capacity. After 1973, however, the problems become greater, for there is evidence that the long run growth rate has changed. This means that, if we are estimating growth rates by drawing lines between cyclical peaks, each cycle (1973-9 and 1979-89) having its own growth rate, it becomes difficult to extrapolate beyond the latest peak. The advantage of such a measure is that it takes account of important evidence which is neglected by the other two methods.

The final panel in figure 6.4 shows an alternative measure of full-capacity output, this time based on the equation that was estimated to calculate the growth rate of total-factor productivity. The method is to calculate what output would have been given actual capital stock and the estimated growth rate of total factor productivity, if employment had been equal to the total labour force (see box 6.1 for more detail). As with estimate (a), the gap between actual and full-capacity output (shown in figure 6.5) depends on the unemployment rate, but there are two differences in the way this is done. The first is that the measure of full capacity is based on the *trend* level of output (with breaks in the trend in 1973 and 1979, as in figure 6.1), not the actual level. The second is that a 1 per cent rise in employment is assumed to produce a rise in output of only two-thirds of 1 per cent: the elasticity of output with respect to labour is assumed to equal two-thirds.

For the period before 1979, this estimate looks similar to estimate (b) above. This is despite its being derived in a completely different way: in deriving estimate (c) we did not make any assumption about which years were ones of full employment. After about 1983, however, the two measures diverge, estimate (c) looking more like estimate (a), failing to show a return to full capacity by 1989 (though the gap between actual and potential output is, for the reason explained above) much smaller than the gap in case (a). This is particularly clear in figure 6.5.

There are two ways to interpret this difference. One is to believe estimate (c) and argue that, despite all appearances to the contrary, output was still significantly below its maximum in 1989. The other is to accept estimate (c) and to argue that estimate (b) is wrong for at least one of a number of reasons. (1) One reason is that, for reasons discussed above, the capital stock has grown more slowly than the statistics indicate: if the capital stock were lower, estimate (c) would be lower too. (2) Another possibility is that the relationship between employment and output changed during the 1980s: that when output started to expand, firms managed to raise productivity, not increasing employment by as much as they would have done in earlier periods. Such a view is consistent with the failure of employment to fall more rapidly after 1982, despite the rapid growth in output, though with a smaller gap between output and full-capacity output. (3) Finally, it could be argued, as many economists have, that the theoretical basis for the use of an aggregate production function is completely untenable, and that production functions such as the ones used here are not worth the paper they are printed on.

It should now be clear that the concept of full-employment, full-capacity, or potential output is fraught with difficulty. Any estimate must be treated with great caution. Of the three measures proposed here, the second seems less likely to be misleading than either of the other two. It is very clearly based on the assumption that certain years were ones of full-capacity output, and if these benchmarks are disputed, it is clear that our estimate of potential output has to be questioned. The theoretical and statistical basis for the last estimate is insufficiently strong for us to disregard the evidence about 1989 being a year when aggregate demand had raised output as high as it could.

6.3 THE PRODUCTIVITY SLOWDOWN OF THE 1970s

The international perspective

During the 1970s there was a significant slowdown in the rate of productivity growth, both in manufacturing and in the economy as a whole, this slowdown usually being dated from around 1973. Both labour productivity and total factor productivity were affected. Before we consider the causes of this slowdown it is important to note that it was a worldwide phenomenon, as is shown by table 6.3. The USA in particular experienced a productivity slowdown very similar to that of the UK. We would, therefore, not expect to find an explanation of the slowdown that made sense solely in Britain.

Table 6.3 International productivity growth rates

	1960-68	1968-73	1973-79	1979-85
UK	3.4	3.8	0.6	3.7
USA	3.2	3.8	0.9	3.5
Japan	9.0	10.4	5.0	6.3
Germany	4.7	4.5	3.1	2.4
France	6.8	5.8	3.9	n.a.

Source: Meen (1988), p. xxvi. Figures are annual percentage growth rates of value added per person in manufacturing.

Several explanations have been proposed for this widespread productivity slowdown. Of the three explanations considered here the first is relevant to the developed world as a whole and the other two apply to Europe. None is specific to the UK.

Energy prices

The first and most obvious explanation is to link the productivity slowdown to the rise in energy prices which took place during and after 1973. There are a number of ways in which this could have worked: the substitution of labour for energy; the need to switch production to export or import-substituting products; capital having to be scrapped sooner; or the result of a reduction in aggregate demand.

❏ As the price of energy rises firms substitute labour for energy. If capital and energy are complements they will also substitute labour for capital. This will raise labour per unit of output, and lower productivity.

❏ The oil price rise of 1973-4 meant that the UK, like most developed economies, was faced with large rise in the cost of its oil imports, which caused a large balance of payments deficit (see chapter 5). Borrowing was only a short-term solution, so it became necessary to increase exports or reduce imports. This necessitated a switch in production away from domestic demand to exports. Such a switch in demand would be costly and the result would be lower productivity.

❏ Rising energy prices may cause capital goods with a particularly high energy-usage to be either scrapped or under-utilized. Plant which is more energy-efficient will be more fully utilized, but the limited supply of such plant means that this cannot compensate for the under-utilization or scrapping of less energy-efficient plant.

❏ The oil shock, because of the way governments responded to it, produced a large 'Keynesian' demand shock, lowering output. Lower output generally causes lower productivity: labour tends to be hoarded (affecting labour productivity), and the incentive to innovate is reduced.

Of these explanations the one that seems most persuasive is the scrapping of energy-inefficient plant. Extensive substitution of other inputs for energy (the first explanation) simply did not occur. Some

Table 6.4 Energy prices and energy-output ratios

	UK		US	
	E/Y	P_E/P_Y	E/Y	P_E/P_Y
1973-81	- 3.4%	+46%	-13%	+220%
OPEC I	0%	27%	0%	82%
OPEC II	- 2.8%	16%	-12%	76%

OPEC I and II denote the oil price rises of 1973 and 1979 respectively.

Source: Ernst R. Berndt and David O. Wood 'Energy price shocks and the productivity slowdown in US and UK manufacturing,' *Oxford Review of Economic Policy* 2(3), 1986, pp. 1-31.

evidence is shown in table 6.4. During OPEC I the energy-output ratio did not change, either for the UK or the US, despite substantial rises in the price of energy relative to the price of output. The explanation must be that switching to more energy-efficient techniques requires new investment and that it is therefore a slow process. Furthermore, because energy use accounts for such a small proportion of costs, it is hard to see how substitution of other inputs for energy could account for such a large fall in productivity growth. The argument about energy and capital being complements, which might explain a large effect, is not supported by empirical evidence. OPEC I was unexpected, energy prices having fallen steadily for 50 years, which meant that firms were not in a position to economize on their use of energy. The option of simply reducing utilization rates for the the least energy-efficient vintages of plant, on the other hand, was something that could happen immediately.

An implication of this view is that what happened during the 1970s was, at least in part, a fall in the effective inputs of capital and, to a lesser extent, labour, rather than a fall in total factor productivity. This is not inconsistent with the estimates presented in table 6.2 which suggest that part of the slowdown could be accounted for by a rise in scrapping beyond that allowed for in the official capital stock figures.

The ending of circumstances favourable to growth

During the 1960s circumstances were, for a number of reasons, particularly favourable to growth in Europe, a situation which changed dramatically during the 1970s. During the 1970s resources became more scarce, concern for the environment increased, scope for technological catching-up with the US was reduced, and export-led growth became more difficult.

❑ Supplies of resources, including not simply energy (discussed above), but also other natural resources and skilled manpower, became less elastic. This, together with over-ambitious attempts at fine-tuning the economy, created inflationary problems. The need to stop accelerating inflation combined with the reluctance of workers to accept a lower growth rate of real wages led to lower profitability and higher interest rates. Investment, and hence the rate of technical progress, were thus reduced.

❑ There emerged a greater concern for 'qualitative' rather than simply 'quantitative' growth, with greater concern for the environment than was shown during the 1960s. This made business more uncertain and more pessimistic. Demands for greater protection of the environment (for example, pollution controls) reduced productivity.

❑ During the 1960s there was still significant scope for Europe to raise productivity by catching up with the United States. By the 1970s many of these opportunities for technological catching-up were exhausted.

❑ Many countries in Europe, together with Japan, experienced a period of export-led growth during the 1960s, this being made possible, at least in part, by the over-valuation of the US dollar. This came to an end in the 1970s.

These factors could account for the slowdown in growth throughout Europe. The first two could also apply to the United States.

Eurosclerosis

A slightly different argument to the one just presented (though the two are not at all inconsistent) is what has been termed 'Eurosclerosis'. The idea underlying it is that the development of the welfare state inhibited the economic adjustments necessary for rapid growth. There are several ways in which this could work. Generous unemployment benefits reduce the incentives for unemployed workers to find jobs and for those in work to moderate their wage demands. Restrictions on hiring and firing inhibit labour mobility and may reduce employment. The power of trade unions is increased. Social insurance charges raise costs relative to take-home pay. Protection and industrial policy inhibit industrial change.

This hypothesis has much to recommend it but there are serious difficulties with it. (1) It provides no explanation of why the slowdown should have come in the early 1970s rather than at any other time. The explanation that has been given is that as long as there were no serious problems, the precarious nature of the European economies' expansion was not revealed. Only when the world become less friendly did these problems become apparent. (2) It cannot be claimed that there has been an increase in government intervention in the 1980s. Slow growth continued in Europe, if not in Britain, for much of the 1980s. (3) The advent of the single European market in 1992 has produced a dramatic change in outlook, with significant growth being expected. If Euro-sclerosis was the fundamental problem its proponents portray it as being, it is hard to see how such a rapid transformation could have come about.

6.4 UK PRODUCTIVITY PERFORMANCE SINCE 1979

The recession of 1980-1

The second oil price rise, in 1979, produced a recession throughout the developed world. For most countries it can be seen as part of the longer period of low productivity growth which started in 1973. In the UK, however, the recession of 1980-1 was exceptionally severe, mainly because of the sudden introduction of a very tight monetary policy. As table 6.2 shows, productivity fell dramatically (the trends in output per head in manufacturing, which are not the same as those in figure 6.1, are shown in figure 6.3).

Output per head in manufacturing, the sector hardest hit by the recession, fell dramatically (see table 6.2). Output and employment fell sharply and, because there was no significant change in the capital stock, the capital-labour ratio rose (see figure 6.6). The result was that total factor productivity, calculated using the simple formula discussed above, fell by 8.1 per cent. What was happening, of course, was that capacity utilization fell sharply, this fall accounting for most of the fall in productivity. When we allow for changes in utilization, the fall in total factor productivity comes down to just under 2 per cent. This is large for total factor productivity but is much smaller than the change attributable to the fall in utilization rates.

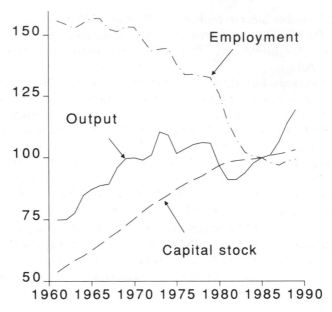

Figure 6.6 Output, employment and capital in manufacturing, 1961-89

Source: Economic Trends and *United Kingdom National Accounts*. Note that capital stock is the stock at the beginning of the year.

One consequence of this enormous fall in utilization was a large increase in scrapping (scrapping can be seen as an extreme case of low utilization) and a fall in the average age of capital equipment. Though there is some evidence which suggests that this may not have been the case, it is natural to assume that it was the least efficient capital that was scrapped. This would have raised the productivity of the capital stock that remained and may account for some of the increase in productivity which has since taken place. The 1980-1 recession has thus been called 'the great shake-out' in UK manufacturing.

Recovery since 1981

Since 1981 there has been a significant improvement in productivity growth, with rates exceeding those observed before 1973 (see table 6.2). This is in sharp contrast to the rest of Europe where productivity growth rates have, on the whole, remained similar to those experienced during the 1970s (see table 6.3 — note that the UK's relative performance would improve if 1980 or 1981 rather than 1979 were taken as the dividing line).

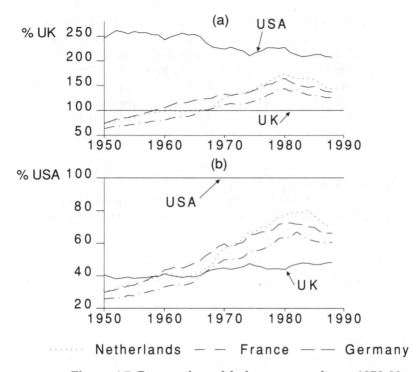

Figure 6.7 Gross value added per person hour, 1950-88

Source. B. van Ark 'Comparative levels of manufacturing productivity in postwar Europe' *Oxford Bulletin of Economics and Statistics,* 52(4), Special Issue, pp. 343-73.

UK productivity levels are compared with productivity levels in the USA and three European countries in figure 6.7. This shows that UK performance was worse than that of France, Germany and the Netherlands from 1950 to 1980, but that after 1980 the UK's relative decline ceased and the UK began to catch up quite rapidly, as is shown in part (a) of figure 6.7. Part (b), however, which shows productivity levels as percentages of US levels, suggests that this catching-up is as much due to European growth being low as to UK growth rates being high.

Several reasons have been put forward to account for this improvement: that it is simply a normal, cyclical phenomenon; that it is because of the scrapping of inefficient plant during the 1980-1 recession; and that it is because of the government's supply-side policies.

❏ The first explanation of the recovery since 1980 is that it is a cyclical phenomenon. The 1980-1 recession was very deep, the strength of the post-1981 boom merely reflecting the depth of the recession. Manufacturing output is still below its 1979 peak. One of the problems with taking 1980 as a starting point, which is essential if we believe productivity performance did change then, is that our estimates include the effects of a strong cyclical recovery.

❏ During the 1980-1 recession, an enormous amount of capital was scrapped. It is natural to assume that plant which is scrapped is of less than average productivity. Though the capital stock would have been reduced by high scrapping, it would have become more modern, permitting a higher growth rate of productivity.

❏ Finally, we have the 'Thatcher effect', with factors such as improved industrial relations, reductions in union power, privatization and deregulation, reductions in direct tax rates and so on.

It is still too early to assess these different explanations. Cyclical factors and the 'shedding of the sub-average' could certainly account for a lot, but the improvement in productivity performance has proved quite long-lasting. Furthermore, if the recession of 1980-1 did result in a large shake-out of old plant it is likely that capital is now increasing *faster* than the figures suggest (capital which is being recorded as being scrapped now was in fact scrapped during 1980-1). This would make total factor productivity growth appear faster than it is. If capital is growing more rapidly the prospects for rapid growth continuing are better. The test of whether the improvement in UK productivity performance is permanent or not is likely to come with the next recession.

FURTHER READING

One of the classic papers on the productivity slowdown is M. N. Baily 'Productivity and the services of capital and labour', *Brookings Papers on Economic Activity*, 1981(1), pp. 1-66, which argues that much of the slowdown in the USA can be explained in terms of a reduction in the effective supply of factor services. Possible errors in the measurement of the UK capital stock are investigated by S. Wadhwani and M. Wall 'The UK capital stock — new estimates of premature scrapping,' *Oxford Review of Economic Policy* 2(3), 1986, pp. 44-55. The role of energy costs in causing the slowdown is analysed in Ernst R. Berndt and David O. Wood 'Energy price shocks and the productivity slowdown in US and UK manufacturing,' *Oxford Review of Economic Policy* 2(3), 1986, pp. 1-31. A wider range of issues is examined in the *Economic Journal* symposium comprising: A. Lindbeck 'The recent slowdown of productivity growth', *Economic Journal* 93, 1983, pp. 13-34; H. Giersch and F. Wolter 'Towards an explanation of the productivity slowdown: an acceleration-deceleration hypothesis', *ibid.*, pp. 35-55; E. F. Denison 'The interruption of productivity growth in the United States', *ibid.*, pp. 56-77; D. J. Morris and S. J. Prais 'The recent slowdown in productivity growth: comments on the papers', *ibid.*, pp. 78-88.

An important reference on UK productivity growth rates during the 1980s is J. Muellbauer 'Productivity and competitiveness in British manufacturing,' *Oxford Review of Economic Policy* 2(3), 1986, pp. 1-25, where data on overtime hours worked are used in an attempt to eliminate the effects of changes in capacity utilization from estimates of total factor productivity growth in manufacturing. A favourable verdict on recent productivity performance also emerges in Bart van Ark 'Comparative levels of manufacturing productivity in postwar Europe', *Oxford Bulletin of Economics and Statistics* 52(4), 1990, pp. 343-74, where British performance is viewed alongside that of Germany, France the Netherlands and the USA. These comparisons are notable because they are based on appropriate purchasing power parity data. A slightly older comparative study is A. Steven Englander and Axel Mittelstädt 'Total factor productivity: macroeconomic and structural aspects of the slowdown,' *OECD Economic Studies* 10, 1988, pp. 7-56. A more pessimistic view is found by emphasising GDP per capita rather than manufacturing productivity, as is done by Charles Feinstein and Robin Matthews 'The growth of output and productivity in the UK: the 1980s as a phase of the post-war period', *National Institute Economic Review*, 133, August 1990, pp. 78-90. International comparisons of productivity levels can be found in many places: Bart van Ark 'Comparative levels of labour productivity in Dutch and British manufacturing,' *National*

Institute Economic Review, 131, February 1990, pp. 71-85; Bart van Ark 'Manufacturing productivity levels in France and the United Kingdom', *National Institute Economic Review*, 133, August 1990, pp. 62-77. The role of educational differences in explaining productivity levels in different countries is explored in a series of papers: A. Daly, D. Hitchens and K. Wagner 'Productivity, machinery and skills in a sample of British and German manufacturing plants: results of a pilot inquiry,' *National Institute Economic Review* 111, 1985, pp. 48-61; S. Prais and K. Wagner 'Productivity and management: the training of foremen in Britain and Germany,' *National Institute Economic Review* 123, 1988, pp. 34-47; H. Steedman 'Vocational training in Britain: mechanical and electrical craftsmen,' *National Institute Economic Review* 126, 1988, pp. 57-70; H. Steedman and K. Wagner 'A second look at productivity, machinery and skills in Britain and Germany,' *National Institute Economic Review* 122, 1987, pp. 84-96.

Cross-section evidence, analysing productivity differences across industries, is provided in R. E. Caves 'Productivity differences among industries', in R. E. Caves and L. B. Krause *Britain's Economic Performance* (Washington DC: Brookings Institution, 1980); S. Prais *Productivity and Industrial Structure* (Cambridge: Cambridge University Press, 1981). Nicholas Oulton 'Labour productivity in UK manufacturing in the 1970s and in the 1980s', *National Institute Economic Review*, 132, May 1990, pp. 71-91. Labour relations are examined as a cause of productivity differences in E. Batstone 'Labour and productivity', *Oxford Review of Economic Policy* 2(3), 1986, pp. 32-43; and William Brown and Sushil Wadwhani 'The economic effects of industrial relations legislation since 1979', *National Institute Economic Review*, 131, February 1990, pp. 57-70. See also Nicholas Oulton 'Plant closures and the productivity miracle in manufacturing,' *National Institute Economic Review* 121, 1987, pp. 53-9; and Nicholas Oulton 'Productivity growth in manufacturing, 1963-85: the role of new investment and scrapping', *National Institute Economic Review*, 127, 1989, pp. 64-75.

Estimates of productive capacity obtained using a CES production function (more general than the one used here) are provided in R. Torres and J. P. Martin 'Measuring potential output in the seven major OECD countries', *OECD Economic Studies* 14, Spring 1990, pp. 127-49. The importance of raising productive capacity is investigated in C. Bean 'Capital shortages and persistent unemployment', *Economic Policy* 8, 1989, pp. 1-53; and Franco Modigliani *et. al.* 'Reducing unemployment in Europe: the role of capital formation,' in Richard Layard and Lars Calmfors (eds.) *The Fight against Unemployment* (Cambridge, Mass. and London: MIT Press, 1987).

7

The labour market, I: real wages, productivity and unemployment

7.1 INTRODUCTION

Since the 1970s one of the major issues in macroeconomics has been the extent to which low output and high unemployment are caused by deficient demand ('Keynesian' unemployment) and how far they are the result of supply-side factors (high real wages, unemployment benefits and so on). Many of these supply-side factors involve arguments about the nature of the labour market: not only is unemployment a major issue in its own right, but wages are a major element in costs, affecting both profitability and inflation. The question underlying most discussions of these problems is how much unemployment is due to supply-side factors and how much is attributable to the level of aggregate demand. The difficulty is that there is no consensus on how such problems should be tackled. We have, instead, a number of possible approaches, each with its own advantages and disadvantages. In this chapter, we adopt one approach, looking at what are called 'wage gaps'. In chapter 8 we approach the problem in a different way.

7.2 REAL WAGES AND PRODUCTIVITY

The real wage rate

The term 'real wage rate' is often used as though it had a single meaning. There is, however, an important difference between the real product wage rate and the real consumption wage rate.

❑ The *consumption wage* is the wage rate measured in terms of consumption goods: the nominal wage divided by the price of consumption goods.

❑ The *product wage* is the wage rate in terms of output: the nominal wage divided by the price of output.

From the worker's point of view it is the consumption wage that matters, whereas firms will be concerned with the product wage. If we are concerned with classical unemployment, therefore, we must use the product wage, not the consumption wage. This gives rise to a further problem, because different sectors of the economy may face very different prices for their products.

Of particular importance is the difference between those sectors producing internationally tradeable goods, which are subject to international competition, and those producing non-tradeable goods. A measure of the relative price of tradeable and non-tradeable goods (the ratio of the price of exports to the GDP deflator) is provided in figure 7.1. Movements in this index will depend on world demand conditions (which will determine the foreign currency prices exporters can charge), the exchange rate (which determines the sterling price they obtain) and the level of UK demand. In 1979-81, for example, the exchange rate rose substantially. However, because there was a world recession, with intense competition in international markets, exporters were not able to raise their prices as much as producers of non-tradeable goods were able to do. Given these changes in relative prices it may be misleading simply to estimate the product wage rate using an aggregate price index such as the GDP deflator.

Different measures of the real wage rate are shown in figures 7.2 and 7.3. The consumption wage, both for the economy as a whole and for manufacturing, is calculated using the retail price index. In addition to this we have two measures of the product wage rate. In figure 7.2 we show the product wage obtained using average earnings for the economy as a whole divided by the GDP deflator. In figure 7.3 average

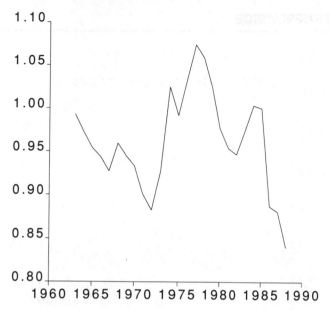

Figure 7.1 The ratio of export prices to the GDP deflator, 1963-88
Source: Economic Trends.

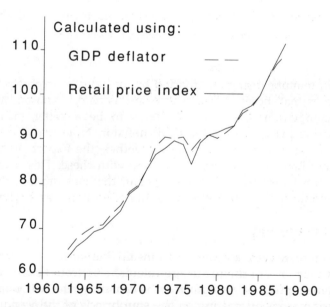

Figure 7.2 The real wage rate (whole economy), 1963-88
Source: based on average earnings, *Economic Trends.*

Figure 7.3 The real wage rate (manufacturing), 1963-88

Source: based on average earnings, *Economic Trends.*

earnings in manufacturing are divided by an index of export prices, on the grounds that because manufacturing is very exposed to international competition this index is likely to be a better measure of manufacturing prices than is the GDP deflator. Note that the RPI and the GDP deflator move fairly closely together: the export price index, on the other hand, has not moved in line with these. This means that divergences between the product wage and the consumption wage are more important in manufacturing than in the economy as a whole.

The real wage gap

If we wish to investigate the relationship between real wages and unemployment it is useful to distinguish between two types of unemployment. *Classical unemployment* is caused by the real wage being too high for reasons originating on the supply side of the economy, and *Keynesian unemployment* is caused by aggregate demand being too low. The distinction between these is clearly of great importance for economic policy: policy designed to cure one type of unemployment might make the other type of unemployment worse. For example, reducing wages would reduce classical unemployment but, if it leads to lower consumers' expenditure, may reduce aggregate demand and exacerbate the problem of Keynesian unemployment.

Actual unemployment may include both classical and Keynesian elements and we need a means of estimating how much unemployment is the result of each cause. The way this is usually done is to calculate what is called the *wage gap*: the difference between the actual real wage rate and the 'full-employment' real wage rate (the real wage at which supply and demand for labour are equal). The idea is that if the real wage rate exceeds the 'full-employment' real wage, employers will be unwilling to employ all the labour that workers wish to supply. This is classical unemployment. The amount of classical unemployment equals the percentage wage gap multiplied by the elasticity of demand for labour. Any unemployment in excess of this is Keynesian unemployment. This is discussed in more detail in box 7.1.

The main problem with measuring the wage gap is that the full-employment real wage rate cannot be observed. The wage gap has to be estimated in other ways. There are several ways we can do this.

❑ Comparing product wage rates with output per head. If real wages are growing faster the wage gap is likely to be increasing; if productivity is growing faster the gap is likely to be falling.

❑ Examining the share of wages in output. The similarity of this to the previous method can be seen by noting that

$$wL/pY = (w/p)/(Y/L)$$

w, p, L and Y denoting the money wage rate, the price level, employment and output respectively. This states that the share of wages in output equals the ratio of the real wage to output per head. In theory, therefore, examining the share of wages in output should give *exactly* the same results as comparing real wages with productivity. In practice the results may be different as the data sources may be different.

❑ Estimating the full-employment marginal product of labour. This can be done in two ways. One is to estimate a production function, relating output to the capital stock and labour employed. Once a production function has been obtained the full-employment marginal product can be calculated. The other is to observe years when the economy was working at full employment (for example 1964, 1973 and 1979) and to use these 'benchmark' years to infer what the real wage would have been in other years had there been full employment. There are great problems with both methods, but they have the advantage that they provide estimates of how low the real wage would have to be in order to eliminate classical unemployment and hence of how much employment is classical and how much is Keynesian.

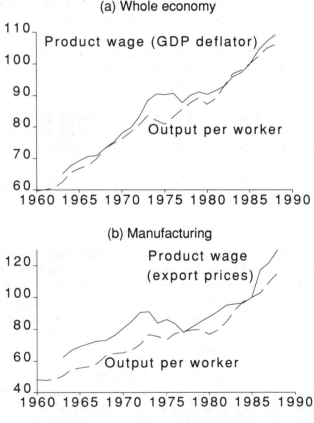

Figure 7.4 Real wages and productivity, 1963-88

Source: Economic Trends.

BOX 7.1 KEYNESIAN AND CLASSICAL UNEMPLOYMENT

We can think of involuntary unemployment as comprising two different types of unemployment.

- ❏ *Keynesian unemployment* — employment is low because firms cannot sell all the goods they wish to produce.

- ❏ *Classical unemployment* — employment is low because high real wages mean it would be unprofitable to produce the full-employment level of output.

In order to provide a full explanation of Keynesian and classical unemployment we would need to consider the goods market as well as the labour market: in particular it would be necessary to explain how a deficiency of demand for goods (and hence Keynesian unemployment) can arise. We can, however, understand the main features of Keynesian and classical unemployment by considering just the labour market.

Before we can consider Keynesian and classical unemployment we need to consider the demand for labour. If firms can sell as much output as they wish at the going price level, they will employ labour up to the point where the real wage rate equals the marginal product of labour. The demand curve will thus be the same as the marginal productivity schedule, shown in figure 7.B1.1. Note that movements along the marginal product curve are associated with changes in output: as firms move from A to B on the marginal product schedule they also move from A to B on the production function shown in the top portion of figure 7.B1.1.

Now suppose that, for some reason, firms believe that they will be unable to sell more than Y_1 units of output. This means that they will not wish to buy more than L_1 units of labour, whatever the real wage. The demand curve for labour will become kinked at B: we thus have the demand curve L^d_1 in figure 7.B1.2. The meaning of the vertical portion of this demand curve is that even if the real wage falls very low, firms will produce only Y_1 units of output: at any point below

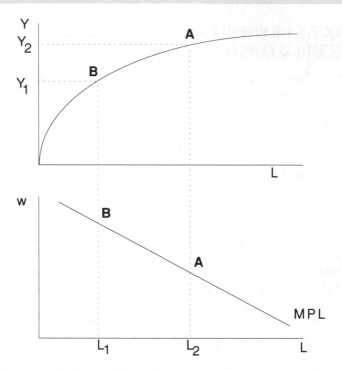

Figure 7.B1.1 The demand for labour

B on the demand curve they will produce at point B on the production function. The demand for labour thus depends not only on the real wage rate but also on the level of output that firms expect to be able to sell. For example, if demand for goods were to increase to Y_2 the labour demand curve would shift to the right, to $L^d{}_2$.

To explain unemployment we introduce a labour supply curve and to keep things simple we assume it is vertical. This is shown in figure 7.B1.2. The 'full employment' real wage rate, w_f, is where the supply curve cuts the marginal product curve. To show Keynesian and classical unemployment suppose that firms believe they will be unable to sell more than Y_1 units of output (shown in figure 7.B1.1) and that the real wage rate is w_2. Firms will employ L_1 units of labour and unemployment (all 'involuntary') will be L_f -L_1. Of this we can say that L_f -L_2 is classical unemployment and L_2-L_1 is Keynesian. The reason is

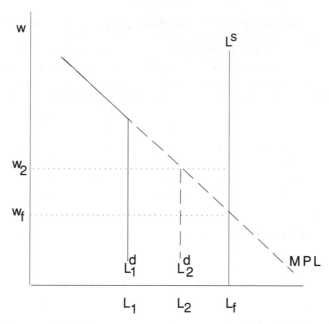

Figure 7.B1.2 Keynesian and classical unemployment

that an expansion of aggregate demand would shift the demand curve for labour to the right and would increase employment up to L_2. For employment to rise beyond L_2, however, would require a fall in the real wage rate.

We can measure the amount of classical unemployment by the difference between the real wage rate and the full-employment real wage. In this simple model where the supply curve is vertical the two are related by the elasticity of the labour demand curve:

$$(L_f - L_2)/L_f = e(w_2 - w_f)/w_f = e(w_2 - MPL_f)/MPL_f$$

where e is the elasticity of demand for labour expressed as a positive number. This gap between the real wage and the full-employment real wage or marginal product is usually referred to as the *real wage gap*.

Table 7.1 Product wage and productivity growth rates, 1963-88

	Whole economy			Manufacturing		
	Product wage	Productivity	Difference	Product wage	Productivity	Difference
1963-69	2.4	3.0	-0.6	3.3	4.3	-1.0
1969-73	4.1	2.8	1.3	4.6	4.2	0.4
1973-75	1.0	-1.6	2.6	-2.6	-2.0	-0.6
1975-79	0.9	2.5	-1.6	-0.3	2.1	-2.4
1979-81	0.6	0.0	0.6	3.6	0.3	3.3
1981-88	2.5	2.5	0.0	5.2	5.5	-0.3

Source: calculated from data used for figure 7.4.

Table 7.2 Wages and productivity in Europe and the US

	France	Germany	UK	US
Product wage				
1962-69	5.1	5.0	3.2	3.1
1969-73	5.5	6.3	3.7	2.6
1973-75	5.1	4.8	4.9	0.2
1975-78	5.2	2.7	1.5	2.3
Output per head				
1962-69	5.2	5.3	3.1	2.7
1969-73	5.7	5.2	3.9	2.6
1973-75	2.6	4.0	0.7	0.3
1975-78	5.0	4.5	2.0	2.1

Source: J. D. Sachs 'Wages, profits and macroeconomic adjustment: a comparative study', *Brookings Papers on Economic Activity*, 1979, pp. 275.

7.3 REAL WAGES AND UNEMPLOYMENT SINCE THE 1960s

Wages and productivity

The behaviour of real wages and productivity is shown in figure 7.4 and table 7.1, which give estimates of product wage rates and output per head, both for the whole economy and for manufacturing. The manufacturing product wage is based on export prices, the assumption being that most manufactured goods are tradeable.

Consider first the whole economy figures. During the 1960s product wage rates were growing at 2.4 per cent per annum, slightly below the growth rate of productivity (3 per cent per annum). After 1969, however, the growth rate of real wages accelerated to 4.1 per cent per annum, substantially higher than the 2.8 per cent per annum growth rate of productivity. From 1969 to 1973, therefore, a wage gap seems to have emerged, the reason being a rapid growth in real wages. The real wage gap continued to grow from 1973 to 1975, but this time the reason was the dramatic fall in productivity caused by the rise in oil prices. Real wage growth slowed to 1 per cent per annum, but even this was high when productivity was *falling* at 1.6 per cent per annum. By 1975 a large wage gap had emerged. Between 1975 and 1979 real wage growth was kept well below the productivity growth rate, the result being that the wage gap was virtually removed.

These figures suggest that a large part of the rise in unemployment which arose after the first oil shock may have been classical unemployment, caused by high real wage rates. A similar story, involving an acceleration of wages in 1969-73 combined with the failure of wages to fall when the oil shock reduced productivity from 1973 to 1975, could be told for most of Europe, as is shown in table 7.2 (note that the data in table 7.2 are for wages and output per hour, rather than per worker, and that they are in 1975 prices). In the USA, on the other hand, real wages fell quickly in response to the rise in oil prices and there is no evidence that any real wage gap emerged. If it were the case that in the late 1970s Europe was experiencing classical unemployment, and the USA Keynesian unemployment, this could explain why European policy-makers were concerned with keeping wages down, whereas their US counterparts were concerned to raise aggregate demand.

It has been suggested that the difference between European and US wage behaviour can be explained by differences in labour market institutions. In the USA wages were fixed by long-term contracts, the result being that when prices rose real wages fell immediately. In Europe, on the other hand, workers were in a strong position to negotiate wage increases to offset price rises, and were able to sustain real wages. In Britain the situation was made worse in 1974, the year when the effects of the oil shock were first felt, by the existence of an incomes policy that index-linked wages: rises in the retail price index automatically triggered wage rises, in complete contrast to what happened in the USA.

The situation after the 1979 oil shock was very different. From 1979 to 1981 productivity growth fell to zero, but real wage growth remained very low, at 0.6 per cent per annum. No significant wage gap appears to have emerged. Since 1981 product wages and productivity have grown at the same rate, 2.5 per cent per annum.

The story for manufacturing productivity looks, at first sight, very different. It is important to remember, however, that because the figures are index numbers it is only *changes* in the gap between real wages and productivity that are significant (the series are constructed so that they are both 100 in 1985). It is also important to remember that the product wage is constructed using an export price index, which may not be appropriate. The figures must be treated with caution. Table 7.1 shows that when we consider manufacturing there was also a rise in real wages relative to productivity from 1969 to 1973, though slightly less than in the economy as a whole. From 1973 to 1975, however, there appears to have been a *fall* in the product wage of 2.6 per cent per annum, because of export prices having risen rapidly (compare the two real wage rates shown in figure 7.3). From 1975 to 1979 wage growth was low relative to productivity growth, as in the economy as a whole. The second major difference between manufacturing and the economy as a whole arises for 1979-81, when the product wage rose at 3.6 per cent per annum, at a time when productivity rose at only 0.3 per cent per annum. The severe world recession and the rapidly rising sterling exchange rate were keeping export prices low, raising the product wage facing exporters very substantially. The gap between product-wage growth and productivity growth rose to 3.3 per cent per annum. Since 1981, on the other hand, product wages have, on average, grown in line with productivity, both growing at over 5 per cent per annum.

The share of wages in output

Figure 7.5 shows the share of wages in GDP. Also shown is a 5-year moving average, which smooths out year-to-year fluctuations. This rose

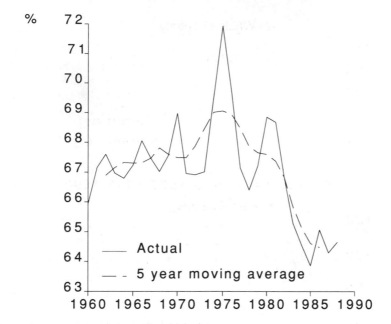

Figure 7.5 The share of wages in national income, 1960-88
Source: Economic Trends.

slowly during the 1960s, and then rose significantly from about 1973 to 1975, after which it declined. What stands out from this graph is that the share of wages fell dramatically after 1980. Thus even if there was a large wage gap, together with classical unemployment, during the 1970s, it is, on the surface at least, hard to see how a wage gap could have persisted into the 1980s: the fall in the share of wages in national income seems too large.

Estimates of the real wage gap

To estimate the real wage gap we need to estimate the full-employment real wage rate. There are two problems here. The first is that productivity data measure output per head: the *average* product of labour, not the marginal product. The second is that we have to work out what productivity would be if there were full employment. The obvious way of doing this would be to estimate a production function, with output depending on the capital stock and the level of employment. Such an approach, however, raises great problems. Instead we adopt a simpler approach.

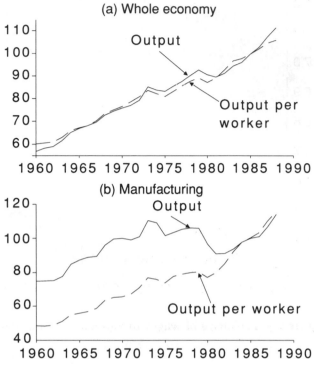

Figure 7.6 Output and productivity, 1960-88

Source: Economic Trends.

Figure 7.6 contains data on total output and output per head. This makes it clear that productivity (output per head) fluctuates over the business cycle. In booms productivity rises and in recessions it falls. The explanation of this is the tendency of firms to 'hoard' labour during recessions. It is expensive to hire and fire workers whenever demand changes and, in addition, there is the danger that if firms fire workers during a recession they may be unable to replace them quickly when the boom comes. This suggests that we can estimate the full-capacity level of output per head by looking at those years when unemployment was at its lowest and output was at its highest. Such full employment years included 1964, 1973 and 1979. We can then estimate full-employment (or full-capacity) output per head in other years by interpolating between these benchmark years.

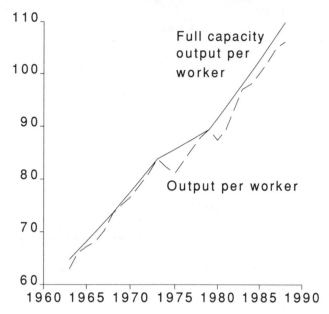

Figure 7.7 Actual and full-capacity output per worker, 1963-88
Source: actual output per worker, figure 7.2.

This is done in figure 7.7. We have assumed that the growth rate of full-capacity output per head was constant for each of the three periods, 1963-73, 1973-79 and 1979-88. For the period after 1979, we have assumed that on average full-employment productivity grew at the same rate as actual output per head.

Using this measure of full-employment or full-capacity output per head we can estimate the real wage gap. It is the percentage by which the product wage rate exceeds full-employment output per head. The gap is adjusted so as to make the wage gap zero on average between 1963 and 1969. The reason for this last assumption is that the 1960s were a period of very low unemployment, by today's standards, when we would not expect there to have been a significant amount of classical unemployment. 1969 is chosen as the end-point as this marks the beginning of the period of wage pressure when we believe the wage gap may have been increasing. The resulting wage gap is shown in figure 7.8. Figure 7.9 brings together the product wage rate and the measure of full-capacity output per head from which the wage gap was derived.

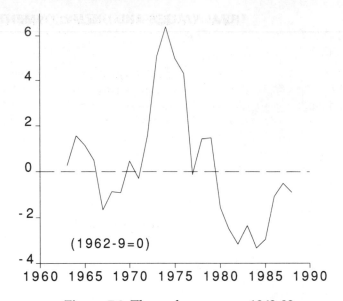

Figure 7.8 The real wage gap, 1963-88

Source: as described in text — real wage is based on average earnings and GDP deflator.

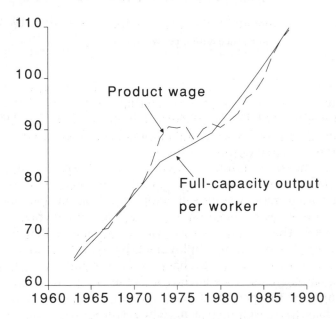

Figure 7.9 Real wages and full-capacity output per worker, 1963-88

Source: as described in text.

These figures suggest that in the mid-1970s a substantial wage gap emerged, amounting to about 6 per cent by 1974. This gap was eliminated by the end of the 1970s. The gap then became negative for a few years, returning nearly to zero by 1987. These figures must, of course, be treated with very great caution. The estimates rely heavily on 1979 being a year of full employment, despite unemployment being much higher than at previous cyclical peaks. The justification for this is the argument that, for various reasons, the equilibrium level of frictional and structural unemployment had risen. There are also similar problems after 1979. Whilst the economy is, in 1989, showing many of the signs associated with full-capacity operation, there is still substantial evidence of unemployment. Rough-and-ready methods such as those used here may be inadequate to deal with situations where large supply- side changes are taking place.

7.4 CONCLUSIONS

The concepts of Keynesian and classical unemployment can be used to ascertain the role of real wages in causing unemployment. The empirical evidence considered in this chapter has to be treated with a great deal of caution, primarily because the estimates of the full-employment real wage are little more than conjectures. It suggests, however, that a large real wage gap did emerge during the 1970s. It seems likely that a significant part of the unemployment which arose in the UK during the 1970s was classical unemployment. After 1975, because of a period of restrictive government policy combined with incomes policies aimed at bringing down wage inflation, the wage gap had been substantially reduced, if not eliminated. Because of the rise in the rate of productivity growth after 1979, high real wage growth during this period does not appear to have led to any large wage gap. Unemployment during the 1980s, therefore, would appear to be Keynesian rather than classical in origin, though this is a conclusion that should be treated with a great deal of caution. It is important to consider other evidence as well. We do this in the next chapter.

FURTHER READING

The main references here are J. D. Sachs 'Wages, profits and macroeconomic adjustment: a comparative study', *Brookings Papers on Economic Activity* 1979(2), pp. 269-319; M. Bruno and J. D. Sachs *The Economics of Worldwide Stagflation* (Oxford: Oxford University Press, 1985); and M. Bruno 'Aggregate supply and demand factors in UK unemployment: an update', *Economica* 53 (supplement), 1985, pp. S35-52. Issues of wage gaps have more recently been discussed in R. M. Coen and B. G. Hickman 'Keynesian and classical unemployment in four countries,' *Brookings Papers on Economic Activity* 1987, 2, pp. 123-206; Bert G. Hickman 'Real wages, aggregate demand and unemployment,' *European Economic Review* 31, 1987, 1531-60; and J. Sachs 'High unemployment in Europe — diagnosis and policy implications,' in C.-H. Siven (ed.) *Unemployment in Europe* (Stockholm: Timbro, 1987). Many of the references cited in chapters 6 and 8 are also relevant to this topic.

Readers wanting further discussion of the theory of Keynesian and classical unemployment, which is not covered in all the standard macroeconomic theory textbooks, could read E. Malinvaud *The Theory of Unemployment Reconsidered* (Oxford: Basil Blackwell, 1977).

8

The labour market, II: unemployment, inflation and the NAIRU

8.1 INTRODUCTION

In chapter 7 we explored the implications of real wages for unemployment from the point of view of rationing models. Estimates of real wage gaps were used to distinguish between classical and Keynesian unemployment. Such an approach can, however, be no more than a first step towards distinguishing between supply-side and demand-side causes of unemployment, its main weakness being that no attempt is made to explain what determines real wage rates. The level of aggregate demand, for example, may affect wage settlements, and thereby influence real wages and unemployment. Real wages and unemployment interact both with each other and with inflation. Our task in this chapter is to examine some of the links between these variables, and thus to explore more fully the role of supply- and demand-side factors in determining unemployment.

When reading these two chapters on the labour market it is important to note that this chapter is not simply building on what was done in chapter 7: the theory discussed here is not just a more complicated version of the theory used in chapter 7. It is rather that, although they are to a certain extent complementary, these two chapters provide alternative ways of viewing the problem of unemployment that are not completely compatible with each other. The reason for using two incompatible approaches is that each appears to throw some light on the problem. There is no single approach to the problem of unemployment that deals adequately with everything. Analysis of wage gaps seems to be able to explain something of what happened to unemployment in the mid-1970s after the first OPEC oil price rise, but it fails to shed much light on why unemployment is now so high, or why real wages have continued to rise during the 1980s, despite a period of persistent high unemployment. To explain these we need a different theory involving a wider range of factors.

8.2 UNEMPLOYMENT AND VACANCIES

The measurement of unemployment

Statistics on unemployment in Britain have to be treated with great caution. The reason is that the official definition of unemployment, and the way the statistics are compiled, have changed so frequently as to make it difficult to discern trends with any confidence. Most of the changes to the definition have been perfectly defensible on the grounds of either improving the accuracy of the statistics or making them easier to collect. Virtually all the changes, however, have reduced the measured total of unemployment. The main change was in October 1982, with the move from statistics based on registration at Jobcentres to one based on numbers claiming unemployment benefit. The change was prompted by a decision to make registration at Jobcentres voluntary, and the movement from a manual count to a computer-based one led to improved accuracy in counting, so there was a strong case for making the change. It did, however, reduce the count of unemployed substantially.

Examples of other changes concern the treatment of school-leavers (now no longer able to claim benefit until the September after leaving school) and the provision of special, higher, long-term benefits to a large number of over-sixties, which caused them no longer to be defined as unemployed, though nothing else had changed. There were also changes in the definition of the workforce, needed to calculate the percentage unemployed. The self-employed and members of the armed forces are now included as part of the workforce, whereas before 1986 they were not. Though this did not alter the figure for the number of unemployed, it reduced the percentage substantially.

Changes such as these make it difficult to obtain long series of consistent unemployment statistics. The statistics shown in figure 8.1 for 1971-89 are based on the current definition: the number un-

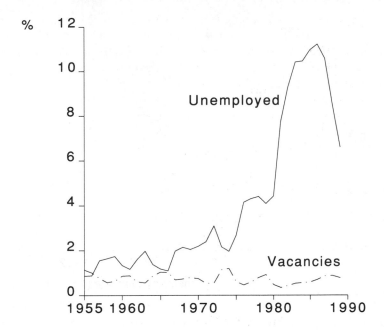

Figure 8.1 Unemployment and vacancies

Source: Economic Trends Annual Supplement. Unemployment and vacancies as percentages
of the workforce. Unemployment is measured using the current definition since 1971.
Figures before 1971 are based on earlier definitions

employed and seeking benefit. Changes in this measure will reflect
changes in the number seeking work only if benefit regulations stay the
same, and if the way in which these are enforced does not change.
Because the statistics calculated in this way go back only to 1971, the
data for the period before 1971 are based on older definitions and are
not strictly comparable with the newer figures (they were calculated
using the published figures for the workforce and employment).
Similarly, there may be large errors in the vacancy statistics which,
according to the Department of Employment's estimates, include only
about thirty per cent of all vacancies.

The *U-V* curve

The main device used for analysing the relationship between unemployment and vacancies is the *U-V* curve. The theory here is that

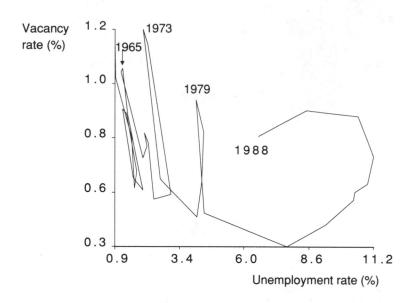

Figure 8.2 The *U-V* curve

Source: as figure 8.1.

there should be an inverse relation between unemployment and vacancies: a rise in the level of aggregate demand will increase the number of vacancies and reduce unemployment. Changes in the level of demand thus cause the economy to move along the *U-V* curve. The position of the *U-V* curve will be determined by supply-side factors (some of which are discussed below). If the labour market is organized in such a way that unemployed workers get matched up with the available jobs very quickly, the *U-V* curve will be relatively close to the origin: if matching of jobs and workers is slower, it will be further out.

Unemployment and vacancies are plotted in figure 8.1 and are graphed against each other in figure 8.2. Throughout the 1960s unemployment and vacancies moved as though they were negatively related to each other. This suggests that fluctuations in unemployment and vacancies were the result of fluctuations in aggregate demand without any major change caused by supply-side factors. During the 1970s and 1980s, however, unemployment increased without any equivalent fall in vacancies, suggesting that supply-side factors had moved the *U-V* curve outwards. This picture of unemployment and vacancies is thus consistent with the view that supply-side factors were responsible for much of the rise in unemployment in the 1980s.

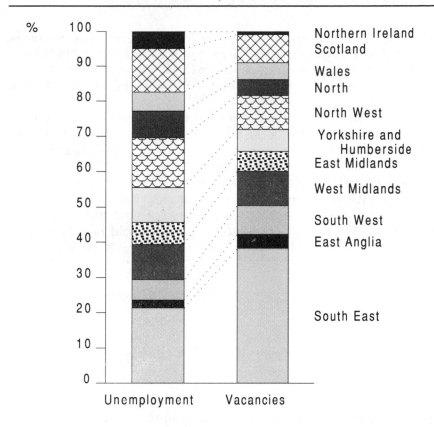

Figure 8.3 Regional shares of unemployment and vacancies, 1988
Source: Employment Gazette.

One important problem in the labour market is that of mismatch between workers and the available jobs. This may take many forms. Workers may not have the skills that employers are wanting, either because they have the wrong educational qualifications or because they are trained to work in one industry, but the available vacancies are in another. In addition, unemployment may be concentrated in certain regions, and vacancies in others. Such effects are likely to be particularly important in times of rapid change, such as the last two decades.

Mismatch in the regional distribution of vacancies and unemployment is shown in figure 8.3, which shows the distribution of vacancies and unemployment across regions. The South East, the South West and East Anglia have a disproportionately large share of vacancies relative to unemployment, whereas Northern Ireland, the North, the North

West and Yorkshire and Humberside have relatively few vacancies compared with unemployment. There is thus a clear regional imbalance in the distribution of unemployment and vacancies: the ratio of vacancies to unemployment is higher in southern regions than in northern ones.

Figure 8.4 shows the balance between unemployment and vacancies in manufacturing relative to the rest of the economy. The main feature here is the sharp fall in manufacturing's share of vacancies after 1977. In 1981 manufacturing still accounted for over 30 per cent of non-agricultural unemployment, but only 16 per cent of vacancies. Thus whilst the ratio of unemployment to vacancies was on average much the same as in the economy as a whole until around 1979, fluctuating between 80 per cent and 120 per cent of the national ratio (see figure 8.4), it rose to over double the national ratio in the early 1980s.

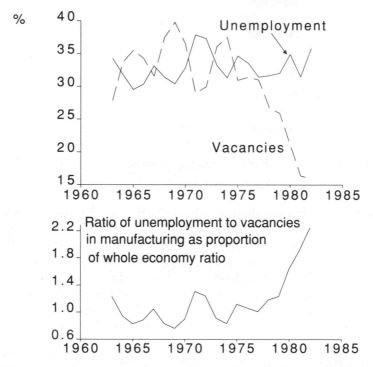

Figure 8.4 Percentage shares of manufacturing in unemployment and vacancies

Source: R. Jackman and S. Roper 'Structural unemployment,' *Oxford Bulletin of Economics and Statistics* 49, 1987, p. 23.

Measuring the extent of mismatch, however, is more difficult. One approach is to use measures based on the difference between unemployment and vacancies in different regions or different industries. One of the simplest measures is to consider each sector of the economy (these 'sectors' may be regions, occupations or industries) and to take the absolute difference between the percentage of total unemployment and the percentage of total vacancies appearing in that sector. If we add these differences across the economy as a whole and divide by two, we get the percentage of the unemployed who would have to move from one sector to another in order to even out the distribution of unemployment and vacancies: to get rid of mismatch. For example, suppose we have just three regions, the South the Midlands and the North. The South has 25 per cent of the unemployed, and 40 per cent of the vacancies, the Midlands has 30 per cent of the unemployed and 35 per cent of the vacancies, with the North having 45 per cent of the unemployed and 25 per cent of the vacancies). The measure of mismatch is thus [(40-25) + (35-30) + (45-25)]/2 = 20.

This measure can be applied to any type of mismatch. In figure 8.5 we use it to measure three types of mismatch: across occupations,

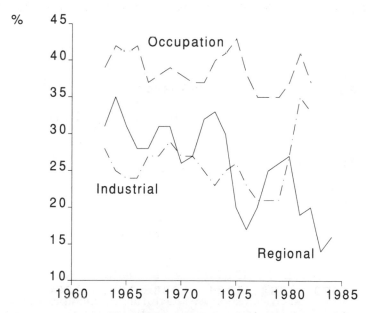

Figure 8.5 Measures of mismatch

Source: R. Jackman and S. Roper 'Structural unemployment,' *Oxford Bulletin of Economics and Statistics* 49, 1987, p. 20.

industries and regions. These three measures suggest that, though mismatch is a serious problem, it has not increased significantly over time. There was a sharp increase in 1981-2, resulting from the recession hitting production industries (especially manufacturing and construction) particularly hard, but this is likely to represent a short-term fluctuation rather than a longer term trend.

A further source of evidence for the existence of mismatch is CBI (Confederation of British Industry) surveys of the percentage of firms that expects output to be limited by labour shortages. Figure 8.6 gives the percentage of firms expecting output to be limited by shortages of skilled labour and by other types of labour. Given the high level of unemployment during this period these figures suggest that there was a significant degree of mismatch.

An even simpler way to obtain a measure of mismatch, very similar to the one used in the Layard-Nickell wage equation equation discussed below, is provided in figure 8.7. This shows the change in the share of production industries (i.e. manufacturing, mining, construction, power and water supply) in total employment. It is thus a crude measure of structural change. The assumption is that if the sectoral composition of output is changing more rapidly there will be a greater degree of mismatch in the labour market. Figure 8.7 suggests that the

Figure 8.6 Percentage of firms expecting labour shortages to limit output

Source: National Institute Economic Review.

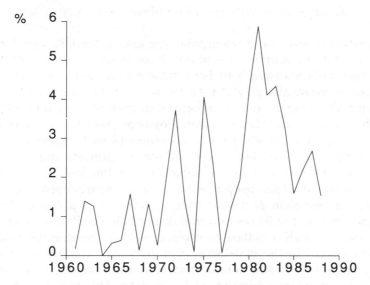

Figure 8.7 A measure of mismatch, 1956-88

Source: percentage change in ratio of manufacturing to total employment.

pace of structural change, and hence the degree of mismatch, has on average been much higher during the 1970s and 1980s than in previous decades. It supports the view that the extent of mismatch in 1981-2 was exceptional.

8.3 TURNOVER IN THE LABOUR MARKET

Inflows and outflows

In all our discussion so far we have focused attention on the stock of unemployment: that is on the number unemployed at any time. This can, however, give a misleading impression, for it neglects the fact that there is continuous turnover in the labour market. Even when unemployment is constant, new jobs are being created, workers are being fired, and unemployed workers are finding jobs. To take account of this, therefore, we need to consider not changes in the *stock* of unemployment, but *flows* into and out of the 'pool' of unemployment. The term *inflows* denotes the number of workers becoming unemployed during a given period of time. The term *outflows* denotes the number of workers who cease to be unemployed during a given period. Outflows and inflows are, of course, related to unemployment by the formula,

Change in unemployment = inflows - outflows.

These flows into and out of unemployment are, in the UK, very large compared with the number unemployed, as is shown in figure 8.8. Inflows and outflows have both been between two and three million per annum, substantially greater than the number unemployed. To put these numbers in perspective, it is helpful to look at what they imply about the average duration of unemployment: namely the average length of time for which people are unemployed. Suppose that outflows and inflows are both three million per annum, and that the stock of unemployment is half a million (as in the late 1960s). This means that on average, people who become unemployed are unemployed for one sixth of a year (two months) — at a rate of three million per annum it will take two months for half a million workers to get jobs (and for half a million to replace them in the unemployment pool). In contrast, in the mid-1980s unemployment was (keeping the numbers simple) about two million, and flows were around 2.5 million. This implies an average duration of 9.6 months. This rise in expected duration is reflected in the rise in the proportion of long-term unemployment, shown in figure 8.9.

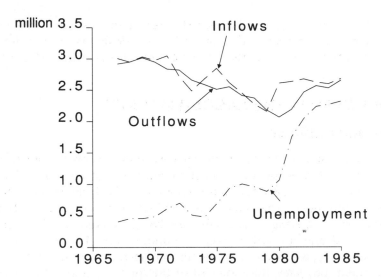

Figure 8.8 Inflows, outflows and unemployment

Source: data provided by Simon Burgess, discussed in 'How does unemployment change?' University of Bristol, Department of Economics Discussion Paper, 1990. Flows are per *annum.*

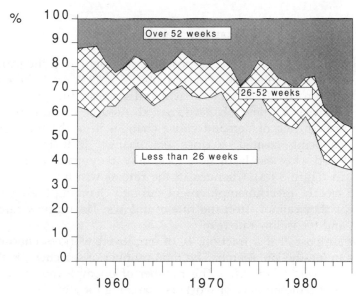

Figure 8.9 The duration of unemployment

Source: Centre for Labour Economics dataset.

The dynamics of unemployment

It has often been argued that changes in the unemployment rate have been dominated by changes in the outflow rate, changes in the inflow rate being of little significance. Evidence for this is shown in figure 8.10. This shows that if we assume the inflow rate to have been constant, we obtain an unemployment rate very similar to the one which was actually experienced. If, on the other hand, we hold the outflow rate constant, letting the inflow rate vary, we completely fail to predict changes in the level of employment. Given that the outflow rate is the inverse of the average duration of unemployment, this evidence can be used to argue that the key to understanding changes in the unemployment rate is understanding why unemployment duration has changed — in other words, that the problem of rising unemployment is not one of increased job losses, but one of failing to create enough new jobs.

Figure 8.10 would seem to provide very strong evidence in favour of the thesis that outflows dominate inflows as the cause of changes in the unemployment rate. We can, however, present the same information in a different way, as is done in figure 8.11. This shows the close

BOX 8.1 UNEMPLOYMENT DYNAMICS

To keep the theory as simple as possible, assume that at the start of the year there is a given stock of 'old jobs', $E = (1 - u)L$ (where L is the labour force), a fraction, δ, of which disappear during the year. During the year nL 'new jobs' are created. Assume that fluctuations in the growth rate of demand cause changes in n, the number of new jobs being created: δ does not change. If it is only the unemployed who search for new jobs, unemployment flows are as shown in figure 8.1(a). Changes in the rate at which new jobs are created clearly affect unemployment through changing the level of outflows: they cannot affect the rate of inflows. The outflow rate, x, is n/u, and the inflow rate is δ.

Now suppose that a fraction, θ, of employed workers choose to engage in 'on-the-job' search. The total number of searchers, is thus $[u + \theta(1 - u)]L$, where uL is the number of unemployed searchers and $\theta(1 - u)L$ the number of workers searching for jobs. To simplify the notation, define $\sigma = [u + \theta(1 - u)]$ as the ratio of searchers to the labour force. If we assume that all job searchers have an equal chance of getting one of the new jobs, a fraction $\theta(1-u)/\sigma$ of the new jobs will go to existing workers, and the rest, u/σ, will go to the unemployed. This gives rise to the flows shown in figure 8.1(b). Outflows will be $(u/\sigma)nL$, the number of new jobs going to the unemployed, and the *outflow rate, x*, will be given by

$$x = n/\sigma.$$

Because of the number of workers moving to new jobs, only $\delta(1 - u)L - [\theta(1-u)/\sigma]nL$ workers will have to lose their jobs: the inflow rate, i, will thus be

$$i = [\delta(1 - u) - \theta(1-u)/\sigma n]/(1 -u) = \delta - \theta n/\sigma.$$

The link between outflows, inflows and the change in unemployment depends crucially on the value of θ and on the elasticity of θ with respect to n.

❑ If $\theta = 0$ (the standard case) all changes in unemployment derive from changes in the outflow rate.

❑ If $0 < \theta \leq 1$ and θ is constant, then both inflow and outflow matter. If $\theta = 1$, for example, all workers stand an equal chance of getting one of the new jobs, and so $x = n$ and $i = \delta - n$.

❑ If $\theta > n$ and $d\theta/dn > 0$ then, if the elasticity of θ with respect to n is sufficiently high, $x = n/[u + \theta(n)(1 - n)]$ may vary very little with n, and $i = \delta - \theta(n)n/s$ may vary substantially with n. Thus changes in unemployment may come about largely through changes in the *inflow* rate. The reason why θ will vary with n is that when new jobs are more plentiful (when n is high), more workers will find it worthwhile to search for a new job.

In deriving this result, we have made some strong simplifying assumptions. In all cases, however, the simplifications would seem to favour the conventional view linking changes in unemployment to the outflow rate.

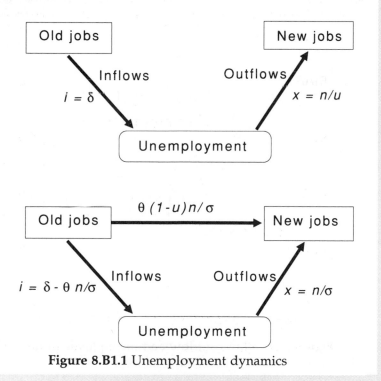

Figure 8.B1.1 Unemployment dynamics

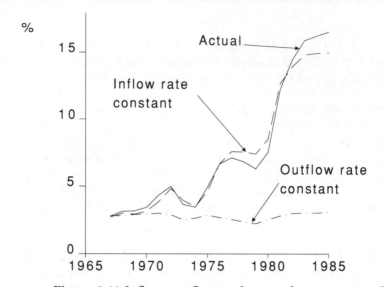

Figure 8.10 Inflow, outflow and unemployment rates, I

Source: as figure 8.8. The constant inflow and outflow series are constructed using the formula in C. Pissarides 'Unemployment and vacancies in Britain', *Economic Policy*, 3, 1986, pp. 499-599.

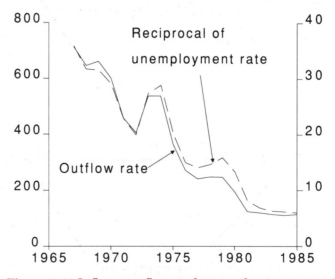

Figure 8.11 Inflow, outflow and unemployment rates, II

Source: as figure 8.8.

correlation between the outflow rate and the unemployment rate. This makes the point that the reason why the outflow rate is highly correlated with the unemployment rate is that it is defined as outflows divided by the number unemployed: over the period covered by figures 8.10 and 8.11, outflows were fairly constant, which meant that the outflow *rate* was highly correlated with the unemployment rate. If we are to draw any conclusions about causation, therefore, we need a theory about how outflows and the outflow rate are determined. Without such a theory we cannot tell whether the correlation between the outflow rate and the unemployment rate arises because there is a causal link, or whether it is simply the result of the way we have defined the outflow rate.

The theory used to justify arguing for a causal link between the outflow rate and the change in unemployment is a job search model in which unemployed workers search for jobs. In such models the outflow rate is equal to the probability that an unemployed person will obtain work. Unemployed job-searchers are assumed to set an optimal reservation wage (the lowest wage for which they are prepared to work), thereby determining the probability of their obtaining a job: if they set the reservation wage very high, they are less likely to become employed than if they set a low reservation wage. It can thus be argued that it is the ratio of outflows to unemployment (the outflow rate) that is determined by the theory. If we assume that all new jobs go to the unemployed, figure 8.10 can be interpreted as suggesting that causation runs from the outflow rate to the unemployment rate.

The problem with this theory is that it ignores the possibility of workers searching for new jobs whilst still working (on-the-job searching). If this is taken into account (see box 8.1), changes in the hiring rate (the rate at which new jobs are created) may affect unemployment through inflows, through outflows or through both, even if the rate at which firms wish to lose existing workers does not change. If the proportion of workers engaging in on-the-job search is sufficiently responsive to changes in the hiring rate, changes in the hiring rate can produce larger changes in the inflow rate than in the outflow rate. In such a case it would make more sense to see the outflow rate as changing in response to changes in unemployment, not the other way round.

There is some evidence (discussed by Burgess, cited in the further reading section) to suggest that the level of job search by the employed is responsive to changes in the hiring rate, and hence that hiring affects unemployment mainly through changing the inflow rate. This is consistent with the data on inflows and outflows shown in figure 8.8, which suggest that, at least between 1967 and 1980, the cyclical behaviour reflected the cyclical pattern of inflows: during this period there was a downward trend in outflows, but there were no significant fluctuations.

The most important conclusion to be drawn from this is that if we are to establish the links between the hiring rate, the inflow rate and the outflow rate it is necessary to do more than simply look at the correlation between the inflow, outflow and unemployment rates. It is necessary to look very carefully at the theory as well.

8.4 SUPPLY-SIDE FACTORS

Unemployment benefits

Before we get involved with the details of a theory of unemployment it is helpful to consider some of the main supply-side factors that have been used in models of the labour market and how they might be expected to affect unemployment. The most controversial of these is probably the level of unemployment benefits. High unemployment benefits are claimed to make employment less attractive compared with unemployment, encouraging workers to opt for longer spells of unemployment. The variable usually used to measure the impact of benefits on unemployment is the so-called *replacement ratio*. This is the ratio of the income received whilst unemployed to the income received when in work. Such a replacement ratio is shown in figure 8.12. It has to be treated with great caution, the reason being that it measures a notional average replacement ratio for the workforce as a whole. It is based on the benefits to which people are theoretically entitled, making no allowance for the fact that if people's contribution records are incomplete they may not be entitled to full benefits, or that not all benefits are taken up. In addition, it may not measure the replacement ratio for those workers who are likely to become unemployed. Notwithstanding such objections, figure 8.12 shows that unemployment benefits became more generous during the 1950s and 1960s. Since 1970, however, the replacement ratio has fallen slightly, albeit with enormous fluctuations in the mid and late 1970s. Since 1982 the replacement ratio has fallen because of the withdrawal of the earnings-related supplement, until then received by a significant number of the unemployed.

Because unemployment benefits are so widely cited as a cause of high unemployment (and a high NAIRU; see boxes 8.3 and 8.4) and because of their political importance the question of the link between unemployment benefits and unemployment deserves further attention.

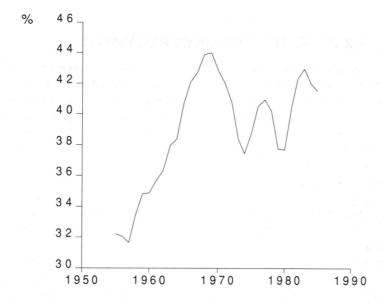

Figure 8.12 The replacement ratio

Source: Centre for Labour Economics dataset.

One type of evidence is derived from macroeconomic time-series models: variables such as the aggregate replacement ratio shown in figure 8.12 can be incorporated into macroeconomic models and the coefficients estimated. We do this in the following section. A different, and probably more reliable, type of evidence is that derived from microeconomic data. Here economists look at evidence provided by a large sample of households. The basic data come from a survey of a large sample (hundreds or, if possible, thousands) of workers: the survey tells us the worker's replacement ratio and how long he has been unemployed together with a long list of personal characteristics (education, class, family size, spouse's income, etc). The use of 'he' here is deliberate, for most studies concentrate on male unemployment, the reason being that the determinants of male and female unemployment are very different: men and women have different attitudes, the social security system discriminates between men and women and the nature of the opportunities provided by the labour market are different. Furthermore, data on female unemployment are harder to interpret.

BOX 8.2 BENEFITS AND UNEMPLOYMENT

Most microeconomic studies of the effects of unemployment benefits on unemployment are based on what are called 'search models'. When a worker becomes unemployed he has to decide how intensively to search for a new job. This will depend on the level of unemployment benefits: if benefits are high he will choose to spend longer looking for a job than if benefits are low. Benefits thus affect the *duration* of unemployment. The size of the effect is found by constructing an equation in which the length of each worker's spell of unemployment depends on the replacement ratio and a list, often very long, of personal characteristics (such as age, education, marital status, dependants, health, region, class, wife's income etc.). The result of such studies is usually a figure for the elasticity of unemployment duration with respect to the replacement ratio. Once we have the elasticity of duration with respect to the replacement ratio we can calculate the effect of the replacement ratio on the level of unemployment.

There are several reasons why this method is difficult to apply. One problem is that the data used often come from surveys such as the General Household Survey or the Family Expenditure Survey, where each household is sampled only once. This means that we observe a large number of uncompleted spells of unemployment, where the worker is still unemployed when the survey is

Several conclusions can be drawn from such microeconomic studies. The first is that the elasticity of unemployment duration, and hence unemployment, with respect to unemployment benefits is either zero or small and positive. A few years ago there was some justification for the claim that a consensus had been reached that the elasticity of unemployment duration with respect to benefits was about 0.6: that a 10 per cent rise in benefits would raise unemployment duration by 6 per cent. Translated into aggregate terms, this means that a 10 per cent cut in benefits would reduce unemployment by about 50,000. In other words, it was thought that some unemployment could be attributed to the level of unemployment benefits, but that the numbers involved were very small. Since then, however, it has been argued that when undertaken, and where we do not know how long the worker is unemployed. This creates technical, econometric problems. To overcome this problem we need a survey in which men are interviewed several times. One such study, the results of which are quoted in the text, was based on taking a group of men who became unemployed at a particular time, and interviewing them after 4, 13 and 52 weeks: the survey is thus of a particular *cohort* of the unemployed. Such data are, however, limited.

A second problem is measuring the replacement ratio. Difficulties here arise for two reasons. The benefits system is very complicated, with a household's entitlement to benefits depending on a large number of factors: benefits change over time whilst someone is unemployed, their level depending on things such as family composition and the worker's contribution record. Earlier spells of unemployment may, for example, have used up a worker's entitlement to unemployment benefit. The other reason is that not all benefits are claimed. This is particularly important with means-tested benefits. For both these reasons it can be argued that aggregate series, such as that shown in figure 8.12, give little idea of what is happening to individuals' replacement ratios. This is a reason for attaching greater significance to properly done micro-economic studies than to aggregate time series ones.

Table 8.1 Benefits and unemployment

Age	Duration < 6 months	Duration > 6 months
Under 20	-0.74	-0.44
20-24	-0.55	0.06*
25-44	-0.37	0.43*
45-64	-0.13*	-0.10*

* Not significantly different from zero.

Source: W. Narendranathan, S. Nickell and J. Stern 'Unemployment benefits revisited', *Economic Journal* 95, 1985, p. 320.

account is taken of the fact that people do not in practice get all the benefits to which they are theoretically entitled, the effect disappears.

A second result from microeconomic studies is that the effect of benefits on unemployment is far from uniform across different groups of workers. For example, one study produced the results shown in table 8.1. The coefficients in this table give the effect of a rise in benefits on the probability of leaving unemployment: a negative sign means that a rise in benefits increases the duration of unemployment through making the worker less likely to become unemployed. Two conclusions emerge from this table. The first is that the effect of benefits on unemployment is strongest for the young, and that it declines with age. The second is that, with the exception of men under 20, benefits have

Table 8.2 Unemployment incidence by replacement ratio

Replacement ratio	Per cent of working population	Per cent unemployed
0-49	16.6	4.0
50-59	19.4	3.2
60-69	23.7	3.6
70-79	19.5	4.6
80-89	11.4	6.1
90-99	5.5	10.0
100-110	2.5	9.9

Source: S. Nickell 'A picture of male unemployment in Britain', Economic Journal 90, 1980, p. 787.

no significant effect on unemployment for men who have been unemployed for more than 6 months.

Such results are consistent with other evidence on unemployment. Table 8.2 shows that, in 1972, high replacement ratios were associated with a higher incidence of unemployment. On the other hand, 90 per cent of those who had little to lose by being unemployed (i.e. with replacement ratios over 90 per cent) were working, despite the absence of any great financial incentive to do so. Furthermore, the proportion of the workforce with such high replacement ratios was very small (8 per cent) and since then is likely to have become even smaller with reductions in benefit levels.

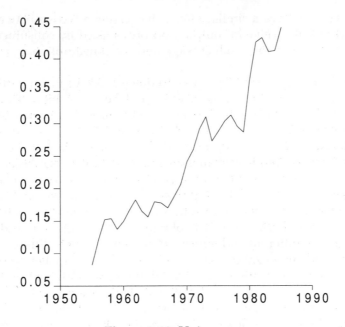

Figure 8.13 Union power

Source: Centre for Labour Economics dataset.

Other factors

In addition to unemployment benefits, there are several other supply-side factors which have been proposed as explanations of the rise in unemployment since the early 1970s. These include taxes, union power, housing costs, company profits and the proportion of long-term unemployed.

❑ *Taxation and import prices.* Taxes on labour, whether paid by workers (income tax and employees' national insurance contributions) or by firms (employers' national insurance contributions) insert a 'wedge' between the amount paid by firms and the amount received by workers. If this tax wedge is borne by the workers in the form of lower real wages this may result in higher inflation. The level of unemployment necessary to keep inflation from accelerating may thus be raised. Since the 1960s, employers' and employees' tax rates have increased, but indirect taxation, which can also lower real wages, shows no such trend. Import prices may have a similar effect: they create a wedge between the prices firms receive for output and prices faced by consumers, and hence between the product wage and the consumption wage.

❑ *Union power*. Union power has frequently been put forward as an explanation of high wage claims, and hence of high unemployment. Union power is, however, very difficult to measure. The percentage of workers who are in trade unions and the level of strike activity have been used to measure it, but neither is adequate. An alternative measure, discussed here not because it is the best measure of union power, but because it plays an important role in the empirical work considered later in this chapter, is the mark-up of union over non-union wage rates. This is shown in figure 8.13. It is obtained from cross section data on wages in different industries: each industry has different wage rates and unionization rates, and the relationship between wage rates and unionization is calculated, the series shown in figure 8.13 being derived from this. It shows a sharp rise around 1970 (after the events of 1968) and, more surprisingly, a rise in 1981. This might be because of the greater ability of unionized workers to withstand the effects of the depression of 1980-1, in which case it might be regarded as measuring union power. Such an interpretation is consistent with evidence from the 1930s suggesting that the union markup tends to rise in times of recession. An equally plausible explanation, however, is that the recession hit certain groups of workers (for example unskilled workers) particularly hard, and that these groups are less unionized than other groups of workers. In this case, the rise in this index does not correspond to any rise in union power. There is also the problem that the markups shown in figure 8.13 are high compared with estimates obtained from other cross-section evidence, which suggests a mark-up of only 7 to 10 per cent. Results based on this index must, therefore, be treated with *great* scepticism. It is given here because it plays an important role in empirical results which are discussed later on.

❑ *Housing costs*. A notable feature of the UK economy during the 1970s and 1980s has been the enormous rise in the price of housing. This rise has been particularly marked in the South-East, creating enormous regional differences in house prices. Figure 8.14 provides a measure of the extent to which house prices have risen relative to wage rates since 1960-1 (see also figure 3.14 for data

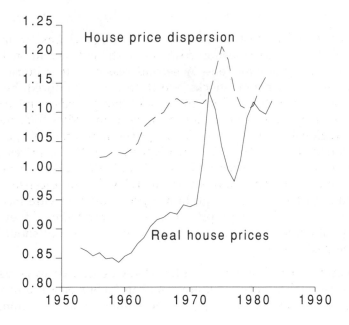

Figure 8.14 Real house prices

Source: Alan A. Carruth and Andrew J. Oswald *Pay Determination and Industrial Prosperity.*
Oxford: Oxford University Press, 1989, appendix 3.2.

covering a longer period). It measures the ratio of the rise in house prices since 1960-1 to the rise in wage rates in the same period. In order to measure the significance of rising house prices for household budgets, the series is adjusted to allow for changes in the proportion of houses that are owner-occupied. What stands out from this graph is the sharp rises in real house prices in 1972-3 and in 1979-80, together with the fact that real house prices have remained very high since 1980, though there has been some fall in house prices in 1989-90.

Figure 8.14 also shows a measure of the regional dispersion of house prices. This is defined as real house prices (as defined above) in the South-East divided by real house prices in the UK as a whole. This shows a very similar pattern: much of the rise in house prices has been in the South-East.

There are several reasons why house prices may be important in the wage-determination process. If house prices are rising because of a shortage of land, the cost of living (which includes the cost of housing) may be rising faster than output prices (which do not).

Given that the cost of living affects wage claims, it may be necessary to use housing costs as well as conventional price indices in wage equations. A second reason is that house prices may reflect demand shocks which are not captured by other measures of demand. Both the cost-of-living wedge and demand shocks may vary from region to region, providing reasons why the regional dispersion of house prices may affect wage determination. Finally, the regional dispersion of house prices affects labour mobility between regions. Not only do workers experience difficulty in moving from regions with low house prices to regions with higher prices, but high house prices may provide incentives to home-owners in high-price regions to stay there: if they move they may find it difficult to return. Lack of mobility should raise unemployment rates.

❑ *Company profits.* There is considerable evidence that wage negotiators use high profits as an argument in favour of wage increases. Furthermore, if we view unions and employers as bargaining over

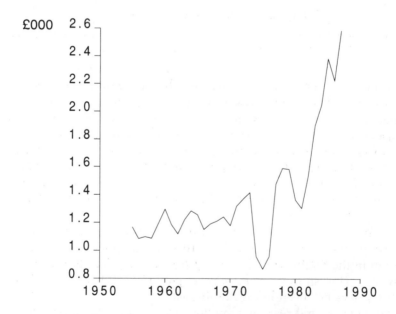

Figure 8.15 Real company profits per employee

Source: Economic Trends Annual Supplement. Gross trading profits of companies, deflated by GDP deflator, divided by workforce.

how income is divided between profits and wages, there are good theoretical reasons why high profits should push wages upwards: higher profits mean that the size of the 'cake' to be bargained over is higher, and that labour's share should be higher. Figure 8.15 shows real profits per employee. The main feature of this graph is the extremely low level of profits in 1974-6, and the unusually high level of profits after around 1982. If high company profits do cause wage bargainers to aim at achieving a higher real wage rate, this will, for reasons explained in section 8.5, cause unemployment to rise.

❑ *The proportion of long-term unemployed.* Figure 8.9 shows how the duration of unemployment has changed since the 1950s. In the late 1950s and the 1960s only about 10-20 per cent of the unemployed had been unemployed for over a year, but during the 1970s this proportion rose to around 30 per cent. Since 1979 the proportion of long-term unemployed has risen to over 40 per cent, a very high level: during the 1930s, for example, the proportion of long-term unemployment did not rise above 25 per cent. If 'long-term' is defined to be unemployment longer than 6 months then it now covers 60 per cent of the unemployed. The duration of unemployment has been argued to affect real wages and hence unemployment because as workers remain unemployed they lose skills and it becomes harder to match them with suitable jobs. As the long-term unemployed become less employable, they exercise less of a restraining influence on unemployment, which tends to raise the unemployment rate.

8.5 WAGE DETERMINATION

The Phillips curve

The simplest framework for analysing the link between inflation and unemployment is the Phillips curve. We could argue that supply-side factors determine the position of the Phillips curve, including the NAIRU (the unemployment rate at which the inflation rate is constant, sometimes called the 'natural' rate of unemployment — for further detail see box 8.3). If we can estimate a Phillips curve we should be able to estimate the NAIRU and hence work out how much unemployment is caused by supply-side factors (causing the NAIRU to rise) and how much is caused by aggregate demand being too low (unemployment rising above the NAIRU). Before we can do this, however, we have to make a number of decisions about how we are going to estimate the Phillips curve: which inflation rate to use; how to model expected inflation; and what other variables to include.

❑ Which inflation rate (wage inflation or price inflation) is to be explained? Either is possible for although the Phillips curve is based on a relationship between wages and unemployment, wages are linked to prices via costs. We would expect the relationship to hold whether we tried to explain wage or price inflation.

❑ How do we model expected inflation? One of two approaches is usually adopted: adaptive or rational expectations. With adaptive expectations it is assumed that expectations adjust to actual inflation with a lag. Expectations are thus modelled by incorporating lagged inflation on the right-hand side of the Phillips curve. Rational expectations involve the assumption that people are forming their expectations in such a way as to make the best possible use of all the information available to them. If people are assumed to know how the economy works, this means that rational expectations should be the same as the predictions generated by the model based on these expectations. Such expectations are, clearly, more complicated to model than adaptive expectations.

❑ What other variables (besides expected inflation and unemployment) should be incorporated? Candidates here are import prices, real wages and productivity growth. This problem is an important one, for it is clear that if we are to make any sense of a Phillips curve for the UK in recent years we have to allow, somehow, for a rise in the NAIRU since the 1960s.

We start with what is almost the simplest possible expectations-augmented Phillips curve: the previous period's inflation rate is used as a proxy for expected inflation. Changes in the NAIRU are allowed for by a time trend (t = date - 1954) and a dummy variable (IPD) to capture the effects of the very severe incomes policy which lowered inflation in 1976 (IPD takes the value 1 in 1976, and 0 in every other year). The following equation is estimated over the period 1955-85.

$$\pi_t = \pi_{t-1} + 3.6 - 7.7\log(U_t) + 0.48t - 13.0IPD$$

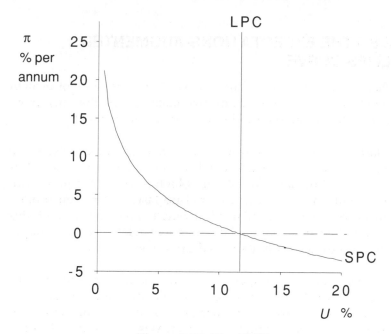

Figure 8.16 The Phillips curve

The logarithm of unemployment is used simply to obtain a curve of the shape we usually associate with the Phillips curve: at low levels of unemployment we expect the Phillips curve to be very steep and at high levels of unemployment we expect it to be fairly flat. To find the NAIRU we set $\pi_t = \pi_{t-1}$ (IPD is, of course, taken as zero). The short-run Phillips curve slopes downwards as expected and because of the time trend the NAIRU is rising over time. For 1986 the NAIRU implied by this equation is 11.7 per cent and the resulting Phillips curves are those plotted in figure 8.16.

Although such an equation might seem to work well, there are major problems with it. One is that it is very sensitive to the choice of period over which it is estimated. To see this, consider the same equation estimated using data for 1965-84:

$$\pi_t = \pi_{t-1} + 8.1 - 14.0\log(U_t) + 1.40t - 12.1IPD$$

This gives a NAIRU of only 10 per cent and it implies that the short run Phillips curve is twice as steep: a 1 per cent fall in unemployment

BOX 8.3 THE EXPECTATIONS-AUGMENTED PHILLIPS CURVE

The theory underlying the Phillips curve is that the rate of growth of money wages (π^W) depends on two main factors: the unemployment rate (U) and the expected rate of price inflation (π^e).

❑ *Unemployment* affects wage inflation because it reflects the state of the labour market: when unemployment is low this means that demand for labour is high relative to supply, with the result that wages will be bid up faster than if unemployment were higher. Similarly if unemployment is very high this means that demand for labour is low relative to the supply and wages rates will not be bid up so fast.

❑ *Expected inflation* is important because both firms and workers are concerned with real wages, not money wages. If firms and workers both expect a higher rate of inflation not only will workers demand higher wage increases, but firms will offer higher wages as well.

The simplest version of the expectations-augmented Phillips curve is

$$\pi = \pi^e - \beta(U\text{-}U^*),$$

where U^* is the so-called 'natural' rate of unemployment, or NAIRU (non-accelerating inflation rate of unemployment). If $U = U^*$ the actual rate of inflation will equal the expected rate, which means that there is no reason for the inflation rate to change.

Given the expected inflation rate we can draw a downward-sloping curve relating inflation and unemployment: this is the *short-run Phillips curve*. Note that in this box a linear relationship is assumed in order to keep the theory as simple as possible. The short-run Phillips curve is usually assumed to have the shape depicted in figure 8.13. If the expectations of inflation change the curve will shift. To see this, consider figure 8.B3.1. If expected inflation is zero ($\pi^e = 0$) the short run Phillips curve is SPC_0, a line with slope -β, cutting the horizontal axis at U^*. If, on the other hand, expected inflation were π^e_1, the short run Phillips curve would be SPC_1: π^e_1 higher than if expected inflation were zero.

It follows from this that if expectations are to be correct (if $\pi = \pi^e$) unemployment must be equal to U^*. This can easily be seen if we re-write the Phillips curve equation as

$$\pi - \pi^e = -\beta(U-U^*).$$

If $U > U^*$ then $\pi < \pi^e$ and vice versa. If we make the quite reasonable assumption that if expectations are incorrect then they will be changing, it follows that the inflation rate can be constant only if $U = U^*$. This is the natural rate hypothesis: th hypothesis that the inflation rate can be constant only if unemployment equals U^*. This is important because if we assume that in the long run the inflation rate cannot either increase or decrease indefinitely, it follows that in the long run unemployment cannot permanently diverge from U^*.

U^* is thus sometimes called the *natural rate of unemployment*. Economists who prefer a more neutral name for U^* refer to it instead as the NAIRU: the *N*on *A*ccelerating *I*nflation *R*ate of *U*nemployment.

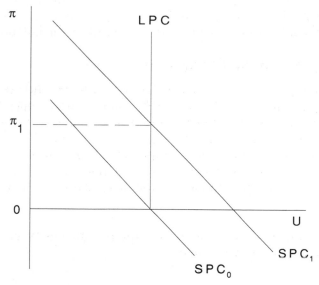

Figure 8.B3.1 The Phillips Curve

produces a 14 per cent rise in inflation, compared with an 8 per cent rise in the previous equation.

A second problem with this equation concerns inflationary expectations. To see how much difference the adoption of rational expectations might make replace π_{t-1} by π^*, where π^* is determined by regressing inflation on π_{t-1} and π_{t-2}. This is, more or less, the best prediction that people could make if they knew simply past inflation rates. In practice we would expect that people might do better than this. Estimating such an equation we obtain

$$\pi_t = \pi^* + 11.9 - 14.1\log(U_t) + 1.58t - 6.0IPD$$

where π^* is the best prediction of π_t that can be obtained from information on π_{t-1} and π_{t-2} (i.e. it is the result of regressing π_t on π_{t-1} and π_{t-2}). Predicting inflation on the basis of just two previous periods' inflation rates is a long way from full rational expectations, but it is a step in the right direction. The lesson to be drawn from this equation is that it gives yet another, very different, estimate of the NAIRU: namely 15.5 per cent in 1986. The fact that such small changes in the way we specify the Phillips curve lead to such large differences in our estimate of the NAIRU suggests that such a simple Phillips curve is inadequate. The major problem with this approach, however, is that it models changes in the NAIRU using a time trend, assuming it is rising remorselessly. We therefore need a theory of how the NAIRU is determined, and a better model of what determines the inflation rate.

Real wages and the Phillips curve

Before turning to a theory of what determines the NAIRU it is worth considering an alternative version of the Phillips curve which brings in the real wages. In addition to providing a link, even if only a weak one, with the ideas discussed in chapter 7, this illustrates an issue that several economists have seen as important. This time we consider a Phillips curve which explains wage inflation, π^W. In addition to unemployment the equation has the following terms on the right-hand side:

❏ Last period's wage inflation, to capture inflationary expectations in the simplest way possible.

❏ The growth in the real wage rate during the previous period ($\pi^W_{t-1} - \pi_{t-1}$). The theory underlying this is that wage bargainers have a target real wage rate which only changes slowly over time. If real wages fell in the previous period, therefore, wage increases will be higher as bargainers attempt to restore real wages to their former level. Similarly, rapidly growing real wages reduce the pressure on wages.

❏ Time trends.

Table 8.3 Estimates of the NAIRU, I

	UK		EC	
	NAIRU	u	NAIRU	u
1966-70	2.4	1.9	3.2	2.4
1971-75	4.0	2.8	3.6	3.2
1976-80	4.7	5.5	4.8	5.4
1981-83	9.2	10.8	7.7	8.8

Source: as described in the text.

The resulting equation is

$$\pi^W_{t-1} = -0.79(\pi^W_{t-1}-\pi_{t-1}) - 2.01U_t + 0.74t + 3.1t^2 + 0.09$$

The negative coefficient on $\pi^W_{t-1}-\pi_{t-1}$ provides some support for the idea that wages increase in response to reductions in real wages (if $\pi^W_{t-1}-\pi_{t-1} < 0$ real wages are falling).

To solve for the NAIRU we need to make some assumption about what would have happened to real wages had the inflation rate been constant. We could, for example, assume that the real wage grows at its 'warranted' rate (see chapter 7). In table 8.3 the NAIRU is calculated by setting $\pi^W-\pi$ equal its average for the period being considered (the results are very similar to using the warranted growth rate of real wages). To provide a comparison, equivalent figures are provided for the European Community as a whole.

Though the dependence of these results on the use of time trends means they must be treated with caution, they suggest the following conclusions.

❏ From 1966 to 1975 unemployment was below the NAIRU and inflation was accelerating, both in the UK and in the European Community as a whole.

❏ From 1976 to 1983 the actual unemployment rate was above the NAIRU, this resulting in falling inflation.

❏ The NAIRU has risen substantially in both the UK and the EC. The experience of the UK has been similar to that of the EC as a whole, the main difference occurring since 1981, when the NAIRU and actual unemployment in the UK have risen well above the EC average.

The problem with such equations is that they do not provide any independent evidence on the NAIRU. The NAIRU is in effect calculated in such a way as to ensure that, as far as possible, it is below actual unemployment when inflation is falling, and above actual unemployment when inflation is rising. To get more solid evidence on the NAIRU we need to bring in other evidence, and to do this we need a theory of what determines the NAIRU. This is done in section 8.5. Before doing that, however, we need to consider wage equations.

Wage equations incorporating supply-side factors

The wage equation that is used in the estimates of the NAIRU discussed in the following section is the one estimated over the period 1956 to 1983 by Layard and Nickell (R. Layard and S. Nickell 'Unemployment in Britain,' *Economica* 53, supplement, 1986, pp. S121-70).

$$\log(W/P) = -0.062\log U + 0.039MM + 0.18RR + 0.50IMP + 0.42\Delta IMP + 0.085UP + 0.18TAX + \text{constant and other terms.}$$

The variables in this equation are MM (mismatch as in figure 8.7), RR (the replacement ratio, figure 8.12), IMP (the ratio of import prices to domestic prices), UP (the union mark-up, figure 8.13), TAX (employment taxes borne by employers) and IPD (an incomes policy dummy variable for 1976-7). The incomes policy dummy variable is a way of capturing the once-for-all effects of the very effective incomes policy imposed at this time. No account is taken of the incomes policies in force at other times, the effects of these being much less clear-cut than in 1976-7.

Although this equation may look fairly complicated, it is easy to interpret. Note that the logarithm of W/P is used simply to get a suitable non-linear relationship between real wages and the variables on the right-hand side: there is no economics behind it. The equation implies a negative relationship between unemployment and real wages: when unemployment rises, real wages fall. This is the 'target real wage' curve discussed in box 8.4. This equation shows that it is shifted up by rises in mismatch, the replacement ratio, the union mark-up, taxes on employment and import prices (the reason that both the change in and the level of import prices appear is simply that it makes the equation fit the data better).

A major problem with wage equations such as this is that they cannot explain why wage inflation should have been so high during the mid to late 1980s, despite the persistence of high unemployment. The only way to explain this would be to argue that the NAIRU has risen enormously, something for which there seems little evidence. It is thus necessary to bring other factors into the wage equation. Three factors which have been brought in are long-term unemployment, real house prices and profit levels (all discussed above). We will consider two such equations. The first, estimated by Muellbauer and Bover (J. Muellbauer and O. Bover 'Housing, wages and UK labour markets', *Oxford Bulletin of Economics and Statistics*, 1988) is

$$\log(RW_t) = -0.031\log(U_t) - 0.075\Delta_3\log(U_t) + 0.067\Delta MM_t + 0.15\log(UD_{t-1})$$
$$+ 0.38HP_{t-1} + 0.0085UCH_{t-1} + 0.57RDHP_{t-1} + \text{constant and other terms}$$

where RW is real wages adjusted for the trend growth rate of productivity, MM is the index of structural change, HP is house prices relative to wages, $RDHP$ is the regional dispersion of house prices (both these are as in figure 8.14), and UCH is an estimate of the user cost of housing (the cost of mortgage payments, repairs and so on). UD is union density, the proportion of the labour force that is in a trade union. This measure was used instead of the union mark-up because of the problems associated with the latter that are discussed above. The 'other terms' include import prices and competitiveness as well as lagged values of different variables. Note that several of the variables are included as two or three year moving averages.

This equation, especially when written out in full, looks very complicated, but it can be interpreted fairly easily. All three aspects of house prices in the equation have the expected effect, raising wages, as do the change in mismatch and union density. More complicated is the second term on the right-hand side, $-0.075\Delta_3\log(U)$. This states that in addition to a higher *level* of unemployment lowering wage increases, *rises* in unemployment keep wages down. Thus if unemployment rises sharply, as in 1979-81, this will have a strong effect on wage increases. But once unemployment has stopped rising, wage increases will rise again, despite a continuing high level of unemployment. To reduce the real wage growth we may need not a high level of unemployment, but a *rising* level of unemployment. This is a phenomenon sometimes known as *hysteresis*: it means that once unemployment has risen it tends to stay high. This could easily be rationalized by arguing that once people become unemployed they lose their skills and become harder to employ. Thus there may be mismatch between workers and jobs, even though this may not appear in measures of mismatch such as those discussed above.

Including the change in unemployment in the wage equation is one way to allow for hysteresis effects. This is the notion that the longer unemployment persists, the smaller is its effect on inflation. This arises because the long-term unemployed have less impact on the labour market: they are less active, having failed to find work for a long time, and they are less likely than people who have been unemployed for a shorter period to have the skills that employers are demanding. An alternative (related) approach is to include long-term unemployment in a wage equation. This is done in the following wage equation, taken from Carruth and Oswald (Alan A. Carruth and Andrew J. Oswald *Pay Determination and Industrial Prosperity*. Oxford: Oxford University Press, 1989).

$$\log(W/P)_t = -0.07\log(U_t) - 0.05\log(PE_{t-2}) + 0.1PLTU_t - 0.17\Delta LTU_t +$$
$$0.22HP_{t-2} + \text{constant and other terms}$$

where *PE* is real profits per employee (see figure 8.15), *PLTU* is the proportion of long-term unemployment (see figure 8.9) and *LTU* is the stock of long-term unemployed. The 'other terms' include import prices and a tax rate but, interestingly, neither the replacement ratio nor any measure of union power. These figures suggest that profits, house prices and long-term unemployment all have significant effects on real wages. The elasticity of real wages with respect to profits per employee (5 per cent) may seem small, but profits are *extremely* volatile, whereas real wages fluctuate very little. The elasticity of real wages with respect to unemployment is very low, implying that a doubling of the unemployment rate would lower real wages by only 7 per cent. This effect is very close to that in the Layard and Nickell equation, discussed above.

These last two equations have important implications for the behaviour of real wages in the early 1990s. A major policy issue concerns what needs to be done about the high level of wage increases. If wage increases have been rising either because of rapidly rising house prices, or because of rising company profits, then wage inflation should, if the relationship is reversible, and provided that nothing else changes, moderate of its own accord as both house prices and company profits have started to fall. The importance of the proportion of long-term unemployed also has policy implications, for it suggests that the long-term unemployed do not exert as great a downward pressure on wage increases as do the short-term unemployed. This has two implications. If higher unemployment involves a higher proportion of long-term unemployed, then it may have little effect on wages. In addition, the fact that the long-term unemployed have a small effect on wages means that policy measures can be targeted at them without there being any increase in wage inflation.

In this section, we have considered a number of competing, though related, wage equations. Though it is difficult to disentangle the effects of different supply-side factors from each other, these equations suggest a number of factors which may be important in determining real wages. Thus although it seems very plausible that factors such as the duration of unemployment, house prices and company profits affect real wages, the results should be treated cautiously, and this should be taken into account when formulating policy.

8.6 THE NAIRU

The determinants of the NAIRU

When we use a simple Phillips curve to determine inflation it is simple to solve for the NAIRU. When we start using wage equations such as those discussed at the end of the previous section, however, we need to bring in other equations as well. In this section, which is based on Layard and Nickell's work, we use the theory outlined in box 8.4 according to which the NAIRU is explained as the outcome of a bargaining process in which wages are determined by a wage bargaining process, and wages are determined by the first of the wage equations discussed above. To complete the empirical model we need to introduce labour demand and price-setting equations.

The labour demand equation is

$$\log(N_t) = AD - 2.9\log(W/P)_{t-1} + \text{constant and other terms}$$

where, once again, the other terms are lagged variables, capturing the fact that employment takes time to respond to disturbances. *AD* is a measure of the level of aggregate demand, and is an appropriately weighted average of the level of world trade, the government deficit and international competitiveness (the ratio of the price of world exports, converted to sterling, to the UK price level). The only economically interesting term not listed is the capital stock, which clearly affects demand for labour.

This demand curve has the conventional slope, and shifts to the right when aggregate demand increases. The latter effect is something that can be explained only if competition is imperfect: if there were perfect competition we would expect demand for labour to depend simply on the real wage rate (and the capital stock), not on the level of aggregate demand. The short run elasticity of demand for labour with respect to the real wage rate is 2.9. Because of the lags involved (these are not reported here) the long run elasticity is smaller (-0.9).

The price setting equation is

$$\log(P/W) = 0.38AD + \text{constant and other terms}$$

where the other terms are mostly lagged values of P, W and P/W, included to capture lagged adjustments in expectations. This equation implies that increases in the level of aggregate demand raise the profit margin and reduce the 'feasible' real wage rate (see box 8.4 for an explanation).

Before we can use these equations to estimate the NAIRU one further decision has to be made. The reason is that when we estimate the NAIRU we are concerned with estimating the equilibrium rate of unemployment, but the wage-setting equation contains import prices and, in addition, competitiveness is one of the factors used to calculate aggregate demand. The level of competitiveness (the ratio of import prices to domestic prices) is subject to large short term variations. We therefore want a way of calculating the equilibrium level of competitiveness. The way to do this is to estimate an equation relating the trade balance to competitiveness and to use this equation to calculate the level of competitiveness that is consistent with a zero balance of trade. The trade balance equation is,

$$B/Y_t^P = 4.68 + 361.0WP_{t-1} + 135.8IMP_{t-1} - 39.8AD_{t-1} + 24.6OIL_{t-1}$$

where Y^P is a measure of permanent income and OIL is North Sea oil production. WP is a is the world price of manufactured exports relative

BOX 8.4 A MODEL OF THE NAIRU

The model of the NAIRU that we shall consider here is based on the notion that wages and employment are the outcome of bargaining between employers and workers. There are three elements in the model: price and wage setting equations, and a demand for labour function.

❏ *Price setting*. Firms determine prices relative to costs. To keep the model simple assume that firms set prices on the basis of a mark-up on variable cost (this makes sense only if firms are imperfectly competitive). If wages are the main element in costs, it follows that

$$\frac{W}{P} = \frac{1}{\text{normal mark-up of prices over wages}}.$$

❏ We will call this the 'feasible real wage rate'. In applying their mark-up firms set prices on the basis of expected wage costs. Thus if firms' expectations are incorrect, the real wage may diverge from this level. If they under-estimate wage inflation, for example, they will set prices too low, with the result that real wages will be higher than they planned: the real wage will be higher than the 'feasible' real wage.

❏ *Wage setting*. The nature of the labour market determines what can best be called the 'target' real wage rate. This depends on unemployment (which reduces the target real wage) and various supply-side factors, such as unemployment benefits, mismatch and so on. This target real wage is the real wage that results from the wage bargaining process. Because people bargaining over wages are concerned about real wages, the money wage that results from the bargaining process will depend on what people expect to happen to prices. If inflation is under-estimated, for example, wages will be set too low and as a result the real wage will end up being below the target real wage.

❏ *Demand for labour*. This depends on the real wage and the level of aggregate demand. The level of aggregate demand is included to allow for the possibility of imperfect competition, where the level of aggregate demand affects the position of firms' demand curves. Under perfect competition, where firms face horizontal demand curves, demand for labour should depend only on the real wage rate.

These three things are put together in figure 8.B3.1. The NAIRU is the level of unemployment at which the feasible real wage equals the target real wage. To show this, labour demand curves are drawn corresponding to three levels of aggregate demand. L^d_1 corresponds to a high level of demand, L^d_2 to a low level of demand, and L^d_0 to an intermediate level of demand. If demand for labour is given by L^d_0 equilibrium is at E_0. The target real wage equals the actual real wage and there is no reason for inflation to change. This is the NAIRU. Suppose instead that aggregate demand is high and demand for labour is determined by L^d_1. Equilibrium will be at a point such as E_1, with accelerating inflation causing both firms and workers to under-estimate the inflation rate. Because firms under- estimate inflation they set prices too low and as a result the actual real wage exceeds the feasible real wage. Because workers under-estimate inflation they set money wages lower than they would otherwise have done, the result being that the actual real wage falls short of the target real wage. Similarly, if aggregate demand is too low, giving labour demand L^d_2, the result will be an equilibrium such as E_2, with a falling inflation rate, resulting in both firms and workers over- estimating inflation.

to the UK price level, a measure of competitiveness. The terms in this equation are all self-explanatory: the balance of trade will improve if competitiveness improves (both *WP* and *IMP* measure foreign prices), if aggregate demand falls or if oil production increases.

Table 8.4 gives the resulting estimates of the NAIRU. Two estimates are shown, one using the actual level of real import prices in the periods in question, the other using the level of import prices that would, using the above equation, give a zero trade balance. Both estimates show a substantial rise in the NAIRU, especially during the

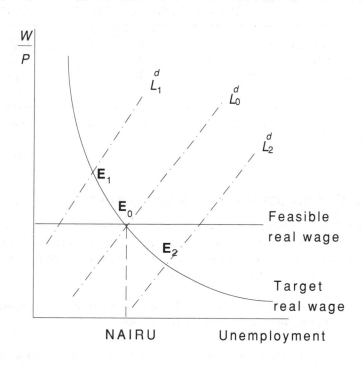

Figure 8.B4.1 The determination of the NAIRU

1970s. These figures are compatible with those shown in table 8.3, derived using a different method. They suggest that during 1967-74 and 1975-79 the NAIRU rose above the actual unemployment rate. This is consistent with the acceleration in inflation during both periods. Since 1979, however, though the NAIRU has risen further, unemployment has risen above the NAIRU, the result being a fall in the inflation rate.

Table 8.4 Estimates of the NAIRU, II

	1956-66	1967-74	1975-79	1980-83
Given real import prices	1.96	4.02	8.20	10.47
Given trade balance	1.96	4.19	7.63	9.07
Actual unemployment rate (percentages)	1.96	3.78	6.79	13.79

Source: R. Layard and S. Nickell 'Unemployment in Britain,' *Economica* 53 (supplement), 1986, p. S158.

Accounting for the rise in unemployment

The advantage of using the relatively complicated theory discussed in this section is that in addition to estimating changes in the NAIRU we can work out what caused it to rise. This is done in table 8.5. Several conclusions can be drawn from these figures.

❏ Increases in the union mark-up have had an important impact on raising the natural rate in all three periods.

❏ The benefits variable contributed to the rise in the NAIRU up to 1967-74, but since then the fall in the replacement ratio has served to lower the NAIRU.

❏ North Sea oil production has kept the NAIRU down in the last two periods.

❏ The rise in raw material prices in 1973-4 had a large effect on the NAIRU.

❏ Incomes policy succeeded in keeping the NAIRU down in 1976-7.

Another way of using these equations is to calculate the influence of various factors on the actual level of unemployment. This is done in table 8.6. Note that when the contributions of the different factors are added up the total is not the same as the actual unemployment rate. The reason is that there is a certain random component which the equations cannot account for. The main feature to stand out from

Table 8.5 Causes of the rise in the NAIRU

Given trade balance	1956-66 to 1967-74	1967-74 to 1975-79	1975-79 to 1980-83
Employers' labour taxes (TAX)	0.29	0.51	0.69
Benefit replacement ratio (RR)	0.64	-0.12	-0.15
Union mark-up (UP)	1.40	1.58	1.25
Oil production (OIL)	-	-0.32	-1.73
Import prices/world export prices (IMP/WP)	-0.29	2.02	-0.17
Mismatch (MM)	0.19	0.27	0.77
Incomes policy (IPD)	-	-0.50	0.78
Total	2.23	3.44	1.44

Source: Layard and Nickell 'Unemployment in Britain', p. S159.

Table 8.6 Causes of the rise in unemployment

	1956-66 to 1967-74	1967-74 to 1975-79	1975-79 to 1980-83
Employers' labour taxes (TAX)	0.25	0.38	0.44
Benefit replacement ratio (RR)	0.54	-0.09	-0.10
Union mark-up (UP)	1.18	1.17	0.80
Real import prices (IMP)	-0.58	1.47	-0.93
Mismatch (MM)	0.16	0.20	0.49
Incomes policy (IPD)	-	-0.36	0.49
Demand factors (AD)	0.12	0.54	6.56
Total	1.67	3.31	7.75
Actual change	1.82	3.01	7.00

Source: Layard and Nickell 'Unemployment in Britain', p. S158.

table 8.6 is the importance of supply factors in causing the rise in unemployment during the 1970s, and the importance of demand factors during the 1980s. Of this fall in demand, 46 per cent was due to fiscal policy, 42 per cent to a reduction in competitiveness and 12 per cent to a decline in world trade. Most of the other entries in table 8.6 correspond to entries in table 8.5 that have been discussed already.

FURTHER READING

A good, very simple, introduction to the issues discussed in this chapter (and many others) is Richard Layard *How to Beat Unemployment* (Oxford: Oxford University Press, 1986). Shorter and more technical, though still very accessible, is R. Layard and S. Nickell 'The labour market,' in R. Dornbusch and R. Layard (eds.) *The Performance of the British Economy* (Oxford: Oxford University Press, 1987). A book which should, based on the authors' track record, be very useful is R. Jackman, R. Layard and S. Nickell *Unemployment* (Oxford: Oxford University Press, forthcoming). Peter Fallon and Donald Verry *The Economics of Labour Markets* (Oxford and New Jersey: Philip Allan, 1988), chapter 8, provides a very helpful survey of empirical evidence on the structure of the labour market — particularly on inflows and outflows and on the relationship between aggregate durations such as used here, and the durations observed in microeconomic surveys.

The model on which much of this chapter is based has been expounded in several places. The easiest is in Richard Layard *How to Beat Unemployment* (Oxford: Oxford University Press, 1986); more thorough than this is P. R. G. Layard and S. J. Nickell 'The causes of British unemployment', *National Institute Economic Review*, 111, 1985, pp. 62-85; most thorough is P. R. G. Layard and S. J. Nickell 'Unemployment in Britain', *Economica* 53 (supplement), pp. S121-70. The wage equation is extended to incorporate house prices in O. Bover, J. Muellbauer and A. Murphy 'Housing, wages and UK labour markets', *Oxford Bulletin of Economics and Statistics*, 1988; and profits are introduced in Alan A. Carruth and Andrew J. Oswald *Pay Determination and Industrial Prosperity* (Oxford: Oxford University Press, 1989). The role of the housing market is also investigated in John Ermisch (ed.) *Housing and the National Economy* (Aldershot and Brookfield, VT: Avebury, 1990). A European perspective is provided in: R. Layard

'European unemployment: cause and cure', LSE Centre for Labour Economics Discussion Paper No. 368, November 1989; *Economica* supplement on unemployment, 1986, reprinted as C. Bean, R. Layard and S. Nickell (eds.) *The Rise in Unemployment* (Oxford and Cambridge, Mass.: Basil Blackwell, 1987).

Though microfoundations have not been discussed in this chapter, the bargaining model used is based on the assumption of imperfect competition. As most textbooks on macroeconomics, if they deal with microfoundations at all, assume perfect competition, it is worth mentioning that Wendy Carlin and David Soskice *Macroeconomics and the Wage Bargain* (Oxford: Oxford University Press, 1990) analyses a model of imperfect competition similar to the one used by Layard and Nickell. Another interesting recent attempt to construct a macroeconomic model based on imperfect competition is Robin Marris *Reconstructing Keynesian Economics with Imperfect Competition* (Aldershot: Edward Elgar, 1991).

Many other explanations of unemployment have been offered. There follows a selection of these: Olivier J. Blanchard and Lawrence H. Summers 'Hysteresis and the European unemployment problem,' *NBER Macroeconomics Annual* 1986, pp. 15-78; R. Cross (ed.) *Unemployment, Hysteresis and the Natural Rate Hypothesis* (Oxford and Cambridge, Mass.: Basil Blackwell, 1988); David Metcalfe 'Labour market flexibility and jobs: a survey of evidence from OECD countries with special reference to Europe', in Richard Layard and Lars Calmfors (eds.) *The Fight Against Unemployment: Macroeconomic Papers from the Centre for European Studies* (London and Cambridge, Mass.: MIT Press, 1987). L. Calmfors and J. Driffil 'Bargaining structure, corporatism and macroeconomic performance,' *Economic Policy* 6, 1988, pp. 13-62; Richard B. Freeman 'Labour market institutions and economic performance', *Economic Policy* 6, 1988, pp. 64-80; Michael Burda '"Wait unemployment" in Europe', *Economic Policy* 7, 1988, pp. 391-426; George S. Alogoskoufis and Alan Manning 'On the persistence of unemployment', *Economic Policy* 7, 1988, pp. 427-69; C. Bean and A. Gavosto 'Outsiders, capacity shortages and unemployment in the United Kingdom,' in J. Drèze, C. Bean and R. Layard (eds.) *Europe's Unemployment Problem* (Cambridge, Mass.: MIT Press, 1989); A. Newell and J. Symons 'Corporatism, laissez-faire and the rise in unemployment,' *European Economic Review* 31, 1987, pp. 567-614; G. Burtless 'Jobless pay and high European unemployment', in R. Z. Lawrence and C. L. Schultze (eds.) *Barriers to European Growth* (Washington, DC: Brookings Institution, 1987). A different perspective on recent European experience is provided in Robert J. Gordon 'Back to the future:

European unemployment today viewed from America in 1939,' *Brookings Papers on Economic Activity* 1988, 1, pp, 271-304. Many of the references cited in chapters 6 and 7 are also relevant here.

The argument that it is outflows from unemployment that are critical in determining the unemployment rate is clearly put forward in Christopher Pissarides 'Unemployment and vacancies in Britain', *Economic Policy*, 3, 1986, pp. 499-559. The contrary view is proposed in S. Burgess 'How does unemployment change' (unpublished paper, University of Bristol, 1990), on which much of the section on flows is based. Discussion of the U/V curve can be found in Pissarides (*ibid.*) and in A. Budd, P. Levine and P. Smith 'Long term unemployment and the shifting U/V curve: a multi-country study', *European Economic Review* 31, 1987, pp. 296-305. The problem of structural unemployment is covered in R. Jackman and S. Roper 'Structural unemployment,' *Oxford Bulletin of Economics and Statistics* 49, 1987, pp. 9-36. A good example of evidence from microeconomic survey data is S. Nickell, W. Narendranathan, J. Stern and J. Garcia *The Nature of Unemployment in Britain: Studies of the DHSS Cohort* (Oxford: Clarendon Press, 1989). Also useful is K. G. Knight *Unemployment: an Economic Analysis (London and Sydney: Croom Helm, 1987)*, especially chapter 6.

An article that was published too late to be taken into account here is R. Jackman, C. Pissarides and S. Savouri 'Labour market policies and unemployment in the OECD', *Economic Policy* 11, 1990, pp. 449-90.

9

North Sea oil

9.1 THE UK AS AN OIL PRODUCER

Oil production

Oil has played a major role in the UK economy during the 1970s and 1980s for two reasons: the price of oil has fluctuated dramatically and, partly in response to higher oil prices, there has been large-scale investment in North Sea oil production, resulting in the UK becoming a major oil-exporting country. The price of oil is shown in figures 9.1 and 9.2. It had been constant throughout the 1960s with, for example, Libyan oil, the price of which is shown in figures 9.1 and 9.2, selling for $2.58 per barrel. Because prices of other goods were rising, however, the real price of oil was falling steadily during the 1960s. By 1972 the price had 'crept' up to $3.37. Then, in 1973, the price rose by over 40 per cent to $4.80 and in 1974 a further rise of 190 per cent brought the price to $13.84 per barrel. The price remained at about this level till 1979, though the real price fell by 29.3 per cent because of the high rates of inflation that industrial countries were experiencing during this period. In 1979 the price rose sharply to over $35 per barrel. During the 1980s the oil price fell sharply, in both real and nominal terms, until the crisis over Kuwait caused the price to rise sharply to around $40 per barrel during 1990.

So far we have considered the world price of oil, both in US dollars and in relation to the price level prevailing in industrial countries as a whole. To obtain the price of oil to the UK we have to convert the price into sterling. This is done in figure 9.1. During this period the value of

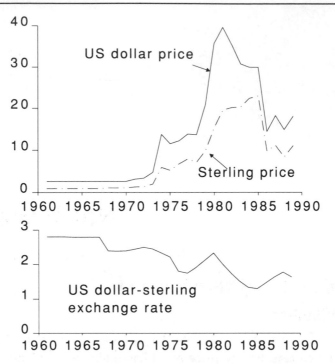

Figure 9.1 The nominal price of oil, 1961-89
Source: International Financial Statistics. Oil price is Libyan oil to 1985 and UK (Brent)
thereafter.

sterling has declined, which has meant that the sterling price of oil has
risen faster than its dollar price. Furthermore, the rise in the value of
sterling during the 1979-80 oil price rise meant that the sterling price of
oil did not reach its peak until 1983: the appreciation of sterling
insulated the UK from the full extent of the oil price rise.

North Sea oil is very expensive, with high development and
production costs, but the price rises of the 1970s made it profitable to
exploit it on a large scale, and a high level of investment took place.
Investment in oil and gas extraction accounted for 6-8 per cent of all
UK fixed investment from 1975 to 1983 (as shown in figure 9.3). During
the 1980s the share of investment being allocated to the oil and gas
extraction has fallen, for two reasons. The first is that, partly because of
the fall in the price of oil, real investment in oil and gas, measured in
1985 prices, fell from over £3 billion per annum up to 1984 to below £2
billion in 1987. The second is that, with the expansion of the economy

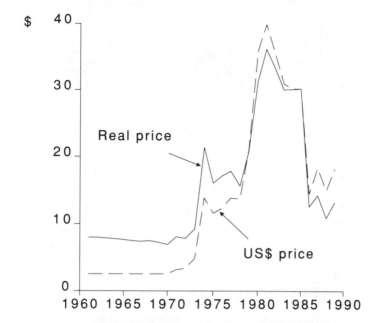

Figure 9.2 The real price of oil, 1961-89

Source: US dollar price from fig 9.1, deflated with industrial countries export price index from *International Financial Statistics.*

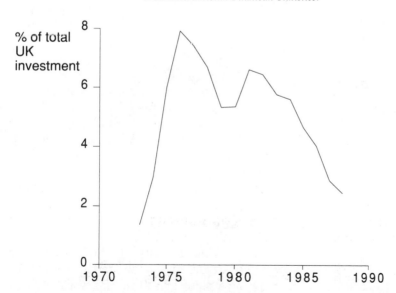

Figure 9.3 Investment in oil and gas extraction, 1973-88

Source: United Kingdom National Accounts.

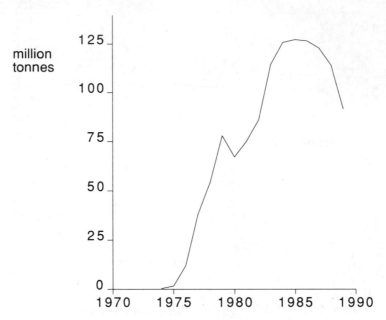

Figure 9.4 UK oil production, 1970-89
Source: Monthly Digest of Statistics.

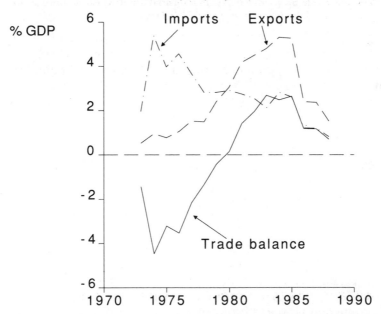

Figure 9.5 The trade deficit in oil, 1973-88
Source: United Kingdom Balance of Payments.

after 1981, real investment in the UK as a whole has risen: this rise in investment has reduced the share taken by oil and gas extraction to under 3 per cent.

The result of this high level of investment was a sharp rise in UK oil production. Oil production was negligible before 1975 but by 1980 it had risen to 603 million barrels per annum, 2.6 per cent of world production. By 1985, partly because of a continued rise in UK production to 953 million barrels a year, and partly because OPEC virtually halved its production in an attempt to keep the price of oil high, UK production accounted for 4.6 per cent of world production. Since 1985 production has fallen slightly. Without investment in discovering and developing new fields current levels of production cannot be sustained and falling oil prices significantly reduced the incentive for the oil companies to undertake such investment in the North Sea.

Oil and the balance of payments

The oil price rise of 1973-4 left the UK, in common with most other industrial countries, with a large balance of payments deficit, because of the sharply increased cost of importing oil. In 1974 the cost of oil imports rose to £4.1 billion, the result being an oil deficit (i.e. imports minus exports of oil) of £3.4 billion, or 4.5 per cent of GDP. The growth of North Sea oil production, together with the effects of high oil prices and measures to economize on oil consumption (it was at this time, for example, that speed limits were introduced for all roads), resulted in this oil deficit being eliminated by 1980: exports rose and imports were reduced, as shown in figure 9.5. As North Sea production rose still further, the UK became a net exporter of oil, the surplus reaching £8.1 billion, or 2.7 per cent or GDP by 1985.

The trade deficit in oil, however, is not the only way in which North Sea oil affects the balance of payments. Three other things have to be taken into account: profits and dividends due abroad; overseas investment in the North Sea; and expectations about the future.

❏ A substantial part of the investment undertaken in the North Sea has been financed from abroad, both through foreign investment in UK oil companies and through direct investment by foreign-owned oil companies. This means that part of the profits earned on oil production accrues to foreigners. These profits, which may be paid as interest, dividends or transfers of profits, are shown in figure 9.6.

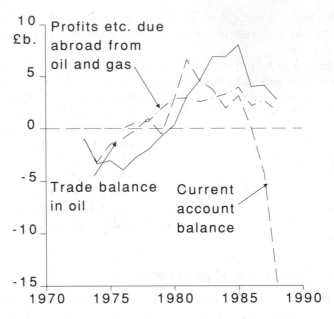

Figure 9.6 Oil and the balance of payments, 1973-88
Source: United Kingdom Balance of Payments.

These profits due abroad and the trade deficit in oil are the two main links between the North Sea and the current account balance of payments. These are shown in figure 9.6, which suggests a close link between developments in the North Sea and the current account.

❏ Overseas investment in the North Sea enters the capital account. This is something on which data are not available, for it is frequently impossible for the CSO to tell whether overseas investments are in the North Sea or elsewhere in the UK (exceptions are, of course, large identifiable items of capital equipment such as oil rigs). This overseas investment will have been large during the mid-1970s when the North Sea oilfields were being developed.

❏ The fact that North Sea oil production improves the current account may affect investors' views about what will happen to the balance of payments and hence their views on the likely value of sterling. If this occurs it will affect the capital account: confidence in sterling will lead to capital inflows simply to benefit from sterling's strength, not for investment in oil. In other words, the North Sea programme may, through altering investors' expectations about the future, affect the capital account of the balance of payments and the exchange rate. Though this effect is clearly something on which reliable quantitative data do not exist, the day-to-day responsiveness of sterling to news about oil production suggests that it is important.

9.2 OIL AND THE STRUCTURE OF THE UK ECONOMY

Structural change in the UK

The main feature of the oil extraction industry is that it is extremely capital-intensive, as is shown in table 9.1. From the point of view of the economy as a whole employment in oil extraction is negligible (26,000 out of a workforce of about 28 million). On the other hand, the capital stock employed is enormous, this being reflected in a capital-labour ratio of £1,370,000 per employee, compared with a national average of only £43,000 (if we exclude housing). Much of this capital has been supplied from overseas and in any case capital is very mobile between countries, which means that the development of North Sea oil is unlikely to have had a significant resource-movement effect (see box

Table 9.1 Capital, labour and output by sector, 1988

Sector	Capital-output ratio	Output per employee	Capital per employee
Oil and gas extraction	3.53	£388,000	£1.37m.
Agriculture, forestry and fisheries	4.78	£18,326	£87,577
Manufacturing	3.04	£16,628	£50,534
Construction	0.72	£21,332	£15,262
Whole economy	4.49	£14,257	£63,997
Whole economy (excluding housing)	3.01	£14,257	£42,895

Source: United Kingdom National Accounts.

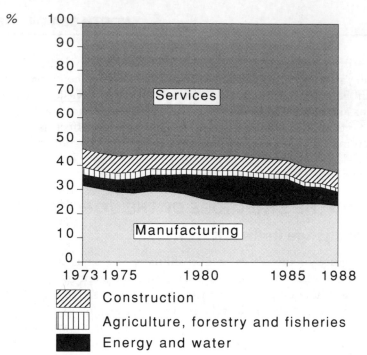

Construction

Agriculture, forestry and fisheries

Energy and water

Figure 9.7 The sectoral composition of output, 1973-87
Source: United Kingdom National Accounts.

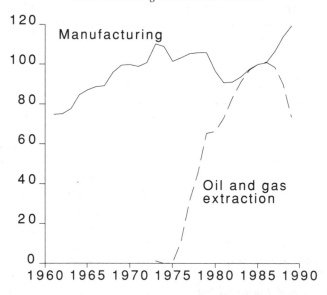

Figure 9.8 Output in manufacturing and oil extraction, 1960-89
Source: United Kingdom National Accounts.

9.1). The main effect of North Sea oil must, in the long run, be the spending effect.

If the theory outlined in box 9.1 is applicable, we would expect the spending effect to cause a shift away from manufacturing towards services. Figure 9.7 shows the behaviour of sectoral shares since 1973, whilst figure 9.8 shows what has happened to real output (GDP) in oil extraction and manufacturing. The main features of this are a rise in the share of output in energy and water supply, and a decline in the share of manufacturing. Over the period covered by figure 9.7 manufacturing fell from 31.7 per cent to 24.2 per cent of GDP. It is tempting to see this as a symptom of the Dutch disease. The problem is, however, more complicated, for there are other factors to take into account.

The decline in UK manufacturing is a long-term phenomenon but, in the period we are considering, the major decline took place between 1978 and 1981 when manufacturing's share of GDP fell from 29.3 per cent to 25.0 per cent — a 4 percentage point drop in three years. There are at least three possible explanations for this: permanent effects of North Sea oil; short-run, temporary effects of oil production; and causes not connected with oil.

❏ There has been a sudden, long-term shift out of manufacturing caused by North Sea oil coming on stream during the late 1970s. It could be argued that the oil price rise of 1979 significantly raised the value of North Sea oil revenues, increasing substantially the wealth effect on spending.

❏ The decline in manufacturing around 1980 was the result of short-run dynamic effects of oil production. It could, for example, be argued that with the introduction of the Medium Term Financial Strategy (see chapter 13) monetary policy ceased to be accommodating: the supply of money failed to keep pace with demand and the result was high interest rates and recession. Alternatively, and this is generally thought a more likely explanation, it could be that the rise in the real exchange rate in 1978-80 (see chapter 11), the timing of which fits very closely with the decline of manufacturing, was caused, at least in part, by the advent of North Sea oil revenues.

❏ Manufacturing might have declined for reasons unconnected with the North Sea. In particular, the decline may have been due simply to restrictive monetary policy. If, as seems highly likely, monetary policy operated primarily via the exchange rate, a restrictive monetary policy would have affected manufacturing worse than sectors less exposed to international competition.

Since around 1985, however, the situation has changed in that manufacturing has recovered, with the share of oil declining. This decline in the share of oil extraction was almost entirely the result of the fall in the price of oil after 1985. This change, however, does not help us tell which of above explanations is the right one: the revival of manufacturing could be caused by the falling share of oil and a reversal of the Dutch disease phenomena, or it could be because of other factors. It is thus necessary to find some way to disentangle these various effects.

Table 9.2 The UK economy in 1976

	Production	Exports	Imports	Consumption
Primary	9	-1.2	8.0	15.8
Manufacturing	48.9	-24.9	22	46
Construction	22.5	-0.2	0.3	22.6
Distribution and services	88.1	-18.8	16.9	86.2
Public administration	13.5	-	-	13.5
	181.9	-45.1	47.3	184.1

Values are £billion.
Source: Forsyth and Kay, *Fiscal Studies*, 1980. Exports are measured, unconventionally, as value added by each sector.

Measuring the effects of North Sea oil

The original analysis of the effects of North Sea Oil production on the structure of the UK economy was undertaken by Forsyth and Kay in 1980. Their methods and assumptions have been heavily criticized, but their work nonetheless provides a useful starting point that is fairly easy to understand. After examining their work we will turn to some of the criticisms.

Forsyth and Kay started with the UK economy as it existed in 1976, the last year before North Sea oil production became significant. The structure of the UK economy is summed up in table 9.2. Column 1 gives production (value added) for each of the major sectors of the economy, total production being £181.9 billion (the whole analysis is at 1980 prices). Columns 2 and 3 give the exports and imports associated with each sector. If we subtract output that is exported and add imports we get the level of domestic consumption corresponding to each of these sectors, as shown in column 4. Note that in 1976 there was a deficit on the balance of trade, amounting to £2.2 billion, and that consumption equals production plus the trade deficit.

Starting from this position Forsyth and Kay worked out the effects of a rise in oil production to £10 billion. This has the following effects.

(1) Primary production rises by £10 billion to £19 billion.
(2) Total production rises to £191.9 billion. Note that this is a rise of 5.5 per cent. If the trade deficit remains unchanged, consumption must rise to £194.1 billion.
(3) Assume that when domestic consumption rises, consumption of all goods rises in the same proportion (this is similar to the movement from A to C in figure 9.B1.2). If we assume that consumption of each sector's output rises by 5.5 per cent we get the results shown in column 4 of table 9.3.
(4) If primary output rises to £19 billion but consumption rises to only £16.7 billion the result is that the primary balance of trade moves from a deficit of £6.8 billion to a surplus of £2.3 billion. This gives us the entry in table 9.3.
(5) At this stage we assume that the overall balance of trade is to remain unchanged at £2.2 billion. If the primary balance improves

Table 9.3 The effects of North Sea oil: stage I

	Production	Exports	Imports	Consumption
Primary	19	-2.3		16.7
Manufacturing				48.5
Construction				23.8
Distribution and services				90.9
Public administration				14.2
	191.9	2.2		194.1

Source: as table 9.2.

Table 9.4 The effects of North Sea oil: stage II

	Production	Exports	Imports	Consumption
Primary	19	-2.3		16.7
Manufacturing	46.3	-22.2	24.4	48.5
Construction	23.8	-0.2	0.3	23.8
Distribution and services	88.8	-16.7	18.8	90.9
Public administration	14.2	—	—	14.2
	191.9	2.2		194.1

Source: as table 9.2.

by £9.1 billion this means that the non-primary balance must deteriorate by the same amount. The simplest assumption is that exports fall and imports rise by the same percentage, which turns out to be about 11 per cent. This gives the figures for exports and imports shown in table 9.4.

(6) The final stage is to add exports to consumption and to subtract imports to obtain levels of production for each sector. These are shown in column 1 of table 9.4.

If we compare column 1 of table 9.4 with column 1 of table 9.2 we obtain the effects of North Sea oil on the structure of production. Primary production rises by 111 per cent, simply because we took a rise from £9 billion to £19 billion as our initial assumption. Because they are barely involved in trade, construction and public administration rise by the same as national income: by 5.5 per cent. The interesting changes are in services (which rise by only 0.9 per cent) and manufacturing (which *falls* by 5.7 per cent). These are the main non-primary sectors producing tradeable goods (notice that, in contrast with the theoretical models discussed in box 9.1, the distinction between manufacturing and services is not the same as between tradeable and non-tradeable goods).

The mechanism which produces the required changes is, of course, the exchange rate. The rise in oil revenues leads to an appreciation of the exchange rate which causes a rise in imports and a fall in exports. Though they admit that there is a large amount of guesswork involved, Forsyth and Kay suggested that, given conventional estimates of demand elasticities, a rise in the value of sterling of about 20-25 per cent would be required to produce these changes.

BOX 9.1 'DUTCH DISEASE' MODELS

There are two related problems commonly associated with a natural resource discovery: De-industrialization — a decline in the manufacturing sector of the economy and a shift towards services; and a rise in the real exchange rate, causing a loss of international competitiveness and a rise in the price of services relative to manufactured goods. These two problems were thought to have arisen in Holland in the 1960s as a result of the discovery and exploitation of natural gas reserves, hence the term 'Dutch disease'. Notice that although we use the term 'disease', and although we are concerned with some of the problems associated with natural resource discoveries, there is no suggestion that such discoveries make an economy worse off. Some sectors may suffer, but overall the economy gains.

Long run 'static' effects

The effects of an oil discovery (we use the term 'oil discovery' as a convenient shorthand, though the arguments refer to any natural resource and though it is the exploitation of the resource rather than just its discovery that matters) are usually analysed in terms of two effects: the spending effect and the resource-movement effect.

❏ *The resource-movement effect*: oil production may take resources away from other sectors of the economy, forcing up factor prices. This effect will be larger for resources which are scarce and cannot be traded internationally.

❏ *The spending effect*: the revenues from oil production will raise incomes and hence spending.

To see how these effects work we divide the economy into two sectors: one producing tradeable goods, the other non-tradeables. Tradeables can be thought of as including manufactures plus oil and non-tradeables as services. Consider first the resource-movement effect. Assume that capital is internationally mobile and that the supply of capital is completely elastic: its price is fixed in world markets. The only scarce resource is labour, the

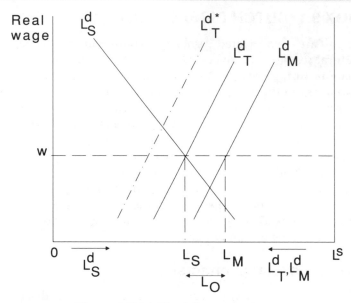

Figure 9.B1.1 The labour market

market for which is depicted in figure 9.B1.1. Demand for labour by the services sector, L_S^d, is measured from left to right, and demand for labour by manufacturing, L_M^d, from right to left. Both sectors have conventional, downward-sloping demand curves for labour. If we add the oil-producing sector's demand for labour to that of the manufacturing sector we have total demand for labour for tradeables, L_T^d. Supply and demand for labour are equal where L_S^d and L_T^d intersect. We can read off employment in each of the three sectors.

Now suppose there is an increase in demand for labour by the oil sector. This will shift L_T^d to the left, leaving the other demand curves unchanged. The result will be a rise in the real wage rate and a fall in employment in both services and manufacturing. Similarly, if there were no oil sector, L_T^d would be identical to L_M^d, and the real wage would be where L_S^d intersects with L_M^d. The oil sector's demand for labour raises the real wage rate, reducing employment in the other two sectors.

To illustrate the spending effect we will eliminate the resource-movement effect by assuming that oil-extraction uses a negligible amount of labour and that any capital can be purchased on

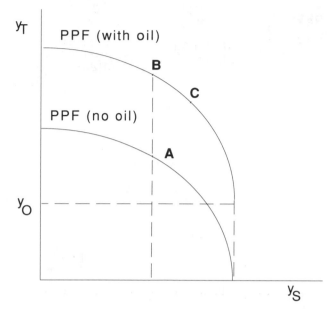

Figure 9.B1.2 The goods markets

international markets without affecting the domestic cost of capital. In figure 9.B1.2 we have drawn a production possibility frontier for tradeables and non-tradeables, both in the absence of oil production and with a given level of oil production. Note that because oil makes no demands on domestic resources, an oil discovery shifts the production possibility frontier vertically upwards. It affects potential output of neither manufactures nor services. Potential output of tradeables rises because it includes manufactures plus oil.

Assume that the socially optimal level of output is at A (though it is not drawn, we could imagine a social indifference curve tangential to the production possibility frontier at A). The oil discovery shifts the production possibility frontier upwards, permitting higher consumption of both tradeables and non-tradeables. For the balance between manufacturing and services to remain unchanged, the economy would have to move to B: in other words, people would have to spend *all* their increased income on tradeable goods (remember that we need not distinguish between oil and manufactures because they can exchanged for each other on the world market). In general people will use higher incomes to increase spending on both tradeables and non-tradeables,

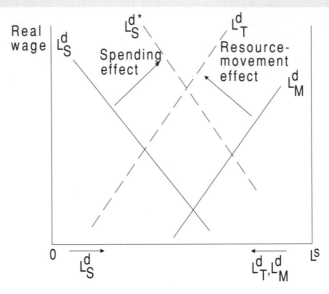

Figure 9.B1.3 The overall effect of an oil discovery

which means that the economy will move to a point such as C. Three things happen in the movement from A to C: (1) output of services rises; (2) output of manufactured goods falls; (3) the price of services rises relative to manufactures (i.e. the production possibility frontier is steeper at C than at A).

The spending effect, therefore, can produce both de-industrialization and a rise in the real exchange rate (a rise in the price of services relative to manufactures).

When the the resource-movement and spending effects on manufacturing are combined the result is that manufacturing will decline, but production of services may rise or fall, depending on whether the resource-movement or the spending effect is stronger. This is illustrated in figure 9.B1.3. The real wage on the vertical axis is now measured in terms of tradeable goods (before, because relative prices were not changing we did not have to specify what the real wage was measured in) and in addition to the leftward shift in L_T^d there is a rise in L_S^d, caused by the rise in the price of services. The real wage in terms of tradeables rises, causing manufacturing to decline, whilst whether services increase or decline depends on whether it is L_S^d or L_T^d that shifts the most.

Short-run dynamic effects

In the static models considered so far there is full employment: oil discoveries affect the way in which resources are allocated between sectors, but they do not cause resources to be under-utilized. However, in addition to these long run effects there are short run effects which may cause unemployment. These include the effects of an expenditure lag; the effects of oil revenues on the demand for money; and real wage inertia.

An expenditure lag: an oil discovery increases expected future real incomes and hence the level of consumption. This rise in consumption raises the level of aggregate demand, thus offsetting the effects of a rising real exchange rate (which lowers demand). Suppose, however, that foreign-exchange markets are forward-looking and take account of oil revenues very quickly, but that consumers respond more slowly. The result would be a rise in the real exchange rate, reducing aggregate demand, without any compensating rise in consumption. This could produce a recession.

Effects on the demand for money: the rise in wealth caused by an oil discovery should raise the demand for money. If there is no rise in the money supply the result will be a rise in interest rates and possibly a recession.

Real wage inertia: there is considerable evidence to suggest that, in the medium term (say 2 to 5 years) nominal wages are flexible, but that real wages are fairly sticky (see chapter 6). Wage-earners consume both manufactured goods and services, so the real consumption wage (W/P_C) is a weighted average of the real product wage rates in manufacturing (W/P_M) and services (W/P_S). Assume that W/P_C is constant (extreme real wage stickiness). An oil discovery will, through the spending effect, produce a rise in the real exchange rate. Because manufacturers face international competition they will have to accept lower (sterling) prices, which causes a rise in W/P_M, reducing employment in manufacturing. At the same time there will be a fall in W/P_S. Because the consumption wage is fixed, the overall wage rate cannot adjust to maintain full employment, and so the overall effect on employment will depend on the relative strength of these two effects. If demand for labour in services is relatively inelastic compared with manufacturing, employment may fall.

FURTHER READING

A good survey of the major issues is C. Bean 'The impact of North Sea oil,' in R. Dornbusch and R. Layard (eds) *The Performance of the British Economy*. Oxford: Oxford University Press, 1987. The classic article on the problem of North Sea oil is P. J. Forsyth and J. A. Kay 'The economic implications of North Sea oil revenues,' *Fiscal Studies* 1, 1980, pp. 1- 28.

Since 1973 oil prices have fluctuated enormously, so prediction is hazardous. Some articles which analyse the effects of oil price changes are: Powell and Horton 'The economic effects of lower oil prices, Government Economic Service Paper, No. 76 (1985); P. Odell 'Back to cheap oil?' *Lloyds Bank Review* April 1985, pp. 1-15; P. Odell 'The prospect for oil prices and the energy market,' *Lloyds Bank Review*, July 1987; S. Hall, S. G. B. Henry and Herbert 'Oil prices and the economy,' *National Institute Economic Review*, May 1986. The treatment of North Sea oil in the main macroeconomic forecasting models is discussed in K. F. Wallis *et al.* 'Modelling North Sea oil', in *Models of the UK Economy: Second Review by the ESRC Macroeconomic Modelling Bureau* (Oxford: Oxford University Press, 1985).

IV

Money and Finance

Money

10.1 THE MONEY SUPPLY

Definitions of the money supply

In theory, money is easy to define. It is the stock of assets that can readily be used to settle debts or to buy goods and services. This property, of being easily and quickly exchanged for something else, is known as *liquidity*, and provides a reason for people to hold money, either to enable them to buy and sell goods when they want to, or as a form of insurance against unforeseen events. In theory, therefore, we simply define money as the stock of all completely liquid assets: of those assets which can *immediately* and *costlessly* be used to buy things. In practice, however, it is extraordinarily difficult to translate this theoretical definition into a satisfactory measure of the money supply. There are several reasons for this: it is impossible to draw a clear dividing line between liquid and non-liquid assets; the liquidity of an asset may be different at different times, and under different circumstances; institutional changes may cause changes in the liquidity of different assets.

❏ The distinction between liquid and non-liquid assets is hard to make precise, because liquidity is a matter of degree, assets being more or less liquid, rather than simply liquid or non-liquid.

❏ An asset's liquidity may vary over time and under different circumstances. Consider the example of a bank account where the bank is entitled to ask for a week's notice for withdrawals. Most of the time the bank may ignore this, allowing customers to withdraw funds on demand, in which case the deposits are very liquid. Sometimes, of if withdrawals are very large, the bank may enforce its entitlement to notice, in which case the deposits are less liquid.

❏ Institutional changes cause the liquidity of different assets to change. For example, when building societies were allowed to issue cheque books, their deposits became more liquid.

It is because there is no clear-cut criterion for deciding what counts as money and what does not, that there are so many definitions of the money supply. In addition, institutional changes mean that it has often been necessary to introduce new definitions of the money supply, and to switch from one definition to another. For example, when the Abbey National became a PLC it changed its status from that of a building society to that of a bank (it became subject to the regulations governing banks instead of those governing building societies). There was an overnight increase in those definitions of the money supply (M1 and M3) which included bank deposits but not building society deposits, even though there was no change in the assets held by the public.

The item which appears in all definitions of the money supply is cash (notes and coin) in the hands of the public (i.e. the private sector, excluding the banking system). In addition, because most transactions are now settled without cash, using cheques or other means of transferring funds from one bank account to another, bank deposits have to be included. This, however, is where the problems start, because there are many types of deposit, ranging from sight deposits (payable on demand) on which no interest is paid and on which cheques can be drawn (which should clearly be included in definitions of the money supply) to interest-bearing deposits on which a long period of notice is required for withdrawals, and on which cheques cannot be drawn (which cannot be used to finance transactions, and thus should not be counted as money). In between these two extremes there are many different types of deposit. Different definitions of the money supply are based on different decisions about which types of deposit to include.

The main definitions of the money supply used in the UK are described in Figure 10.1. The starting point is non-interest-bearing

(NIB) M1, which comprises notes and coin held by the public (i.e. excluding cash held by banks) plus deposits that (a) are with banks, (b) are in sterling, (c) can be withdrawn on demand (without giving any notice) and (d) on which no interest is paid. The reason why only sterling deposits are included is that we are normally concerned with money kept to finance transactions within the UK. The presumption is that foreign currency deposits are, where they are not purely an investment, held to finance overseas transactions. If we add interest-bearing sterling bank sight deposits, we obtain M1.

M1 is (apart from M0, which is discussed below) the smallest measure of the money supply. It might be thought that everything included in M1 clearly counted as money, but this is not the case. There are some bank sight deposits which earn interest and on which cheques cannot be drawn. It can be argued that where such deposits are large they must be held as a form of saving rather than to finance transactions. This is the reason why M2, the next definition of the money supply, starts with just the non-interest-bearing component of M1: the part which is clearly being held to finance transactions. To this is added 'retail' sterling deposits, these being defined as deposits on which cheques can be drawn, deposits under £100,000 and with less than one month's notice of withdrawal. Because the distinction between banks and building societies is becoming increasingly blurred, deposits with both banks and building societies are included. There are two things to note about this definition of M2. (1) It includes some time deposits (where notice of withdrawal is required) as well as some deposits on which cheques cannot be drawn. (2) Because it includes building society deposits M2 can be larger than M3 (which includes only bank deposits).

Proceeding down from M1 in figure 10.1 we come to M3. Like M1, this includes only bank deposits (as well as cash), but unlike M1 it includes all sterling bank deposits and certificates of deposit. Certificates of deposit are like bank deposits, the difference being that the bank provides the depositor with a certificate, ownership of which can be transferred from one person to another. In that it comprises cash in circulation with the public, plus all sterling bank deposits, M3 is the most straightforward definition of the money supply. When the difference between banks and building societies was very clear cut, with each engaging in different types of business, and with little competition between the two types of institution, there was some rationale for using M3 as a measure of the money supply. With de-regulation and the greater freedom given to building societies under the Building Societies Act of 1986, however, the distinction between

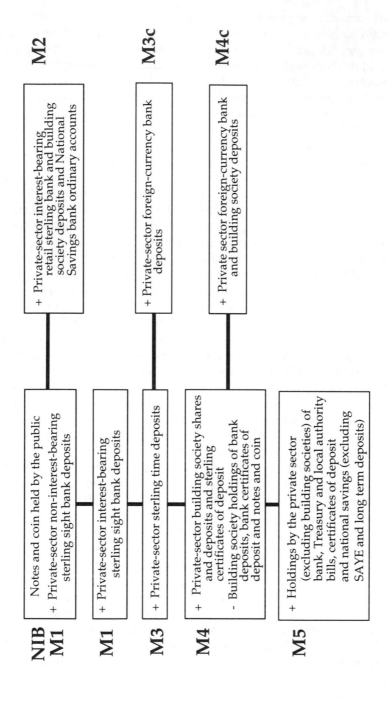

Figure 10.1 UK monetary aggregates

banks and building societies has considerably diminished, and it no longer makes sense to include bank deposits but not building society deposits. It is thus better to focus on M4, which includes all sterling bank and building society deposits. Indeed, since the summer of 1989, with the conversion of the Abbey National into a PLC (and hence from a building society into a bank), the Bank of England has ceased to publish figures for M3.

Figure 10.1 also shows M3c and M4c. These are like M3 and M4, except that they include foreign currency as well as sterling deposits. The reason why building societies' holdings of cash and bank deposits are subtracted is to avoid double-counting. It is worth noting at this point that there was a change in terminology concerning M3 in May 1987. Prior to this what we have called M3 was known as 'sterling M3' (£M3) whilst what is now M3c was known simply as M3. The change in terminology was to bring that for M3 into line with that for other definitions of the money supply.

Finally we have the broadest definition of the money supply, M5. This includes not only bank and building society deposits but also a range of other short-term financial assets. The rationale for this is that many of these assets are, for many purposes, highly liquid, and are held by many firms as a substitute for deposits with financial institutions. Note that M5 was previously known as PSL2, where PSL stood for private-sector liquidity.

The behaviour of the main monetary aggregates is shown in figures 10.2 and 10.3. Several conclusions can be drawn from these figures: that there have been great differences in the behaviour of different financial assets; that the rate of growth of the money supply has at times fluctuated very sharply; that there was a pronounced increase in the average growth rate of most monetary aggregates after about 1970; and that since around 1970 the differences between different measures of the money supply appear to have increased.

❑ There are enormous differences between the growth rates of different definitions of the money supply. In 1972-3, for example, M3 and M4 grew at nearly 25 per cent per annum, and M5 grew at over 20 per cent per annum, whereas M1 grew at only around 10 per cent per annum. After this M1 grew more rapidly than M3 and M4 for a few years. The 1980 recession saw a very sharp fall in the growth of M1, and a slight fall in the growth rate of M5, but the growth of M3 and M4 accelerated.

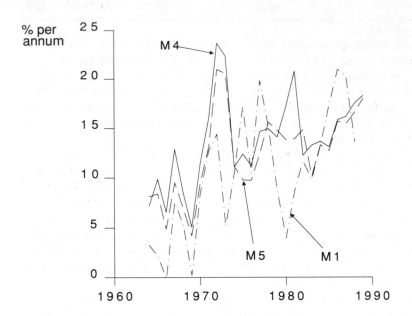

Figure 10.2 Growth rates of M1, M4 and M5, 1964-89

Source: Economic Trends.

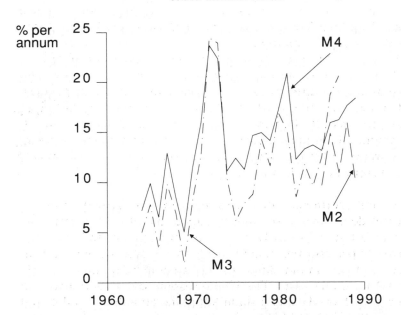

Figure 10.3 Growth rates of M2, M3 and M4, 1964-89

Source: Economic Trends and Financial Statistics.

❑ There have been sharp fluctuations in the growth rate of the money supply, growth rates often changing by as much as 10 percentage points in a couple of years.

❑ Prior to 1970 monetary growth rates were rarely above 10 per cent per annum, whereas since 1970 the average rate of growth has been closer to 12 per cent per annum, this applying to all five measures of the money supply.

❑ The divergence between different measures of the money supply appears to have been greater since the early 1970s than before. Until about 1972, though broad measures of money were growing faster than M1, the cyclical pattern appears to have been similar for all monetary aggregates (uncertainty about this arises because there are so few observations in this period). The same cannot be said for the period after 1972. The explanation for this is presumably institutional changes, which started with Competition and Credit Control in 1971.

The velocity of circulation

The simplest way to explore what has happened to the demand for money is to look at the behaviour of the velocity of circulation. This is calculated as the ratio of nominal GDP to the money supply: it measures the volume of transactions financed by each unit of money or, in other words, the frequency with which money changes hands. Although it is conventional to look at statistics on velocity, it is exactly the same as looking at figures on money per unit of output. If demand for money is a proportion, k of nominal income, Py, we will have $M = kPy$. Re-arranging this gives velocity as $Py/M = 1/k$. In examining velocity, therefore, we are, indirectly at least, investigating the demand for money.

Statistics on the velocity of circulation for three definitions of the money supply are given in figure 10.4. The first point to note is that velocity has, whichever definition of the money supply we take, been far from constant. Consider first M4 and M5. There is some evidence that velocity may have risen when monetary policy was restrictive (tight monetary policy means high interest rates which will reduce the demand for money, raising velocity). It rose in the recession of 1970-1; it then fell as the money supply was expanded in the boom years of 1972 and 1973; after which it rose during the recession which followed in 1974-5. Since the mid-1970s, on the other hand, these velocities have

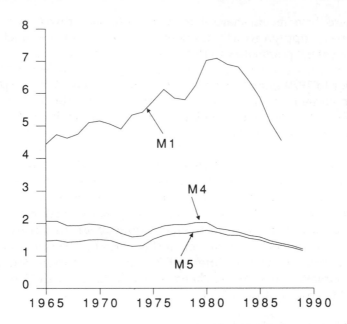

Figure 10.4 The velocity of circulation, 1965-89

Source: calculated using M1, M4 and M5 and GDP at market prices from *Economic Trends.*

not behaved as we would expect: there was no fall in the 1978-9 boom and no rise even during the very severe recession in 1980-1. On the other hand, the fall in velocity since 1981 is what we would expect: the economy has been growing rapidly.

When we turn to M1, on the other hand, we get a very different picture. Up to 1972 the picture is similar to that for M4 and M5, though the fluctuations are larger, but in the 1973 boom, when the velocity of both M4 and M5 continued to fall, the velocity of M1, which had been falling, started to rise. Apart from an interruption in 1976-7, the rise continued until 1981. Up to 1981 the overall picture was of a more or less steady increase in the velocity of M1, from 4.5 in 1963 to over 7 in 1981. Since then velocity has declined rapidly, returning to the level of the mid-1960s within the space of six years.

This evidence suggests that if we are to explain changes in velocity or the demand for money we must look not only at income and interest rates but also at the institutional changes which took place during the period. The main feature of the graphs for the velocity of M4 and M5 is the decline in 1972-3, something that could be attributed to the reforms, which went under the name of 'Competition and credit control', introduced in 1971, which liberalized the financial system. These reforms caused an expansion of broad monetary aggregates, lowering velocity. Over the succeeding years this sharp decline, which did not affect M1, was reversed.

If we try to go beyond looking at velocity to estimate demand functions for the various definitions of money and to obtain estimates of elasticities of demand, we run into a number of problems. There a very serious identification problem (how do we know that what we have is a demand function, not a supply function or some meaningless hybrid?). Another problem is that we would expect the demand to fluctuate a lot: it depends on expectations and, because it is, by definition, easy to switch between holding money and other assets, the amount of money to hold is a short-term decision that can be changed rapidly as expectations change. Finally, it is hard adequately to take account of the many institutional changes which have taken place, most of which have probably had a major impact on the demand for money. Such institutional changes include changes in the way the financial system is regulated, changes in the roles of different financial institutions (such as banks and building societies) and changes in technology (the spread of credit cards, electronic payments systems and so on).

Thus although demand for money functions have been estimated, they need to be treated extremely cautiously. For this reason, and because it is so difficult to find a simple 'demand' function that fits the data well, no estimates will be provided.

10.2 THE DETERMINATION OF THE MONEY SUPPLY

Money and high-powered money

The simplest theory of the money supply is the money multiplier theory (see box 10.1). According to this there should be a clear relationship between the money supply and the quantity of reserve assets, variously termed *high-powered money* or *monetary base*. This raises the issue of what constitutes high-powered money in the UK. In a primitive banking system where cash means gold coins and where banks held gold as reserves, the answer would be simple: gold. Similarly, if the commercial banks' reserves comprised simply Bank of England notes and deposits with the Bank of England, it would be clear that high-powered money should be defined as the total monetary liabilities of the Bank of England. In a modern banking system,

BOX 10.1 THE MONEY MULTIPLIER

Assume that the money supply (M) comprises cash in the hands of the public (C) plus bank deposits (D):

$$M = C + D.$$

The banking system does one of two things with the money deposited with it: it either holds it as reserves (R) or it lends it to the public as bank loans (L). We thus have,

$$D = R + L.$$

Lastly we define the stock of high-powered money as cash plus bank reserves:

$$H = C + R.$$

So far all we have is definitions. To get a theory of the money supply we need to make assumptions about the behaviour of the public and the banking system. Assume that the public wishes a fraction c of its money holdings to be cash, so that $C^d = cM$. Similarly assume that banks desire to hold a fraction b of their deposits as reserves: $R^d = bD$. It follows that demand for high-powered money is

$$H^d = C^d + R^d = cM + bD$$

$$= [c + b(1 - c)]M.$$

If we assume that supply and demand for high-powered money are equal, we have

$$M = mH \text{ where } m = 1/[c + b(1 - c)] > 1.$$

Here m is the *money multiplier*, which is greater than 1. The usefulness of this theory depends on whether b and c are fairly stable. If b and c are constant we can predict that a £1 increase in H will lead to an increase in M of £m. If, on the other hand, b and c are very unstable and change when H changes, the money multiplier will be less useful in explaining changes in the money supply.

however, commercial banks hold a wide spectrum of assets as reserves, not simply Bank of England notes and deposits. Though many of these short-term liquid assets, readily convertible into cash, are created by the Bank of England or the Treasury, many of them are created within the private sector.

If the commercial banks' lending activities were controlled simply by a single reserve ratio (for example if their only consideration was a legally imposed requirement that they hold x per cent of their liabilities in a specified list of assets) the concept of high-powered money would have a clear meaning. In practice, however, banks are constrained not simply by legal reserve ratios, but by considerations of risk. It is the structure of their balance sheets that matters, not just their holdings of one particular type of asset.

The main measure of monetary base, or high-powered money, that the UK authorities publish is called M0. This comprises notes and coin plus deposits at the Bank of England. It is sometimes referred to as the 'broad' measure of monetary base, the 'narrow' definition comprising merely notes and coin. Despite this, however, it can be argued that M0 is still a very narrow definition of monetary base, for it excludes the bulk of the short-term, liquid assets that commercial banks use as reserves. Only if quantities of these other liquid assets vary in line with the quantity of M0 will M0 be related to the money supply in the way suggested by the money multiplier theory.

Money multipliers for M1, M4 and M5 are given in figure 10.5. This shows that there has been a clear long-term upward trend in all the money multipliers. The multiplier for M1 has more than doubled, whilst that for M4 has increased nearly four-fold. During this period, the rates at which these money multipliers have grown have been very variable, as is shown in figure 10.6, which gives the growth rates of the three money multipliers shown in figure 10.5. The size of the changes in these money multipliers provides an indication of the problem facing the Bank of England, if it were to try to control the money supply through controlling the supply of high-powered money.

The enormous growth in money multipliers means that a large part of the rise in the money supply over the past 20 years has not been caused by increases in the quantity of high-powered money (assuming we define this as M0). This point is made more forcefully by figure 10.6. If we assume that (a) M0 is the right measure of high-powered money and that (b) money multipliers would have been the same had M0 been growing at a different rate (which is admittedly not very likely), the growth rates in figure 10.6 give the rates at which the various definitions of the money supply would have grown had the

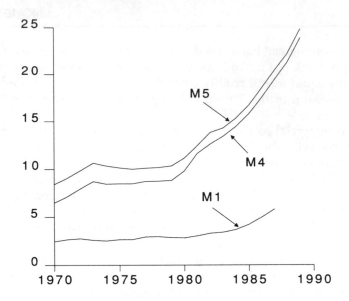

Figure 10.5 Money multipliers for M1, M4 and M5, 1970-89

Source: Economic Trends. M1, M4 and M5 are end-year figures, and M0 is the average for the last quarter of each year.

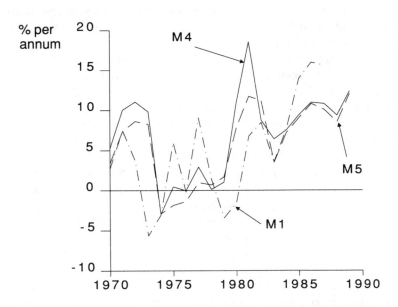

Figure 10.6 Growth rates of money multipliers, 1970-89

Source: as figure 10.5.

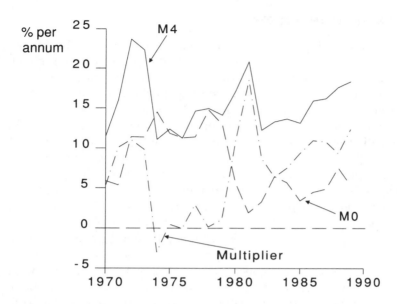

Figure 10.7 The growth rate of M4, 1970-89
Source: as figure 10.5.

stock of M0 remained constant. Thus even if the monetary base (M0) had been kept constant, the money supply would have grown by at least 5 to 10 per cent per annum during the 1980s. In figure 10.7 the growth in M4 is broken down, in this very crude way, into the component 'due to' the change in M0 and that 'due to' a rise in the money multiplier. This shows that although M4 has been growing at around 10 to 15 per cent per annum for most of the past 20 years, it was growth in the monetary base, not changes in the money multiplier, that 'caused' it to grow during the mid to late 1970s. In contrast, during the 1980s changes in the money multiplier (presumably connected with the liberalization of financial markets and other institutional changes) have been more important than changes in M0 in 'causing' M4 to rise. Note that 'cause' has been placed in quotation marks, for accounting relationships such as these cannot show the direction of causation: it may run from M0 to M4, the other way round, or a mixture of both.

The variability of money multipliers makes it clear that if we are to explain the money supply, we must consider other factors. Two things to consider are interest rates and the many institutional changes which have taken place over the past 20 years.

Money and interest rates

For the money multiplier theory to work as a theory of the money supply, with changes in monetary base causing changes in the money supply, it is necessary (a) that the ratios b and c be independent of changes in the monetary base and changes in the demand for money (the simplest case is if they are constants) and (b) that the quantity of high-powered money be independent of the demand for money. In practice neither of these is true. The most important problem is that the Bank of England does not simply fix the quantity of high-powered money, leaving the markets to determine interest rates. Though it may have targets for monetary base, it buys and sells assets in the financial markets and can influence interest rates as much as the quantity of monetary base.

The policy objectives of the Bank of England are quite complicated in that they have targets for the exchange rate and the money supply. In addition, the government is concerned that interest rates are as low as possible. The two polar cases are *interest rate control* (where the Bank sets a target interest rate) and *monetary base control* (where the Bank fixes the monetary base irrespective of interest rates - note that to achieve strict monetary base control the Bank would have to change its methods of operating in the financial markets: this involves technical issues that we shall not explore here). In either case there is a determinate money supply (see box 10.2). These two cases correspond to horizontal and vertical supply curves for high-powered money respectively. In addition to these polar cases, we have others. For example, if the Bank of England were to fix the interest rate subject to the condition that monetary base fell within a given range, we would have the supply curve shown in figure 10.8(a). If on the other hand the Bank fixed the quantity of high-powered money subject to maximum and minimum interest rates we would have the supply curve shown in figure 10.8(b).

In practice, of course, the range of options open to the Bank of England is even greater than this. They can set targets for any monetary aggregate, not simply for monetary base. In addition, they have a variety of interest rates to which they can respond. The difference is that they have more success in controlling some variables than others. Control over short-term interest rates is easier than control over long-term rates and controlling rates on government securities is easier than controlling yields on equities, because the Bank faces constraints imposed by the markets in which it is able to operate. Under normal circumstances, for example, the Bank of England does

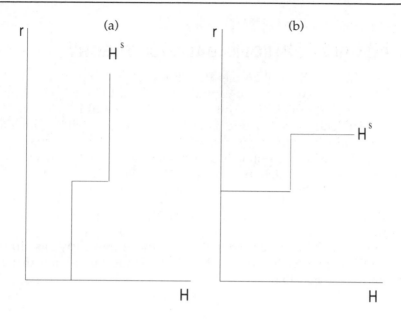

Figure 10.8 The supply of high-powered money

not buy and sell equities. If it wishes to influence this market it has to do so indirectly, operating in markets which will have an influence on equity markets.

Methods of monetary control

Since the 1960s there have been several substantial changes in the way the financial system has been regulated. Prior to 1971 the emphasis was not on controlling the money supply (before 1963 the government did not even compile statistics on the money supply) but on controlling the level of credit. This was done using a variety of methods, including interest rates and quantitative controls on credit. There were restrictions on what banks could lend to various categories of borrower. Hire-purchase regulations (governing, for example, the minimum deposit and the maximum repayment period) were frequently varied as a means of regulating the level of consumer credit. In addition, banks were subject to *two* required reserve ratios. This regime was ended in 1971.

BOX 10.2 PORTFOLIO BALANCE THEORY

Assume that the public has the choice of holding money (M) or other assets (equities, real capital, government bonds etc). Demand for money depends on income (Y) and the rate of interest on these non-monetary assets (r): demand for money rises with income and falls with the rate of interest. If we assume that the quantity of money held by the public is determined by demand (banks always accept money which people deposit with them) it follows that demand for high-powered money will be determined by

$$H^d = (1/m)M^d,$$

where H and m are defined in the same way as in the money-multiplier theory (see box 10.1). From the identity that $D = L + R$ it follows that

$$L^s = D - R^d$$

$$= (M^d - C^d) - R^d$$

$$= M^d - H^d.$$

Using these results we can draw demand curves for money and high-powered money, as in figure 10.B2.1. Assume for the moment that there is a fixed stock of high-powered money, H_1. The supply curve for high powered money is vertical. The equilibrium interest rate must, therefore, be r_1, where $H^d = H^s$. For complete equilibrium, however, it is also necessary that the market for bank loans be in equilibrium. This is shown in the left-hand part of figure 10.B2.1. The *supply* of loans, L^s (the amount that banks wish to lend), is the same as the gap between M^d and H^d. To complete the model assume that the demand for bank loans depends on two interest rates: the rate of interest on bank loans (r^L) and the rate of interest on 'other assets' (r). When r increases (e.g. because lending to the government or investing in real capital becomes more profitable) demand for bank loans will rise. L^d slopes upwards.

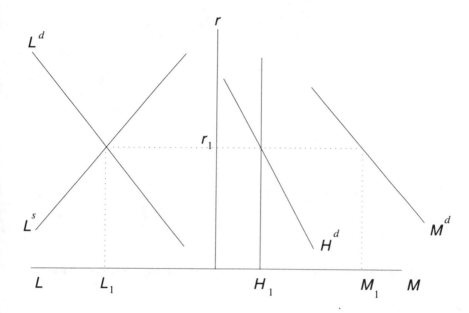

Figure 10.B2.1 The determination of the money supply

Equally important, the position of L^d will depend on r^L: rises in r^L will reduce L^d, shifting the curve to the right. For equilibrium, r^L must be such that $L^s = L^d$ at r_1. Equilibrium in the markets for high-powered money and for bank loans determines two rates of interest: r and r^L.

This diagram can now be used to show a number of things. In figure 10.B2.2 we can see the effects of a change in the quantity of high-powered money. H^s shifts to the right and the equilibrium interest rate falls to r_2. For equilibrium in the market for bank loans L^d must increase, which means that r^L must fall. A rise in H, therefore, leads to a

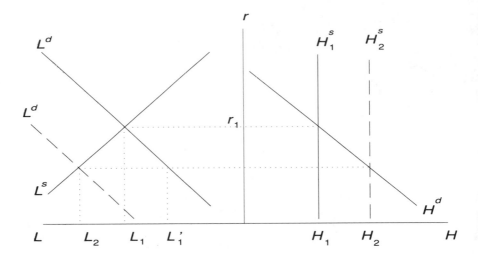

Figure 10.B2.2 An increase in the supply of high-powered money

fall in both r and r^L and to a rise in the money supply from $H_1 + L_1$ to $H_2 + L_2$.

Figure 10.B2.3 shows the effects of a rise in the demand for money (suppose, for example, income has risen) under two assumptions: (a) that the quantity of high-powered money is fixed and (b) that the quantity of high-powered money is completely elastic at rate of interest r_1 (that the interest rate is fixed, either by the government or by international capital markets). In case (a) the result is a rise in both interest rates, with no change in the money supply. In case (b), on the other hand, the quantity of high-powered money increases in response to demand. In addition, because L^s rises, r^L has to fall in order to cause L^d. The result is a rise in the money supply and a fall in r^L, even though the rate of interest on 'other assets' is unchanged.

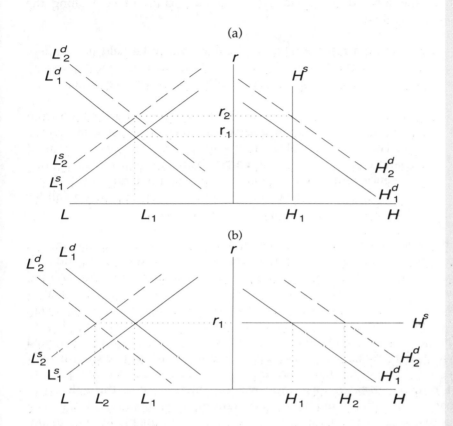

Figure 10.B2.3 A rise in the demand for money

1971: *Competition and credit control*. The aim of this package of reforms was to make the financial system more competitive. It contained two main measures designed to assist the authorities in controlling the banking system.

❑ A minimum reserve ratio of 12.5 per cent, to be held in a variety of assets: deposits at the Bank of England; treasury, local-authority and commercial bills; and certain other short-term securities.

❑ Special deposits, which the Bank of England could demand from the commercial banks in addition to their 12.5 per cent reserve ratio. The idea was that by asking for special deposits the Bank of England could force the commercial banks to reduce their lending and hence reduce their deposits. The required ratio of 12.5 per cent would prevent the commercial banks from meeting a call for special deposits by running down their reserves.

This is a system that could be understood in terms of the money multiplier theory where high-powered money is defined to include the whole range of assets that counted towards commercial banks' 12.5 per cent reserve ratio. The problem with this method of monetary control was that this 'high-powered money' included many assets that were not under the Bank of England's control. In particular supplies of commercial bills and other very short term assets were determined within the private sector. The private sector could thus create its own reserves. The authorities were therefore forced to control the quantity of reserves through their influence on interest rates: through open-market operations and minimum lending rate. Because of the way reserve assets were defined, the authorities were unable to operate any form of monetary base control — they had to operate a policy of interest rate control (see figure 10.8).

1973: *The 'corset'*. The system introduced in Competition and credit control proved unable to control the money supply. M3, for example, rose by 12 per cent in 1971, 23 per cent in 1972 and 26 per cent in 1973. To increase the authorities' control, ceilings were imposed on banks' deposits. If a commercial bank's deposits grew faster than was permitted by this ceiling it had to hold what were termed 'supplementary special deposits' with the Bank of England. The greater the amount by which deposits exceeded the ceiling, the greater the supplementary special deposits it had to hold. No interest was payable on such deposits. This system was known as the corset.

1981: Attempts to move towards monetary base control. A number of changes were introduced to enable the government to move in this direction.

❏ The 12.5 per cent ratio was abolished.

❏ In addition to the funds they kept voluntarily at the Bank of England for clearing purposes (about 1.5 per cent) the commercial banks were required to keep 0.5 per cent of their liabilities as deposits at the Bank of England.

❏ The clearing banks agreed to keep an average of 6 per cent of their liabilities as call money in the disount market and to discuss with the Bank of England, in advance, any changes in their policies regarding holdings of liquid assets.

❏ Minimum lending rate was abolished, to reduce the Bank of England's role in determining interest rates.

These changes in the way the banking system was regulated provide a possible explanation of the changes in the money multipliers shown in figure 10.5. Competition and credit control resulted in an increase in the multipliers, especially for the broader aggregates, M3 and M5. The corset reduced the multipliers and kept them down; with the abolition of the corset and other forms of deregulation money multipliers were free to rise.

10.3 STOCKS, FLOWS AND CHANGES IN THE MONEY SUPPLY

Some accounting identities

So far in this chapter we have focused exclusively on the *stock* of money: the amount of money in existence at a specific time. In accounting terminology, we have been concerned with money as an item in a balance sheet. An alternative way of approaching the problem of the money supply is to look at *flows* rather than stocks: in other words, to consider the causes of *changes* in the money supply. The value of this approach is that it links changes in the money supply to the PSBR and the balance of payments. The reason for this link between deficits and stocks of assets is that deficits have to be financed. The only way a sector can spend more than it is receiving is through

increasing its indebtedness to other sectors: in other words, by selling
financial assets. There is thus an unavoidable link between sectoral
deficits and changes in stocks of financial assets. The best way to see
the implications of this for the money supply is to consider a few basic
accounting identities. The starting point is the need to finance both the
government deficit and the foreign exchange transactions implicit in a
balance of payments deficit.

❏ Government deficits have to be financed in one of four ways:
  selling bonds to the public; selling bonds to the commercial banks;
  borrowing from abroad; or borrowing from the Bank of England,
  thus creating high-powered money. Conversely, of course, government surpluses imply buying bonds or reducing lending from the
  Bank of England.

❏ The balance of payments deficit (the balance for official financing)
  causes changes in the Bank of England's reserves of gold and
  foreign exchange. This has to be financed.

Starting with the government deficit, we have the following identity.

$$PSBR = \Delta H + \Delta B_b + \Delta B_p,$$

where ΔB_b and ΔB_p are sales of bonds to the banking system and the
public and ΔH is the change in the stock of high powered money.

This is the basic identity linking PSBR to changes in stocks of assets.
To turn it into a relationship between PSBR and the money supply we
have to bring in the commercial banking system's balance sheet.
Assume that banks have the simplified balance sheet shown in table
10.1. Because assets must equal liabilities, we can obtain the following
equation:

$$\Delta R + \Delta B_b = \Delta D - \Delta L + \Delta N,$$

where Δx denotes the change in x.
  Finally we require the two identities:

$$\Delta M = \Delta C + \Delta D$$

$$\Delta H = \Delta C + \Delta R.$$

Using these we can derive the relationship

$$\Delta M = \text{PSBR} - \Delta B_p + \Delta L - \Delta N.$$

The derivation of this may seem a little complicated, but its meaning is simple. Because of the identity that banks' liabilities and assets must be equal, the rise in the money supply must equal the rise in banks' holdings of government debt (including bonds and reserves of high-powered money) plus their lending to the public (ΔL), adjusted to allow for any increase in non-deposit liabilities (ΔN). The increase in banks' holdings of government debt is PSBR minus whatever bonds the government sells to the public (ΔB_p).

Table 10.1 A simplified Banking Sector Balance Sheet

Assets	Liabilities
High-powered money (R)	Sterling deposits (D)
Other public sector debt (B_b)	Non-deposit liabilities —
Sterling loans to the private sector (L)	bank capital etc. (N)

To complete the relationship between the change in the money supply, the government deficit and the balance of payments we have to bring in changes in foreign exchange reserves. There are two complications here. The first is that the government may finance spending by borrowing abroad, thus reducing the need to borrow at home. The second is that there are many foreign currency transactions which, because the money supply is defined as involving *sterling* deposits, must be taken out of the above equation. For example, bank lending in the UK may be financed by foreign-currency deposits, which do not form part of the money supply. Rather than go into a large amount of detail that is not very informative, we will sum up these effects by the term *external and foreign currency counterparts* of the change in the money supply, which covers both external financing of the government deficit plus UK banks' external and foreign currency transactions. We thus have

$$\Delta M = \text{PSBR} - \Delta B_p + \Delta L - \Delta N + EFC,$$

where *EFC* is external and foreign currency counterparts (ΔL and ΔN refer to sterling transactions, all foreign currency transactions being included within *EFC*). The first three items on the right-hand side are termed the *domestic counterparts* of the change in the money supply.

In explaining these identities, we have referred to 'the banking system', 'banks' and 'the money supply'. If we define the 'banking system' to include banks and not building societies, we have a relationship between the change in M3 and its domestic and external and foreign currency counterparts. If we define the 'banking system' to include building societies as well as banks, we have the relationship between the change in M4 and its domestic and external and foreign currency counterparts. (Note that when counterparts to the change in M3 were published, changes in non-deposit liabilities were included amongst the domestic counterparts; in recent figures on counterparts to the change in M4, they are not included, but appear as an item separate from both domestic and external and foreign currency counterparts.)

Changes in the money supply

The contributions of the domestic and external and foreign currency counterparts to changes in M4 are shown in figure 10.9. Two conclusions can be drawn from this: that on the whole, changes in M4 have followed the domestic counterparts; and that there is a tendency for domestic and external and foreign currency counterparts to move in opposite directions.

❏ On the whole changes in M4 have moved fairly closely together with the domestic counterparts. This has been true not only during the period of flexible exchange rates since 1972, but also before that. In other words, it would appear that it is domestic factors that are primarily responsible for monetary growth in the UK. Since 1986 there has been a sharp rise in the domestic counterparts, which explains the rise in the growth rate of M4.

❏ The domestic and external and foreign currency counterparts tend to move in opposite directions. The explanation for this is the obvious one: tight monetary and fiscal policies (which reduce the domestic counterparts) lead to an improved balance of payments, which in turn leads to a rise in external and foreign currency counterparts. This effect was particularly marked in 1977 when extremely tight monetary and fiscal policies, aimed at reducing the domestic contribution to the money supply, produced a large balance of payments surplus. The result of the balance of payments surplus was that, despite the restrictive policy, M4 grew by more than in 1976.

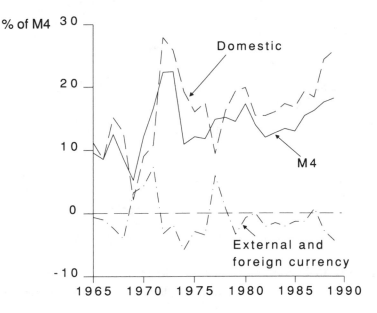

Figure 10.9 Counterparts to changes in M4, 1965-89

Source: Economic Trends.

The main domestic contributions to the rise in M4 are distinguished in figure 10.10. Debt sales are net sales of public sector debt to the public (the private sector excluding banks and building societies, sometimes referred to as 'M4 private sector'). Lending is sterling lending to the public (the 'M4 private sector') by banks and building societies. PSBR rose with inflation during the 1970s and fluctuated greatly. This was offset by increased sales of debt to the public. Since 1983 both PSBR and sales of bonds to the public have declined rapidly. The main source of monetary growth during the 1980s has thus been increased bank lending. Figure 10.10 thus shows that the sources of monetary growth were very different in the 1970s and 1980s: in the mid-to-late 1970s it was a high PSBR that was sustaining the growth of the money supply, whereas since 1980, because of restrictive policy, the government has contributed little towards monetary growth, the stimulus coming instead from the private sector.

The implication of this is that such connexion as there may have been between PSBR and the growth of M4 disappeared during the 1980s. Indeed, as figure 10.11 shows, this link was never very strong. During the 1970s both rose, but this trend can be accounted for by inflation.

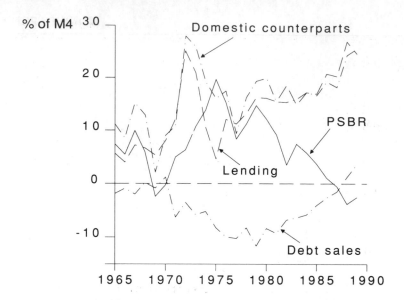

Figure 10.10 Domestic counterparts to growth of M4, 1965-89

Source: Economic Trends. Variables are as defined in the text, as percentages of previous year's M4.

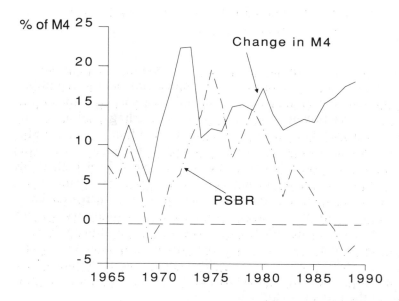

Figure 10.11 PSBR and the growth of M4, 1965-89

Source: Economic Trends. Variables are as percentages of previous year's M4.

During the 1980s it is hard to see any close link, with PSBR (measured relative to M4) falling, and the growth of M4 rising, this divergence being accounted for, as explained above, by increased bank and building society lending to the public.

When using data such as this, it is important to remember that the equations from which they are derived are merely accounting identities: they are not based on any assumption about behaviour and hence can tell us little about causation. For example, if we were to accept a rigid money multiplier theory, with a constant money multiplier, it would follow that changes in the quantity of high-powered money caused changes in bank lending, even though accounting identities used here would attribute part of the rise in the money supply to a rise in bank lending. The fact that part of the rise in the money supply was due to a rise in bank lending would not mean that it had not been caused by government policy. These accounting identities are, nonetheless, useful, for they provide a means of isolating where the main problems lie. For example, these data make it clear that if we are to explain the recent growth in M4, it is important to explain why lending to the private sector has increased so rapidly. For much of the 1970s it would have been much less important to explain movements in such lending, the direct effects of government deficits being more important.

10.4 MONEY AND INFLATION

Our main treatment of inflation is contained in chapter 8. However, because inflation is so often attributed to rises in the money supply it is worth pausing to consider, very briefly, the relationship between money and inflation. The behaviour of inflation and the growth rate of M4 are shown in figure 10.12. There is little evidence in this for any clear link between the growth rate of M4 and either the inflation rate (measured by the RPI) or the growth rate of nominal GDP. There was a dramatic rise in the growth rate of the money supply in 1972-3, followed two years later by a similar rise in inflation, with the result that, looking at this evidence from the late 1970s, there appeared to be some evidence that changes in the growth rate of the money supply affected inflation with a two-year lag. From the perspective of the 1990s, however, it is hard to see such a link. In the early 1980s the peak in the growth rate of M4 came *later* than the peak in inflation, not before it.

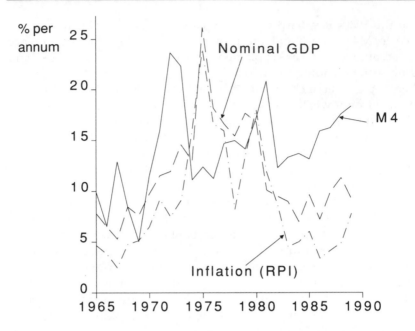

Figure 10.12 Inflation and the growth rate of M4, 1965-89

Source: Economic Trends. GDP is at market prices, average estimate.

FURTHER READING

Christopher Johnson *Measuring the Economy: a Guide to Understanding Official Statistics* (London: Penguin Books, 1988), chapter 7, provides a good introduction to the issues covered in this chapter. Policy is discussed in S. Fischer 'Monetary policy,' in R. Dornbusch and R. Layard (eds.) *The Performance of the British Economy* (Oxford: Oxford University Press, 1987). An interesting recent appraisal of monetary policy is J. C. R. Dow and I. D. Saville *A Critique of Monetary Policy: Theory and British Experience* (Oxford: Oxford University Press, 1988. Paperback edition with new preface, 1990). A critique of this critique has been offered in D. Laidler 'Dow and Saville's critique of monetary policy: a review essay,' *Journal of Economic Literature*, 27(3), 1989, pp. 1147-59. The title of *The Development and Operation of Monetary Policy, 1960-83: a Selection of Material from the Quarterly Bulletin of the Bank of England* (Oxford: Clarendon Press, 1984) is self-explanatory, and the *Bank of England Quarterly Bulletin* should be consulted for more recent developments. Note that many of the references given in chapter 13 are concerned with the appraisal of monetary policy during the 1980s.

Interest rates and exchange rates

11.1 INTRODUCTION

It is conventional in macroeconomics textbooks to see the interest rate as the price of money and to consider it in the context of the supply of and demand for money. Here, however, we consider the interest rate alongside the exchange rate. The reason for this is that because capital can move freely into and out of the country, UK interest rates are closely linked to interest rates in international markets, particularly those in the USA, Europe and Japan. Because investors, in deciding where to place their funds, are choosing between assets denominated in different currencies, this leads to a close connection (explored in detail later in this chapter) between interest rates and exchange rates. In an open economy such as the UK, the link between interest rates and exchange rates is stronger and more direct than the link between interest rates and the money supply. We start with interest rates, and then consider exchange rates.

11.2 INTEREST RATES

The term structure of interest rates

When we consider interest rates it is important to note that there is not just one interest rate, but many. A selection of such interest rates is given in figure 11.1. This shows that whilst there is obviously a

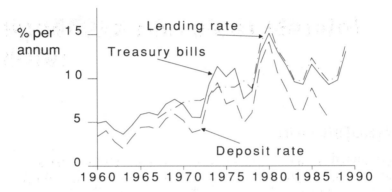

Figure 11.1 Nominal interest rates, 1960-89

Source: International Financial Statistics Yearbook. Figures are averages over the year.

tendency for interest rates to move together, there are considerable differences between different interest rates. Note that the deposit rate will normally be lower than the lending rate charged by financial institutions, for institutions have costs to cover and they need to make a profit.

Further detail on different interest rates is provided in figure 11.2 which illustrates the *term structure* of interest rates: this is the way that interest rates change as the term of the debt changes. It shows what is usually termed the *yield curve*, relating the yields on government securities to their term — to the time before the security matures. Figure 11.2 shows yields on government securities of different maturities at each of the three dates shown. These curves are calculated using the limited range of stocks for which yields are published in *Financial Statistics*, and so should be treated as approximations to the

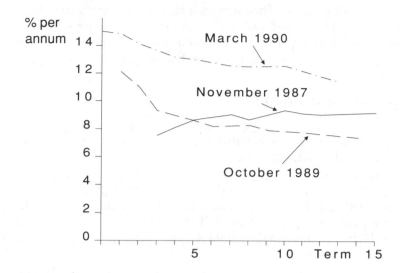

Figure 11.2 The yield curve

Source: Financial Statistics.

true curves. As we move from left to right we move from short-term debt to long-term debt.

There is no particular significance attached to the choice of these particular dates as the ones for which to plot yield curves. November 1987 is interesting, however, in that it illustrates the form we would normally expect the yield curve to take if the overall level of interest rates were expected to remain constant. We would expect the interest rate over a long period to be related to the average short-term interest rate over the period covered, but as uncertainty is greater the further ahead we look, long-term rates should be higher than short-term rates to compensate for the additional risk involved. In recent years, however, the yield curve has frequently had a negative slope, as in October 1989 and March 1990, something which has been true of many countries, not simply the UK. There are a number of reasons for this.

The main reason put forward for downward-sloping yield curves is concerned with expected inflation. Interest rates are, as is explained below, linked to inflation, so if inflation rates are expected to fall this means that short-term interest rates will be expected to fall, thus lowering the long-term interest rate. If the long-term inflation rate were expected to rise, this would raise long-term interest rates, giving the

yield curve a positive slope. The difference between the yield curves for
November 1987 and October 1989 could be explained in the following
way. Short-term interest rates have been raised and because the
markets expect this to lower inflation in the longer term, long rates
have fallen.

Interest rates and inflation

Figure 11.1 shows that there was a significant and sustained rise in
interest rates around 1973. It is natural to explain this as the result of
rising inflation. The standard theory is that the real interest rate (the
nominal interest rate minus the inflation rate) will be determined by
savings and investment, and that this will be fairly stable over time.
The relation between two interest rates (the treasury bill rate and the
rate on long-term government debt) and the inflation rate is shown in
figure 11.3. There are three main points to note about this graph.

❑ The rise in interest rates above their 1960s levels came around
   1973, at the same time as inflation increased dramatically.

❑ The decline in interest rates after 1980 was associated with
   declining inflation.

❑ The real interest rate, defined simply as the difference between
   either of these interest rates and the inflation rate, has not been
   constant. It was positive during both the 1960s and the 1980s, and
   negative during the 1970s. These two real interest rates are shown
   in figure 11.4.

❑ Real interest rates were higher during the 1980s than during the
   1960s.

So far, we have talked of the real interest rate as being the difference
between the relevant nominal interest rate and the current inflation
rate. The problem with this is that it does not take account of
inflationary expectations. This is important because the real interest rate
relevant to spending decisions should be the difference between the
interest rate and the expected inflation rate. One way to measure this is
to measure the real rate of interest on index-linked debt. Unfortunately
such debt was introduced only in 1981, which means that we have no
figures for the 1970s, the period for which we would most like to have
them. Figures for a selection of such real interest rates are shown in
figure 11.5. The two longer-term interest rates, those for debt maturing

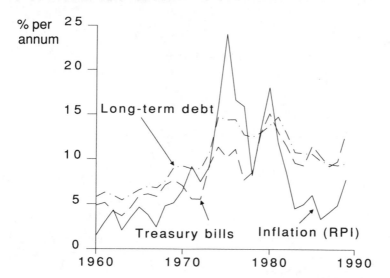

Figure 11.3 Interest rates and inflation, 1960-89
Source: figure 11.1 and *Economic Trends*.

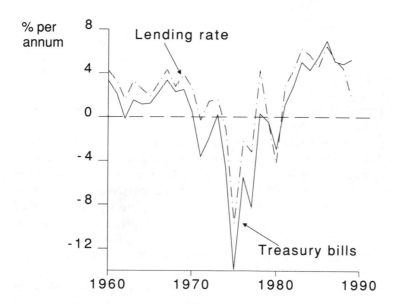

Figure 11.4 Real interest rates I, 1960-89
Source: as figure 11.3.

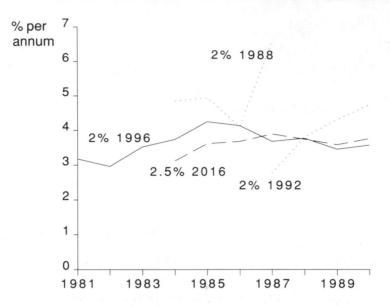

Figure 11.5: Real interest rates II, 1981-90

Source: Financial Statistics.

in 1996 and 2016, fluctuate only slightly compared with the real interest rates shown in figure 11.4.

In interpreting the data in figure 11.5 it is important to note that as we move from left to right along any of these curves, there are two factors to take into account. There are the normal changes in the economic environment (changing expectations and so on) which cause interest rates to change. In addition, the maturity of the relevant security shown is falling. In 1981 debt due to mature in 1996 had a term of 15 years, whereas by 1990 this had declined to 6 years. When first quoted, in 1987, 1992 stock had a term of 5 years, but by 1990 this had declined to 2 years. It is the latter factor which explains the sharp rise in 1988 stock in 1987: by the end of 1987, 1988 stock had only a month or so before it matured, which meant that it will have had a price (and yield) appropriate to a very liquid asset.

Although we do not do this here, it is possible to use the yields on index-linked and non-index-linked stock to calculate the implicit inflation rate expected by the market (such an inflation rate was used in estimating the inflation tax in chapter 4).

Interest rate parity

Capital can nowadays move freely between the world's main financial centres, which means that we would expect rates of return on similar assets to be the same in different countries: if they were not, then investors would move funds from the low-yielding asset to the high-yielding one. Because assets are denominated in different currencies, however, it is not enough to compare interest rates. We have to take account of exchange rate changes as well. The reason is that if an investor from Britain invests in the USA, and the dollar depreciates 5 per cent relative to sterling, the investor will make a capital loss of 5 per cent which has to be subtracted from the US interest rate in order to find out the return which the investor obtained from holding his or her funds in the USA. Had the funds been held in sterling there would have been no exchange rate loss. Thus if there is to be equilibrium in capital markets, the interest rate obtained abroad must equal the corresponding UK interest rate, *plus* the expected appreciation or depreciation of sterling. This is known as *uncovered interest rate parity*.

What makes the notion of interest rate parity usable is the existence of *forward markets* for foreign exchange. The reason for considering forward markets here is that they provide us with a means of measuring the expected change in the exchange rate (see box 11.1). The forward premium on sterling measures the amount by which investors expect sterling to appreciate. We thus have what is known as *covered interest rate parity*, which means that the interest rate obtained abroad must equal the UK interest rate *plus* the forward premium on sterling. It is called 'covered' interest rate parity because exchange rate movements are covered by forward contracts.

Some statistics on covered interest parity are shown in figures 11.6 and 11.7. Figure 11.6 shows the interest rates on UK (sterling) and US (dollar) Treasury bills, together with the forward premium on sterling, expressed as a percentage per annum. The gap between the two interest rates is the *interest rate differential*. The extent to which the interest rate differential equals the forward premium, as would be the case if covered interest parity held exactly, is shown in figure 11.7. Part (a) shows the yield on US Treasury bills together with the UK Treasury bill rate adjusted for the forward premium on sterling. Part (b) shows essentially the same information, but this time it is the US Treasury bill rate that is adjusted for the forward premium. The top panel thus shows US interest rates, and the bottom panel UK rates.

There are five main conclusions to draw from figures 11.6 and 11.7.

Box 11.1 FORWARD MARKETS AND EXPECTED CHANGES IN THE EXCHANGE RATE

On forward markets investors make contracts to buy and sell foreign exchange at a specified price at a specified date in the future (usually 1 or 3 months in advance). For example, if an investor sells £100 forward on 1 March at a 3 months forward price of £1 = $1.53 he or she is undertaking a commitment to sell £100 on 1 June in exchange for $153. Forward markets are useful to firms as they enable them to avoid the risks associated with fluctuations in exchange markets. If a firm knows that it is going to require foreign exchange in 3 months' time to pay for an import order, if can buy foreign exchange on the forward market: this way the firm can know the price it is going to have to pay for foreign exchange in 3 months' time.

To see the relation between forward and spot markets, consider an example. The *spot price* of sterling is $1.5270 and the 3 months *forward premium* on sterling is 0.87 cents. What does this mean?

❑ If you want to buy or sell sterling *now* you can do so at the spot price, of £1 = $1.5270.

❑ If you want to buy or sell sterling in 3 months' time you can do so at a price of £1 = $1.5357: this is the *forward price*, obtained by adding the forward premium ($0.0087) to the spot price. The forward premium is the difference between the forward price and the spot price.

If the forward premium is negative, on the other hand, we refer to sterling being at a *discount*, with the forward price being less than the spot price.

The forward premium is often expressed as a percentage per annum. For example, 0.87 cents divided by $1.527 gives 0.57 per cent. As this is over 3 months, it corresponds to a rate of 2.3 per cent *per annum*.

If the foreign exchange market works efficiently, and if investors are concerned simply with the expected value of their wealth, the forward exchange rate must equal whatever investors expect the spot rate to be in 3 months' time. To see this, consider another example. On 1 March the forward price of sterling is $1.54. Suppose an investor expects the price of sterling to be $1.50 on 1 June. This would mean that if he or she bought dollars (sold sterling) on the forward market, he or she would expect to make a profit: for each £100 sold forward, he or she would get $154 on 1 June; but the investor expects sterling's spot price to be $1.50 on 1 June, which means that he or she would expect to be able to sell these dollars for £102.67, a profit of £2.67. Thus if the forward price were not equal to the expected future spot price, speculators would immediately buy or sell foreign exchange in order to make a profit in this way, with the result that the forward price would change until it equalled the expected future spot price. If follows that the forward premium is, given certain assumptions, a measure of the expected change in the exchange rate.

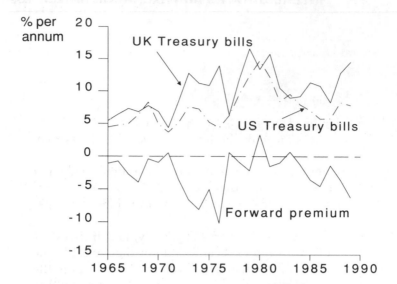

Figure 11.6 Interest rates and the forward premium, 1965-89

Source: Financial Statistics. Figures are for the last working day of the year shown.

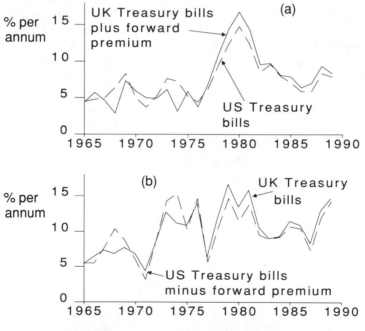

Figure 11.7 Covered interest rate parity, 1965-89

Source: as figure 11.6.

❏ UK and US interest rates move together fairly closely. Covered interest rate parity seems to hold in general, though there are marked differences in individual years.

❏ For most of the period sterling has been at a discount relative to the dollar. Because UK inflation has persistently been higher than US inflation, sterling has, on average, been depreciating against the dollar, and this is reflected in the forward discount.

❏ During the mid-1970s UK interest rates rose very sharply, without any corresponding rise in US interest rates, the difference being accounted for by the enormous forward discount on sterling. Sterling was, from around 1973 to 1976, expected to depreciate substantially, and hence UK interest rates had to exceed US rates by an equivalent margin.

❏ At the end of the 1970s there was a sharp rise in interest rates in both the USA and the UK, this being followed by a decline during the first half of the 1980s.

❏ At the end of the 1980s interest rates rose much more in the UK than in the USA, this being reflected in sterling being at a discount relative to the dollar.

For this illustration we have taken treasury bill rates. A similar exercise could have been undertaken using other interest rates. Had we taken other short-term money market rates (such as the inter-bank rate) interest rate differentials would have been low, reflecting the high degree of international capital mobility between the UK and the USA.

Entry into the exchange rate mechanism of the EMS (see section 11.5) will not mean the disappearance of risk premia, though they should be reduced. This is for two reasons. The EMS rules allow currencies to fluctuate within a limited range. In addition, there is still the risk that a currency may be devalued within the EMS.

11.3 EXCHANGE RATES

Real and nominal exchange rates

Some of the main exchange rates against sterling are shown in figure 11.8. The problem with using any individual exchange rate to talk about what has happened to the value of sterling is that an exchange

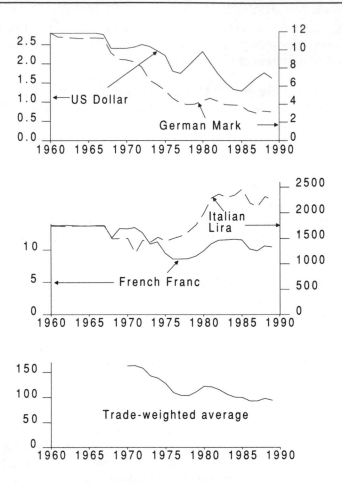

Figure 11.8 Exchange rates, 1960-89

Source: Financial Statistics. Bilateral rates are units of foreign currency per £. Average is an index number, 1985=100.

rate may change either because of what is happening to sterling or because of what is happening to the other currency. To get round this problem we use the *effective exchange rate*, shown in the bottom panel of figure 11.8. This is a weighted average of different exchange rates, the weights corresponding to the importance of the currencies concerned in the UK's international trade. It is, for obvious reasons, calculated only for the years of floating exchange rates. Movements in these exchange rates are discussed in the next section.

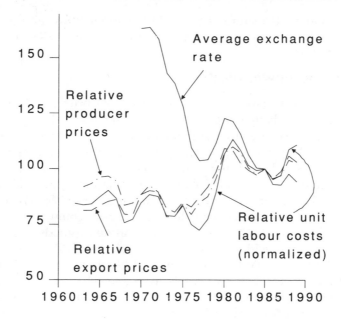

Figure 11.9 Measures of the real exchange rate, 1962-89

Source: Economic Trends.

Movements in an exchange rate, even the effective exchange rate, do not tell the full story of what is happening to the value of a currency. When considering trade between two countries, the important thing is not the rate at which two currencies exchange for each other, but the rate at which the two countries' goods and services are exchanged. This is the *real exchange rate*. There is, of course, no unique way to measure this. Some of the most common measures of the real exchange rate were discussed in chapter 5 under the heading 'measures of competitiveness', and are shown in figure 11.9, together with the effective exchange rate from figure 11.8. The indices are all constructed so as to be 100 in 1985, so the levels of the different indices relative to each other are of no significance, just the changes.

Figure 11.9 immediately shows that the dramatic fall in the value of sterling from 1970 to the late 1980s is mainly the result of relative price changes: the exchange rate has fallen, but this is compensated for by higher sterling prices. There has been no similar decline in the ratio at which UK goods are exchanged with other countries' goods. Indeed, the most noticeable feature of figure 11.9 is the fact that all measures of the real exchange rate were *higher* for most of the 1980s than in the 1960s and 1970s.

Purchasing power parity

Purchasing power parity, a concept introduced briefly in chapter 1, is defined as the exchange rate at which a given commodity, or bundle of commodities, costs the same in two countries. For example, suppose we wish to calculate the purchasing power parity for hamburgers, and a hamburger costs £1 in Britain and $1.50 in the US, whilst the market exchange rate is £1=$2. The dollar price of hamburgers is $1.50 in the US and $2 in the UK. The PPP for hamburgers is $1.50, the exchange rate at which a hamburger costs the same in both countries.

This definition of PPP means that different goods, or different bundles of goods, will in general have different PPPs. A selection of PPPs is shown in table 11.1, together with the comparative dollar price levels they imply. The two parts of table 11.1 provide the same information in two different ways. Take private consumption, for example. In part (b) of table 11.1 we see that goods which cost $100 in the US will cost $76 (at the 1985 exchange rate) in the UK. The 1985 exchange rate was $1 = £0.779 (£1 = $1.28) which means the goods cost £76 × 0.779 = £59. In other words, PPP is £59 = $100, or £0.59 = $1, the figure given in part (a).

It is worth noting that the greatest price differentials arise in non-traded goods. The balance of trade by definition covers only traded goods, and dollar price levels are virtually the same in all four countries. Other goods listed, apart from transport, are cheaper in Europe than in the USA, the cheapest being medical care and government consumption. For GDP as a whole dollar prices in Britain were only 73 per cent of US prices. (Note that many categories of expenditure are not listed here.)

The source of this information was a survey undertaken in 1985, which collected prices of a wide range of goods. These prices were used to calculate PPP figures for 1985. From this starting point PPPs for other years were calculated using relative inflation rates according to the following formula.

$$\text{PPP}_{k,t} = \text{PPP}_{k,1985}(1+\pi_{k,t})/(1+\pi_{US,t})$$

$\text{PPP}_{k,t}$ is the PPP for country k in year t and $\pi_{k,t}$ is the inflation rate in country k between year t and 1985. US inflation appears in all cases because the USA is taken as the benchmark. If we want the PPP

Table 11.1 PPPs and comparative dollar price levels in 1985

(a) Purchasing power parities (£/US$)

Private consumption		0.590
Food, beverages, tobacco	0.613	
Medical care	0.306	
Transport/communication	0.958	
Government consumption		0.428
Gross fixed capital formation		0.670
Construction	0.715	
Machinery/equipment	0.645	
Stocks		0.681
Balance of trade		0.772
GDP		0.567

(b) Comparative dollar price levels (US = 100)

	UK		Germany	France	
Private final consumption		76	87		84
Food, beverages, tobacco	79		80	79	
Medical care	39		62	49	
Transport/communications	123		117	123	
Government consumption		55	79		71
Gross fixed capital formation		86	84		83
Construction	92		85	82	
Machinery/equipment	83		83	85	
Stocks		87	93		91
Balance of trade		99	99		99
GDP		73	84		81

Note: the exchange rate in 1985 was £0.779=$1 (£1=$1.28).

Source: OECD *National Accounts*, supplement on purchasing power parities.

between two other currencies, say sterling and the German mark, we simply take the ratio of the relevant two dollar PPPs.

It is worth noting that these measures of the real exchange rate, or competitiveness, are similar to measures of purchasing power parity (see chapter 1). The notion that there is an equilibrium real exchange rate is the same as claiming that there is an equilibrium relationship between the exchange rate and purchasing power parity. Define P as the domestic price level in sterling, P_W as the world price level (in foreign currency) and e as the exchange rate (value of sterling). Purchasing power parity is thus measured by P_W/P. Let α denote the ratio of the exchange rate to PPP, so that

$$\alpha = e/\text{PPP} = eP/P_W.$$

The right-hand expression here is simply the price of domestic goods divided by the price of foreign goods, both expressed in foreign currency. α is thus a measure of competitiveness, similar to relative producer prices. This means that we can interpret measures of competitiveness as measuring the gap between the exchange rate and PPP.

In a simple world, where both countries produced and consumed identical goods, and in which there were no transport costs or other barriers to trade, the equilibrium value of α would be 1. In practice, however, because of measurement problems and the fact that we are using price indices, there is no reason to expect the equilibrium value of α to be 1. This is equivalent to saying that we could not necessarily expect the equilibrium exchange rate to equal PPP.

PPP and measures of competitiveness have been introduced in this chapter because, though there are great practical problems in knowing what the equilibrium exchange rate might be, these concepts do provide a long run theory of the exchange rate. If the exchange rate rises a long way above PPP (for an appropriate bundle of goods) this means that competitiveness is falling, a situation which should not be sustainable indefinitely (though it may well persist for a long time). The same applies, of course, to downward movements away from PPP, for such movements imply that another country's exchange rate is rising above PPP.

The reason for economists' attachment to PPP as a theory of the exchange rate is not that it as been used successfully to explain exchange rate movements — attempts to test the PPP theory have usually failed. The reason is the theoretical argument that, even if currency speculation causes exchange rates to depart from PPP for long periods, there must be *some* limit to the extent to which a country can lose competitiveness and still enter into international trade. The fact that the link between PPP and exchange rates is in practice so weak, however, means that great care must be taken in interpreting statistics on PPP or competitiveness. PPP and measures of competitiveness must be used alongside other evidence in order to assess whether a country's exchange rate is at, above or below its long run equilibrium level.

11.4 THE HISTORY OF THE EXCHANGE RATE

It is worth providing a brief history of the exchange rate, because in doing so we provide a summary of the main aspects of macroeconomic policy-making in the UK, so central have exchange rate problems been. In such a history we have to divide the post-war period into two main periods: the period up to 1971, when exchange rates were regulated by the Bretton Woods system, established after the war; and the period of floating exchange rates since 1971.

The Bretton Woods system

Under the Bretton Woods system governments were committed to maintaining their currencies close to a par value. From time to time, however, par values became unsustainable, and new parities were established, with currencies being devalued. In the UK the Bretton Woods period falls into two parts: before and after 1967.

From 1949 to 1967 the par value was £1 = $2.80, with the exchange rate being kept within the range $2.78-2.82. During the 1960s, however, sterling came under pressure for a number of reasons. The two main ones were that competitiveness was deteriorating and there was thought to be a large problem with the current account.

❑ Competitiveness was deteriorating because UK wages and prices were rising faster than US wages and prices. The rise in real exchange rates, shown in figure 11.9, from 1963 to 1966 may not look much by more recent standards, but it was nonetheless significant.

❑ There was perceived to be a large balance of payments problem, with the official figures showing a current account deficit from 1964 right through to 1967. Although there had been balance of payments deficits in every business cycle since the war, these had always been eliminated fairly quickly once the boom had finished. This time the deficit was thought to be persistent.

In this paragraph we have focused on contemporaries' perceptions of the balance of payments situation as the cause of problems with the exchange rate. This is very deliberate, the reason being that the current account was, according to subsequent figures, in fact in *surplus* for much of the period from 1965 to 1967. The published balance of payments figures were, if subsequent estimates are to be believed, substantially in error, mainly because exports were systematically under-recorded. This shows the importance of confidence and expectations in exchange rate determination. What appears to have happened during this period was that people *believed* there was a current account problem, which caused problems with the capital account, putting pressure on sterling.

Believing the problem to be with the current account, the government imposed the appropriate policies. Prices and incomes policy, whereby firms had to get government approval before they could raise prices and wage rates, was used to reduce inflation and prevent competitiveness from deteriorating. Strict foreign exchange controls were imposed. Fiscal policy was restrictive. All these were aimed at increasing exports and reducing imports, with a view to strengthening the current account and enabling the government to maintain the value of sterling at £1 = \$2.80.

In October 1967 it became clear that this policy could not be sustained, and sterling was devalued by 14 per cent, to £1 = \$2.40. Competitiveness, as shown by figure 11.9, improved. This, however, did not lead to an end to restrictive policies, for two reasons. The first was that it was important that the competitive advantage given by devaluation was not eroded too quickly by high inflation. If the higher import prices brought about by devaluation were to lead to wage and price rises, competitiveness would deteriorate and the stimulus to increase exports and decrease imports would be reduced. The second was that it was necessary that resources be made available for export industries, which required that domestic demand had to be kept low.

The monetary and fiscal policies pursued after devaluation were thus as restrictive as before: the government budget was in surplus by 1970. The result was an improvement in the balance of payments, which moved into surplus.

Floating exchange rates, 1971-1976

In 1971 the exchange rate floated, at first upwards, and then downwards against all major currencies except the Lira, until 1976. There were three main reasons for this depreciation: a rapid demand expansion; high oil prices; and rapid inflation in the UK.

❏ In 1972 the government made a deliberate decision to expand the economy rapidly, so as to achieve a growth rate of 5 per cent per annum, a high rate by UK standards. By doing this the government expected to reduce unemployment from 1 million to 500,000 by the end of 1973 (a target they achieved). It was hoped that the announcement of such a large and sustained rise in demand would encourage investment and raise productivity, improving prospects for the longer term. Exchange rate policy was a key aspect of this policy. Previous booms had always ended in a balance of payments crisis, so the government announced that it would let the exchange rate float downwards if this were necessary to keep the expansion going.

❏ The oil price rise of 1973-4 led to massive balance of payments deficits for oil-importing countries. At the same time, a miners' strike had disastrous effects on production, with the imposition of a 3-day week to conserve fuel.

❏ In 1974-5 the UK inflation rate rose to around 25 per cent per annum, a rate much higher than in most other industrial countries.

This culminated in the sterling crisis of 1976. This was resolved with a package of restrictive monetary and fiscal policy measures and assistance from the International Monetary Fund.

Floating exchange rates, 1976-1990

1977 saw a dramatic turn-around in the UK's financial situation. A very severe incomes policy, combined with tight monetary and fiscal policies succeeded in bringing down inflation from 25 per cent to under 10 per cent. At the same time unemployment stopped rising and the balance of payments moved into surplus. This, together with the government's perceived determination to stick to its monetary targets, introduced in 1976 at the time of the sterling crisis, led to a slight rise in the exchange rate.

The next few years saw a dramatic rise in the value of sterling, the unprecedented nature of this rise being revealed by the behaviour of the real exchange rate. Relative unit labour costs, often considered the best measure of the real exchange rate, rose by over 55 per cent from 1977 to 1981, an unparalleled increase. This was due to two factors: North Sea oil, and very tight monetary policy.

BOX 11.2 EXCHANGE RATE OVERSHOOTING

To show how exchange rate overshooting can occur, we will consider a very simple example. Many of the assumptions will sound very artificial — they are introduced solely in order to keep everything as simple as possible. Our starting point is an economy which is in equilibrium with a constant inflation rate of 10 per cent per annum. The growth rate of the money supply and the world inflation rate are also equal to 10 per cent per annum. The exchange rate is constant and is not expected to change. At time t_0 the government suddenly announces a new policy: that for the next τ years it is going to reduce the growth rate of the money supply to 6 per cent per annum, after which it will return to 10 per cent. Assume that this will reduce the inflation rate by the same amount for this period.

In this artificially simple economy there is no reason for competitiveness to change at all. If competitiveness is to remain constant we must have

$$\Delta e / e = \Delta P_W / P_W = \Delta P / P$$

where e is the exchange rate (defined as units of foreign currency per unit of domestic currency — as in £1 = \$2), P_W is the world price level and P the domestic price level. For competitiveness to remain constant for the τ years after t_0, the exchange rate must appreciate at 4 per cent per annum.

At this stage we introduce two crucial assumptions: that capital markets are perfect, so that interest rate parity holds, and that investors in financial markets have rational expectations, which in this simple model means that their expectations must be correct. If competitiveness is to remain unchanged, the exchange rate must appreciate at 4 per cent per annum. The exchange rate would follow the path labelled (i) in figure 11.B2.1. If investors anticipate this correctly, interest rate parity requires that domestic interest rates fall by 4 per cent. There is no reason for this to happen: indeed, we would expect a monetary contraction to *raise*, not lower, interest rates.

If interest rates are to stay the same, interest rate parity will hold only if the exchange rate immediately rises to a level such that investors no longer expect it to appreciate: in other words, if the

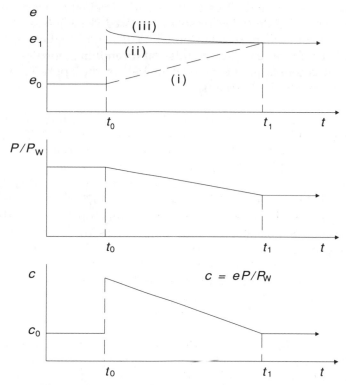

Figure 11.B2.1 Exchange rate overshooting

exchange rate follows the path labelled (ii) in figure 11.B2.1. Even if the exchange rate jumps in this way at time t_0, however, there is no reason to think that prices will do the same. Prices are likely to follow a path such as that shown in figure 11.B2.1. If so, we find that competitiveness jumps up at time t_0 and then falls steadily, returning to its original level after τ years.

If the reduction in the growth rate of the money supply were to raise interest rates, interest rate parity would require the exchange rate to rise to a level high enough for investors to expect it to depreciate: the expected capital loss caused by the depreciation would cancel out the rise in the rate of interest. In this case the exchange rate would follow a path such as (iii) in figure 11.B2.1. This is *exchange rate overshooting* — where the exchange rate overshoots its new equilibrium level.

❏ North Sea oil production was increasing from an insignificant amount in the mid-1970s to the point of self-sufficiency in oil by 1980 (see chapter 9). For reasons discussed elsewhere, increased oil production will have contributed to the appreciation of sterling. Such estimates as exist of this 'oil premium', however, suggest that it accounts for no more than half of the appreciation which occurred, and perhaps less.

❏ The other main factor was the very tight monetary policy which followed the Conservatives' election victory in 1979. The government committed itself to a 'medium term financial strategy', involving a gradual reduction of the growth rate of the money supply over several years. In practice, however, there was a remarkably severe monetary squeeze in 1979-80. This was for a number of reasons, one of the main ones being that the government focused on sterling M3 as its monetary target. Because sterling M3 grew much faster than other monetary aggregates (including M1 and M5) it under-estimated the tightness of monetary policy. Another reason was that the rapid rise in inflation in 1980 made the monetary squeeze even tighter: the *real* value of the money supply fell dramatically.

The commonly accepted argument is that the introduction of this tight monetary policy led to *exchange rate overshooting*, the theory of which is discussed in box 11.2. Such behaviour is needed to account for the exceptionally sharp rise in the real exchange rate which took place from 1979 to 1981. It was a problem made worse by the removal of exchange control regulations which had taken place in the second half of the 1970s. With strict foreign exchange controls, such as existed during the 1960s, the capital flows needed to produce such overshooting would have been less likely to occur.

Since 1981 there has been a decline in the exchange rate. There are three reasons why this may have taken place.

❏ A natural reaction to the overshooting of 1979-81.

❏ Declining North Sea oil revenues, due in part to falling production, but due mainly to the fall in the price of oil.

❏ The inflation rate, though it has fallen substantially, has remained high compared with that of many industrial countries, and has recently started to rise. Since the mid-1980s sterling has been at a substantial discount on the forward market, reflecting the fact that people expect it to depreciate due to rising inflation.

The EMS, since 1990

On 5 October 1990 the government announced its intention to join the exchange rate mechanism of the EMS (which is discussed in detail in the next section) with sterling pegged to a rate of 2.95 German marks to the pound, and a six per cent band on either side. This was accompanied by a cut in interest rates of one per cent. The reason for this interest rate cut was the belief that, once sterling joined the exchange rate mechanism, investors would no longer expect its value to fall relative to other EMS currencies, notably the German mark. If interest rates did not fall this would make the expected yield on investments in sterling (the sterling interest rate less any expected depreciation) very high compared with, say, interest rates in Germany. If this happened funds would flow into sterling, pushing sterling to the top of its allowed range. For the first few days this appeared to be happening, with sterling rising well above 2.95 German marks, but within a few weeks this upward pressure had stopped and sterling was close to its minimum value.

Under the EMS the ability of the government to keep sterling within its allowed range depends crucially on whether or not it can persuade investors that it is going to take whatever action is necessary to achieve this. This in turn will depend on two things: whether or not sterling is over-valued at 2.95 German marks; and how soon UK inflation comes into line with inflation in the other major European Community countries. This issue is discussed further at the end of this chapter and in chapter 13. Before then we need to discuss the EMS in more detail.

11.5 THE EUROPEAN MONETARY SYSTEM

The mechanics of the EMS

The European Monetary system was established in 1979, and has three main elements: the European Currency Unit; the exchange rate mechanism; and the European Monetary Cooperation Fund.

The European Currency Unit (ECU). This is a basket of the currencies of European Community member countries, with the quantity of each country reflecting the size of the corresponding economy. The composition of the ECU is shown in table 11.2 and figure 11.10. Notice that the weight of different currencies in the ECU depends on their values. Thus if, for example, the German Mark appreciates, this will raise its weight within the ECU. The quantity of each currency in the ECU has changed twice: in September 1984 and again in September

Table 11.2 The composition of the ECU

	Units of currency			Weights		
	1979	1984	1989	1979	1984	1989
German mark	0.828	0.719	0.6242	33.0	32.1	30.1
French Franc	1.15	1.31	1.332	19.8	19.1	19.0
Sterling	0.0885	0.0878	0.08784	13.3	14.9	13.0
Guilder	0.286	0.2560	0.2198	10.5	10.2	9.4
Lira	109.0	140.0	151.8	9.5	10.1	10.15
Belgian Franc	3.80	3.85	3.301	9.6	8.5	7.9
Krone	0.217	0.219	0.1976	3.1	2.7	2.45
Punt	0.00759	0.00871	0.008552	1.2	1.2	1.1
Drachma*		1.15	1.44		1.3	0.8
Peseta			6.885			5.3
Escudo*			1.393			0.8

Source: ECU-EMS Information. 1984 refers to the revised basket established in September 1984; 1989 to the basket established in September 1989. Asterisks denote currencies not yet in the exchange rate mechanism. Luxembourg's currency is linked to Belgium's.

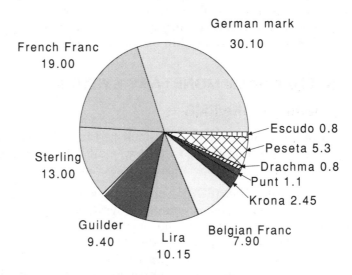

Figure 11.10 Currency weights within the ECU since September 1989

Source: as figure 2.

Table 11.3: EMS divergence indicators

	%
German Mark	1.176
French Franc	1.362
Guilder	1.528
Lira	1.516
Belgian Franc	1.551
Krone	1.645
Punt	1.669
Sterling	3.915
Peseta	4.271

Source: Financial Times.

1989. Again taking the German Mark as an example, the reduction in the number of Marks in the basket has offset the effects of their rising value. Note that sterling is included in the ECU even though it is not part of the exchange rate mechanism.

The ECU is important for a number of reasons. One is that it is used in European Community transactions, such as payments under the Common Agricultural Policy. Another is that it forms the centre of the exchange rate mechanism of the EMS. Finally, the ECU has increasingly been used in commercial markets, particularly as a denomination for bank deposits and certain types of bond issue.

The Exchange Rate Mechanism (ERM). When people talk about whether the UK should participate fully in the EMS what they have in mind is participation in the exchange rate mechanism of the EMS. This is a system designed to peg the values of the European currencies together, paving the way towards eventual monetary unification. Each currency has a *par value* in terms of the ECU.

Around this is constructed a *parity grid* which gives the set of bilateral exchange rates implied by these par values. This parity grid is very important because countries are required to keep their bilateral exchange rates within 2.25 per cent of their par values, except for Spain and the UK which have a limits of 6 per cent (Italy used to have a 6 per cent limit). Eventually, as a further step towards European monetary union, all countries are required to move to a narrow band, the wider band being allowed as a temporary arrangement to ease the transition to a fixed exchange rate. If one bilateral rate reaches this limit, *both* countries are required to take action to stop the exchange rate from exceeding it. This requirement applies to the country whose currency is above the parity as much as to the one whose currency is below parity. This mechanism, focusing on bilateral exchange rates, is the main mechanism for keeping the EMS currencies in line with each other.

This mechanism of bilateral action to maintain bilateral exchange rates works as long as the problem is not that one currency is seriously out of line with all the others. Under these circumstances it is necessary for that country to take unilateral action. The necessity for this is indicated by *divergence indicators*. Currencies are permitted to diverge from their parity against the ECU by only 75 per cent of the maximum permitted by the parity grid (6 per cent for Spain and the UK, and 2.25 per cent for other countries). There is a technical problem here, because when, for example, a currency appreciates, this raises the value of the ECU. For currencies such as the Irish Punt or the Belgian Franc, this is insignificant, because these currencies make up such a small proportion of the ECU. For the German Mark, on the other hand, this is a major problem as it makes up about a third of the ECU: if the German Mark were to appreciate by 1 per cent relative to *all* other currencies, the ECU would appreciate by 0.32 per cent, and so the German Mark's appreciation relative to the ECU would be only 0.68 per cent. If all countries could fluctuate by the same percentage relative to the ECU, therefore, currencies that carry high weights in the ECU would be able to fluctuate much more than those with low weights. To overcome this, divergence indicators are constructed as $0.75(1 - W)$ times either 2.25 per cent or 6 per cent of par values, where W is the weight of the currency concerned in the ECU. When a currency reaches its divergence indicator, unilateral action is called for. Divergence indicators for March 1990 are shown in table 11.3.

The European Monetary Co-operation Fund. This fund assists countries in maintaining their exchange rates, and has been financed by countries lending 20 per cent of their gold and foreign exchange reserves to the fund in return for a corresponding amount of ECUs. At present the system is constructed so that national central banks retain ownership of these funds, but the intention was that the EMCF would be extended into a European Monetary Fund, which could operate as the central bank.

The operation of the EMS

The institutions of the EMS have changed remarkably little since its inception, but the way in which the system has in practice been operated has changed substantially. At first, currency realignments

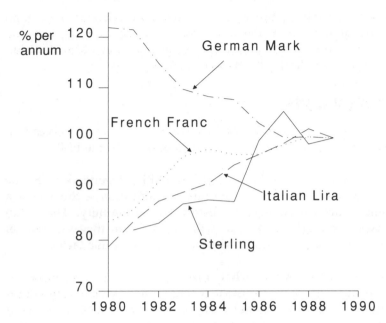

Figure 11.11: Currencies in relation to the ECU, 1980-9

Source: *International Financial Statistics.*

were frequent, with the German Mark and the Guilder usually going up, and the French Franc, the Lira and the Punt going down. Some of these changes are shown in figure 11.11. Since 1987, on the other hand, there have been no realignments at all, which is reflected in all the exchange rates shown in figure 11.11 (except sterling's) remaining approximately the same after 1987. In other words, what has happened is that the system has moved from being effectively a 'crawling peg' system, where par values change gradually, to a fixed exchange rate system. This has been accompanied by greater consensus about how policy is to be conducted. On the other hand, this shift towards a fixed exchange rate system has been to some extent inevitable. With the abolition of many of the controls on capital movements that took place during the period, scope for speculative activity has increased with the result that the earlier system of periodic realignments might have become unworkable. Rumours of realignments might nowadays set up speculative pressures which would prevent realignments from happening in an agreed, orderly manner. It can thus be argued that the EMS has been successful in that it has achieved its main goal, of stabilizing the exchange rates of member countries. The costs, however, have been high for some countries. Spain, for example, experienced very high levels of unemployment in the late 1980s in order to bring inflation down to a rate closer to the inflation rates of the other EMS countries. The UK may face similar problems in the 1990s.

11.6 CONCLUSIONS

Any discussion of interest rates and exchange rates now involves two issues: the future of the EMS; and sterling's position in the EMS.

❏ The exchange rate mechanism of the EMS is intended to be the first step towards European monetary unification -- the use of a common currency within the European Community. This is an intensely political issue and will depend on the outcome of political negotiations rather than on purely economic factors.

❏ Sterling is in the EMS at what some commentators and business-men believe is an unrealistically high rate. At the same time, inflation is high and it is not clear (in November 1990) how fast it is going to fall. There are clearly many possible outcomes, these including, amongst others: an early realignment of sterling; a fairly rapid fall in inflation; and a period of prolonged, high unemployment as the government seeks to reduce inflation.

FURTHER READING

Exchange rates are the subject of *Oxford Review of Economic Policy* 5(3), 1989. The implications of international capital flows are discussed in A. K. Chrystal 'Have recent high capital flows harmed Britain?' *The Economic Review*, September 1985, pp. 24-8; and A. K. Chrystal and K. Dowd 'Two arguments for the restriction of international capital flows,' *National Westminster Bank Quarterly Review*, November 1986.

The EMS is discussed in F. Giavazzi and A. Giovannini 'The EMS and the dollar,' *Economic Policy* 2, April 1986, pp. 456-85; G. Zis 'The EMS, 1979-84: an assessment,' *Journal of Common Market Studies*, September 1984. The implications of the EMS for the UK are examined in M. J. Artis and M. Miller 'On joining the EMS,' *Midland Bank Review*, Winter 1986, pp. 11-20; F. Giavazzi 'The impact of EEC membership,' in R. Dornbusch and R. Layard (eds.) *The Performance of the British Economy* (Oxford: Oxford University Press). The EMS is one of the issues discussed in *Oxford Review of Economic Policy* 3(3), on 'Policy options for the UK', D. Currie 'Options for UK macroeconomic policy' and R. Dornbusch 'Prosperity or price stability' are particularly worth reading.

V

The Economy as a Whole

Models of the whole economy

12.1 INTRODUCTION

Running a model of the UK economy can be a large task, requiring considerable financial support. There are thus a fairly small number of organizations, many receiving government funding, that run them. These include the National Institute of Economic and Social Research (NIESR), the London Business School (LBS), City University Business School, Liverpool University, Her Majesty's Treasury (HMT) and the Bank of England. Some of these models are very large: the NIESR model, for example, has 320 variables; the LBS model has 770; the Bank of England model has 800; and the Treasury model 1275 variables. In contrast the Liverpool model has only 50 variables. As we shall see later on, each of these models has its own distinctive characteristics.

Why are the models so large?

In principle a model of the UK economy could be very small. We could, for example take the basic income-expenditure model, based on the identity $Y = C + I + G$, estimate the consumption function and take investment and government spending to be exogenous. If we thought we knew what was going to happen to investment and government spending we could then use this model to forecast the level of income. This model would perhaps not be very interesting (everything depends on what we expect to happen to autonomous spending, which is determined outside the model), and we might hesitate before calling such a simple model a model of the whole economy, but what is going on here is essentially the same as what is going on in more complicated models.

To clarify what is going on, and to explain why models of a real economy can rapidly become more complicated than textbook models, suppose we were to use an income expenditure model to predict output using some of the equations discussed in earlier chapters. To keep things simple, suppose that we want to use a consumption function from chapter 2 and an import function from chapter 5, and that we are content to take investment, government spending and exports as exogenous. We would then obtain a model such as the following one.

$$TFE = Consumption + Investment + Government\ spending + Exports$$

$$GDP = TFE - Imports$$

$$RPDI = GDP - Taxes + Subsidies$$

$$Consumption = 9.0 + 0.86RPDI$$

$$Imports = 0.34TFE_{t-1} + 0.39RULC_{t-2} - 0.55(GDP - Full\text{-}capacity\ GDP) - 78.7$$

In this model we have:

❑ Twelve variables, of which five are endogenous (determined by the model — *TFE, Consumption, GDP, Imports* and *RPDI*) and seven are exogenous (we take them as given, determined outside the model — *Investment, Government spending, Exports, Taxes, Subsidies, RULC* and *Full capacity GDP*).

❑ Two behavioural equations (the consumption and import functions).

❑ Three identities (describing relationships that are true by definition — the definitions of *TFE, GDP* and *RPDI*).

This shows that even in a model which is essentially nothing more than the simplest income-expenditure model we are beginning to get something that, at first sight, looks more complicated than many textbook models. We have three identities, for example, because we have what are essentially three definitions of income, each relevant for a different purpose. As models become more complicated such identities proliferate.

All the models listed above, however, have far more than 12 variables. These additional variables arise because several things need to be introduced to get a useful model.

❏ *Disaggregation.* All the components of GDP in the model we have just discussed are often broken down into smaller components. Consumption, for example, is usually broken down into spending on durable goods and non-durables, on the grounds that the determinants of these are quite different from each other. Investment is divided into housing, fixed investment and stock-building. Housing can in turn be divided into public and private, and the other categories of investment into government, manufacturing and non-manufacturing. Similarly, exports and imports are often subdivided into manufacturing, oil and other items. Thus, instead of five categories (C, I, G, X and M) we already have 16. In some models the level of disaggregation is taken even further. The Treasury model has a particularly detailed treatment of the public sector, which is the main reason why it has so many more variables than any of the other models.

❏ *The financial sector.* Interest rates and the exchange rate are important variables which have to be determined. Here too, it is possible to disaggregate, having equations to determine not simply 'the' interest rate, but a whole spectrum of interest rates and asset prices.

❏ *The labour market.* Employment and unemployment are key variables in any forecast, and equations are needed to link these to output. In addition, factors such as labour scarcity may feed back into output and prices.

❏ *Prices and wages.* Here too there is not just one wage rate and one price level to be determined. Important price levels include the GDP deflator, wholesale prices and the retail price index. Prices may be linked to costs, bringing in import prices and the exchange rate, productivity and the level of productive capacity (high capacity utilization may cause prices to rise faster). Wages may be different for different types of labour (e.g. manual and non-manual) and for different sections of the workforce (e.g. men and women).

When all, or even some, of these factors are taken into account it is easy for models to become quite large. Of the models mentioned above, the Liverpool model stands out because there is virtually no disaggregation in it: this is the reason why it is so much smaller than all the other models.

Why do the models differ?

One reason why models differ is that economists can easily form different views about which equations provide the best account of the data. Different statistical techniques give different results, and even where modellers can agree on what are the appropriate techniques, there is still scope for disagreement as to what constitutes the best model. It may be, for example, that we can capture the effects of inflation on consumption by bringing either the inflation rate, or some measure of the inflation tax into the consumption function. However, even if these worked equally well in explaining past consumption behaviour, they may cause us to obtain different predictions in the future.

A more important reason why the models differ is that different modellers have different views as to the structure of the economy, and as a result they construct different models. Consider three examples.

❏ *The LBS model* is centred around the identity whereby GDP is determined by adding up the various components of aggregate demand. It has a very detailed financial sector, in which there is a demand equation for each of a large number of assets, these demand equations determining the prices of different assets, and hence both interest rates and the exchange rate. Rational expectations are assumed in financial markets, but not in the economy as a whole. North Sea oil appears in the model, but does little more than affect tax revenues.

❏ *The NIESR model* is, like the LBS model, centred on the identity linking components of aggregate demand to GDP. It differs from the LBS model in that the exchange rate depends not on demands for assets, but on interest rate differentials, expectations of future exchange rate movements and changes in the balance of trade. As with the LBS model, North Sea oil production is separated out, oil production affecting tax revenues. In addition, the value of oil reserves (which depends on the price of oil) can affect the exchange rate.

❏ *The Liverpool model* is different from these two models in that it is a 'New Classical' model, based on the assumption that individuals have rational expectations and that supply and demand are equal in all markets, including the labour market. All the equations are thus constructed so as to embody rational expectations: wherever behaviour depends on expectations, these expectations are the same as what the model forecasts. Thus people expect inflation to be what the model forecasts that it will be. Other features that are distinctive in the model are that consumption depends on wealth, not on income, and that the PSBR and the average tax rate, not the level of government spending, are taken as exogenous.

This gives an idea of the nature of the differences between the models, though to describe the differences in any detail would take a lot more space. In addition, a catalogue of differences would mean very little without some indication of what these differences mean in practice. To see the significance of differences between models, therefore, it is best to see what happens when the models are used to predict the effects of various changes in the exogenous variables (those describing either the world economic situation or government policy). This is done in the following section.

12.2 COMPARISONS BETWEEN THE MODELS

Government expenditure

The first change to be considered is the effect of a £2 billion rise in government current expenditure (i.e. not government investment). Government current spending is assumed to be £2 billion higher than it would otherwise have been in 1989 and every year after that. The multipliers resulting from the three models we shall be considering here are shown in table 12.1. All the multipliers are positive, but the

Table 12.1 Government expenditure multipliers

Time period	1 year	5 years
LBS	1	2
NIESR	1.4	0.4
HMT	1	1

Source: G. A. MacDonald and D. Turner *The PC-Ready Reckoner Program Manual.* Coventry: University of Warwick, Macroeconomic Modelling Bureau, 1990, p. 47.

way in which government spending affects the economy is different in each of the three models.

To explain why these multipliers differ, figure 12.1 shows the effects of the rise in government spending on the growth rate of GDP, the inflation rate and the real exchange rate (the nominal exchange rate multiplied by UK prices relative to world prices). What is shown in figure 12.1 is the difference between what the models forecast with and without the £2billion rise in government spending.

❑ *The LBS model.* The rise in government spending raises output. This means that the real exchange rate must fall, and because the model assumes forward-looking behaviour in financial markets, this means that there is a substantial, immediate fall in the real exchange rate. This raises net exports, stimulating demand and raising the multiplier. Inflation responds only slowly, which means that the fall in the real exchange rate is not reversed by inflation, and that the rise in demand is sustained. This explains why in the LBS model the multiplier after 5 years is twice as large as the multiplier after 1 year.

❑ *The NIESR model.* In this model there is a large and immediate fall in the real exchange rate, similar to that which occurs in the LBS model, and output initially grows more rapidly as a result of the rise in government spending. In this model, however, the fall in the exchange rate causes a sharp rise in the inflation rate (because of its effects on import prices), which in turn leads to a reduction in the multiplier: from 1991 to 1993 growth is *lower* than it would have been had there been no rise in government spending. After 5 years the multiplier is only 0.4.

❑ *The Treasury model.* This contrasts with the other two models in that it does not predict any fall in the real exchange rate. There is thus no immediate effect on inflation. However, the fall in unemployment which results from the rise in GDP does eventually produce a rise in inflation.

The major reason why these three models produce different predictions of the effects of a rise in government spending is their different treatments of the exchange rate. This can be demonstrated by going through the same exercise, but instead of allowing the exchange rate to be determined by the model, assuming a constant real exchange rate.

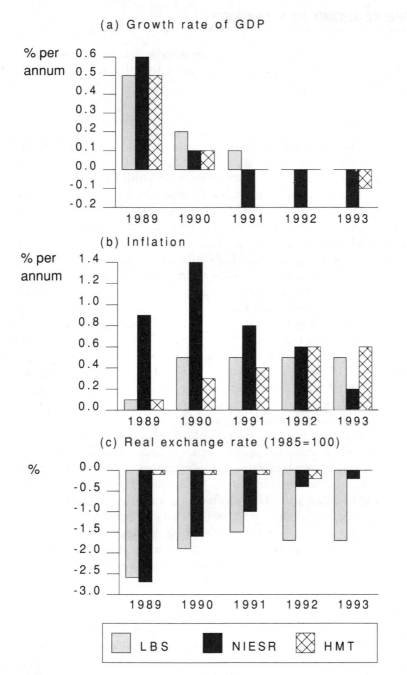

Figure 12.1 The effects of a £2 billion rise in government spending

Source: Calculated using PC Ready Reckoner.

This cuts out the effects of real exchange rate changes on demand. When this is done, the multipliers produced by all three models are much closer together (all around 1).

Interest rates

Interest rates, represented in these models by the interest rate on 3-month treasury bills, have direct effects on aggregate demand (particularly consumption and investment). In addition, interest rate changes have indirect effects through affecting variables such as wealth and the exchange rate, both of which have strong effects on demand. The direct effects are strongest in the LBS model, followed by the Treasury model, with the weakest effects being in the NIESR model. Furthermore, for some categories of spending, the effects of interest rate changes on spending are felt only after a long period of time.

Figure 12.2 shows the effect of a 1 percentage point cut in interest rates in the three models. In all of them the effect is a rise in the growth rate of GDP of about 4 per cent in each of the first two years. From the third year onwards the effects are much smaller, and in years four and five they are negative in all three models. Notice that although the *growth rate* of GDP falls in later years, the *level* of GDP is still higher than it would otherwise have been, for in all the models this fall in GDP is smaller than the initial increase (to get the overall effect on GDP we add up the changes shown in figure 12.2).

In the NIESR model an interest rate cut has effects on GDP similar to those in the other models, despite the NIESR model's very low interest-elasticities of consumption and investment. The reason for this is that the interest rate cut produces a fall in the exchange rate, which in turn stimulates demand. The mechanism whereby this happens is worth considering in detail, because it is very similar to what is happening in the exchange rate overshooting model discussed in box 11.2. The model assumes that interest rate parity holds, so that the domestic interest rate plus the expected appreciation of the exchange rate equals the world interest rate. It is further assumed that the interest rate cut will last for the five years that are being forecast, and that interest rates will revert to their normal levels after that. For interest rate parity to hold, therefore, the exchange rate must immediately fall (i.e. in 1989) just far enough that it can rise at 1 per cent per annum for the next four years and return to its original level. This means that the exchange rate has to fall by very nearly 4 per cent in 1989, rising at 1 per cent a year from 1990 to 1993. This is

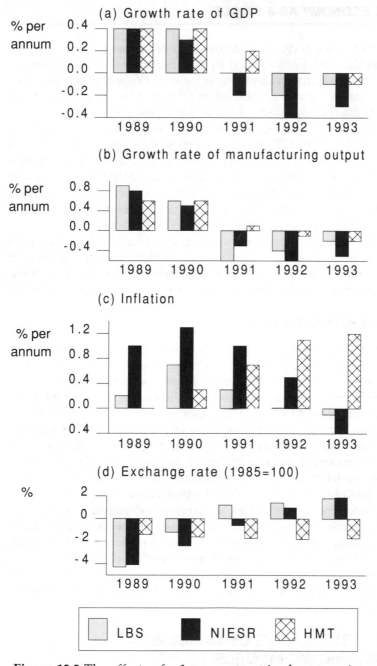

Figure 12.2 The effects of a 1 per cent cut in short term interest rates
Source: Calculated using PC Ready Reckoner.

approximately what is shown in figure 12.2(d) (because other things are going on in the model as well as this, the effects are slightly different).

It is worth noting that in the Treasury model the exchange rate effects are small, but against this interest rate cuts have larger effects on demand via the income effects of lower mortgage payments.

In all the models lowering interest rates raises inflation, as is shown in figure 12.2(c). The LBS model assumes that prices are relatively sticky, so the inflation effect is very small. In the NIESR model there is a large initial effect, because the exchange rate affects import prices. The Treasury model predicts increased inflation towards the end of the five-year period, this being the result of lower unemployment. Note that the inflation rate given here is the consumer price index (i.e. it covers those items of consumer spending which enter GDP). Normally this gives results similar to the RPI, but in this case the two indices behave differently, the reason being that interest rates affect mortgage costs, which appear in the RPI but not in the consumer price index.

North Sea oil production

In view of the discussion in chapter 9 it is interesting to consider the effects of changes in oil production in these models. Figure 12.3 shows the effect of a cut in oil production of 10 million tonnes (about 10 per cent of production). We do not consider the effects of a change in the price of oil because, although it appears in the models, an important aspect of any change in oil prices is its effect on the world economy. These models contain no means of predicting how a change in oil prices will affect either world inflation or the level of world demand.

In all the models the fall in oil production produces a fall in GDP of about 0.4 per cent. This is the direct effect caused by oil production being a component of GDP. There are then small effects in subsequent years, these being the result of the fall in the real exchange rate (figure 12.3d) stimulating demand. There is a small fall in the real exchange rate in the LBS model, a larger one in the NIESR model, and none at all in the Treasury model. If the real exchange rate were held constant, changes in North Sea oil production would have virtually no effect on the rest of the economy.

12.3 THE USEFULNESS OF LARGE-SCALE MACROECONOMIC MODELS

Evaluating macroeconomic models such as those discussed in this chapter is a very complicated exercise. The obvious way of doing this is

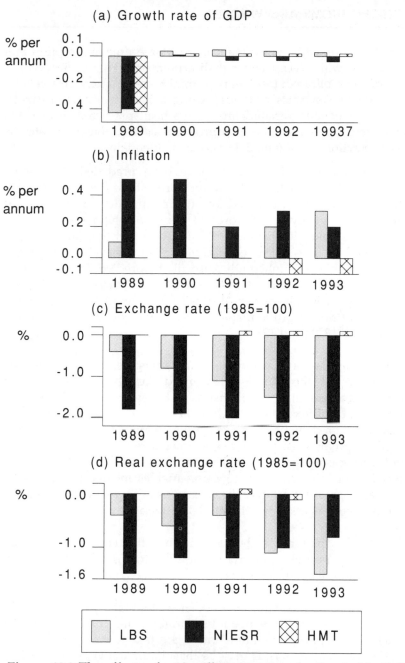

Figure 12.3 The effects of a 10 million tonnes reduction in North Sea oil production

Source: Calculated using PC Ready Reckoner.

through their forecasting performance, working on the assumption that a better model will forecast better than a poor one. This is, however, a much more complicated task than it might seem. There are several reasons why the forecasts produced using a particular model can be wrong: the exogenous variables may have been predicted incorrectly; the forecasters may have made inappropriate *ad hoc* adjustments to the models' predictions; or the models may be inadequate.

❏ The exogenous variables may have been predicted incorrectly. This is not always the fault of the forecasters. For example, the NIESR's forecasts are based on the assumption of unchanged government policy. If the forecast is of, say, high inflation, this may cause policy to change, with the result that the forecast is not fulfilled. This does not reflect badly on the forecasters. In addition, some variables are inherently difficult to predict. Movements in the price of oil, which depend on political factors, are a good example: it would have been difficult for economists to predict the extent and timing of the major oil price changes which took place during the 1970s and 1980s.

❏ The forecasters may have made *ad hoc* adjustments to the forecasts generated by the models. The need for this arises because forecasters frequently have reasons to believe that the outcome is going to be different from what the model predicts. They thus adjust the predictions, using extra information to improve on the model's predictions. Usually this process reduces forecast errors, but if forecasters get it wrong it contributes to them. This and the problem of forecasting exogenous variables means that assessing forecasts made by a forecasting team using a particular model is not the same as assessing the model's forecasts.

❏ The model may be inadequate in that the equations may be incorrectly specified, important variables may have been left out or estimates of coefficients may be incorrect.

If the model is inadequate in the sense that its predictions are inaccurate even when the exogenous variables are correctly forecast and when any inappropriate adjustments are taken away, this may be due to a number of reasons. It may be that the model is wrong, in that the equations simply do not describe the way the economy works. Alternatively, it may be that crucial data have been changed. GDP figures, for example, are estimates and are routinely revised, sometimes by substantial amounts. Or it may be that there has been a structural change in the way the economy works: that the model was adequate, but is so no longer.

A further problem arises in that we are concerned with a range of macroeconomic variables. Any assessment of different models thus depends on how these variables are weighted: on which of them is most important. During the mid-1980s, for example, the LBS was the best at predicting growth and inflation, whereas the NIESR was best at predicting unemployment.

The result of this is that it is difficult to use forecasting performance to say with any degree of certainty which model provides the best analysis of how the economy works. This does not mean that these models cannot be used to draw conclusions about economic policy. They can. It means rather that great care must be exercised when drawing conclusions from the models: results should not be accepted without understanding what features of the models generated them.

FURTHER READING

Straightforward introductions to forecasting models and to the major UK models are given by Giles Keating *The Production and Use of Economic Forecasts* (London: Methuen, 1985); K. Holden, D. A. Peel and J. L. Thompson *Modelling the UK Economy* (Oxford: Martin Robertson, 1982); M. J. C. Surrey 'Modelling the economy', in D. Morris (ed.) *The Economic System in the UK*, 10th edition, 1985, chapter 14. The major work on evaluating and comparing different forecasting models is undertaken by the Macroeconomic Modelling Bureau at the University of Warwick. The most recent assessment of comparative model properties is P. G. Fisher, D. S. Turner, K. F. Wallis and J. D. Whitley 'Comparative properties of models of the UK economy', *National Institute Economic Review*, 133, August 1990, pp. 91-104. The previous such survey was in the *National Institute Economic Review*, 129, August 1989, pp. 69-87. Before that the surveys, together with other exercises in evaluating the different models, were published in a series of books under the title *Models of the UK Economy: a [Second/Third/Fourth] Review by the ESRC Modelling Bureau* (Oxford: Oxford University Press, various dates).

Anyone wishing to understand the way the models can be used to evaluate the effects of changes in macroeconomic policy and in the world environment should explore the 'Ready Reckoner' programme produced by G. A. MacDonald and D. Turner, available from the Macroeconomic Modelling Bureau for (at the time of writing) a nominal charge. Accompanying the programme is *The PC-Ready Reckoner Program Manual* (Coventry: University of Warwick, Macroeconomic Modelling Bureau, 1990). This is more than just a programme manual, for it explores what is happening in the model. The important parts of chapter 12 were based on this manual.

Recent macroeconomic performance and policy

13.1 THE 1979-1989 BUSINESS CYCLE

Output and employment

The behaviour of output during the 1979-89 business cycle is shown in figure 13.1 and table 13.1 (which includes figures to 1988). Figure 13.1 reveals a very marked cycle, with *falling* output (and not simply a lower rate of growth) in 1980 and 1981, followed by a long period of sustained growth to the new peak in 1989. Table 13.1 gives average growth rates for the cycle as a whole and for the period of recovery, together with equivalent figures for the previous two business cycles. These make the point that the unusual feature about growth during the 1979-89 business cycle was not the growth rates achieved: the average growth rate of 2.1 per cent per annum was below the average rate of 2.6 per cent per annum achieved during the period 1960-79; and the rate of 3.2 per cent per annum during the recovery was little higher than the equivalent figure of 2.9 per cent achieved during the 1973-79 cycle. What was remarkable about the 1979-89 boom was the length of the recovery: seven years of sustained growth, compared with two and four years in the previous two business cycles.

Apart from the length of the recovery, the main feature of the UK's growth performance from 1979 to 1989 was an unusually high growth rate of manufacturing productivity. During the cycle as a whole manufacturing productivity rose at 4.2 per cent per annum, whilst during the upswing it rose at 5.5 per cent. This performance was better than that achieved by any of the other major economies listed in table

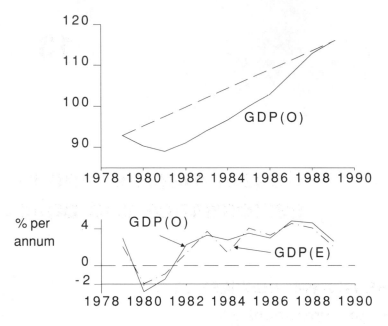

Figure 13.1 Real GDP, 1979-89

Source: Economic Trends.

13.2. In addition, although output per head in the whole economy was growing at only 1.9 per cent per annum, less than the 2.6 per cent achieved from 1960 to 1973, this growth rate was, with the exception of Japan, higher than those of all the other countries listed in table 13.2. Not shown in these tables, there has also been a marked improvement in the growth rate of total factor productivity (see chapter 2).

Since 1979 employment has been growing surprisingly rapidly, the rate of 0.4 per cent per annum from 1979 to 1988, comparing with an average rate of 0.3 per cent per annum for the previous twenty years. Despite this, however, unemployment rose dramatically from 4 per cent of the workforce in 1979 to 11 per cent in 1986: even while output was growing fast, unemployment continued to rise, albeit at a slower pace than in 1980-2. From 1987 to 1989, unemployment fell even more rapidly than it had risen, reaching just over 6 per cent by 1989. It is worth noting that during this period the official definition of unemployment has changed many times: originally it was all those registered as unemployed and seeking work, whereas now it comprises only those claiming unemployment benefit, a more restrictive category

Table 13.1 Performance indicators

Per cent per annum	Average	Cycle averages			Trough-to-peak averages		
	1960-79	1968-73	1973-79	1979-88	1971-73	1975-79	1981-88
GDP	2.6	3.3	1.4	2.1	5.3	2.9	3.2
Employment	0.3	0.2	0.2	0.4	1.4	0.4	1.1
GDP deflator	8.4	7.4	16.0	7.6	7.4	13.7	5.4
Output per head							
Whole economy	2.1	2.6	1.1	1.9	3.2	2.5	2.4
Manufacturing	2.7	3.9	0.7	4.2	7.1	2.1	5.5

Per cent of GDP	1960-79	1968-73	1973-79	1979-88	1971	1973	1975	1979	1981	1988
Current account	-0.2	0.5	-1.0	0.5	1.9	-1.3	-1.4	-0.3	2.7	-3.2
Unemployment	2.7	2.5	3.9	9.5	2.9	2.1	3.6	4.5	9.1	8.3
Government deficit	1.5	-0.3	3.8	2.5	-1.3	2.7	4.5	3.3	2.6	-0.8

Source: OECD Economic Surveys - United Kingdom, 1988-89, p. 57.

Table 13.2 International productivity growth rates, 1979-88

| | Output | | | | | | Productivity | | | | | |
| | Whole economy | | | Manufacturing | | | Whole economy | | | Manufacturing | | |
	1960-73	1973-79	1979-88	1960-73	1973-79	1979-88	1960-73	1973-79	1979-88	1960-73	1973-79	1979-88
UK	3.1	1.4	2.1	2.8	-0.7	0.8	2.6	1.1	1.9	3.6	0.7	4.2
USA	3.9	2.6	2.5	5.3	2.9	2.8	1.9	0.0	0.8	3.8	1.8	3.3
Japan	9.6	3.6	4.1	12.5	2.0	3.9	8.2	2.9	3.0	8.9	3.4	2.4
Germany	4.4	2.3	1.7	5.1	1.1	0.8	4.2	2.9	1.6	4.5	2.5	1.4
France	5.4	2.8	1.9	6.1	1.6	0.3	4.7	2.5	1.9	4.9	2.6	2.1
Italy	5.3	2.6	2.3	6.6	2.6	1.5	5.7	1.8	1.6	5.9	2.5	2.9
Canada	5.4	4.2	3.0	6.1	2.5	2.5	2.4	1.3	1.1	3.5	1.0	2.2
Average	5.5	2.8	2.7	6.3	2.1	2.4	4.2	1.5	1.6	4.9	2.4	3.0

Source: OECD Economic Surveys - United Kingdom, 1988-89, p. 58. Per cent per annum.

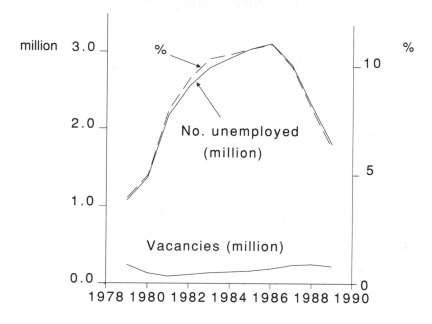

Figure 13.2 Unemployment, 1979-89

Source: Economic Trends. Note that unemployment is calculated from the quarterly, seasonally adjusted series, in which the current definition of unemployment is used throughout the period.

bearing in mind that not everyone who is unemployed qualifies for unemployment benefit. Figures on unemployment must, therefore, be treated with caution. The data shown in figure 13.2 are based on the current definition and are not affected by changes in the definition of unemployment. Also shown in figure 13.2 are vacancies. These fluctuated as we would expect, the significant feature being the downturn in 1989. This is consistent with the economy having reached a turning point in 1989.

Inflation and the balance of payments

During the 1979-89 business cycle the rate of inflation fell dramatically, as shown in figure 13.3. Despite this, inflation remained above the average for the OECD as a whole. In 1986, the year when inflation was at its lowest, inflation had fallen to 2 per cent per annum in the USA, 2.6 per cent in France and was negative (-0.3 per cent) in Germany. Furthermore, from 1987, as unemployment started to fall, inflation

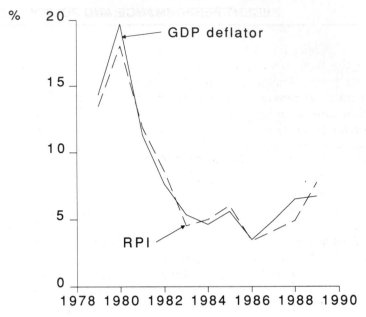

Figure 13.3 Inflation, 1979-89

Source: Economic Trends.

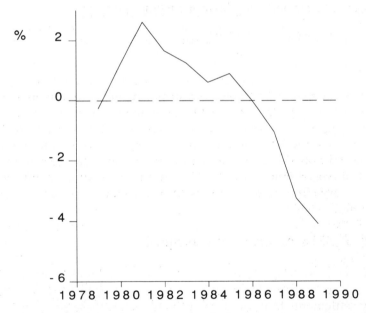

Figure 13.4 The current account balance as a percentage of GDP, 1979-89

Source: Economic Trends.

began to rise. Notice that although they move fairly closely together on the whole, the GDP deflator and the retail price index sometimes move in different ways. The most marked difference occurred in 1988-9, when the inflation rate as measured by the RPI rose sharply, whereas the inflation rate according to the GDP deflator rose by only a little. The reason for this is that the RPI included mortgage interest payments, which became more expensive in 1989 because of rises in interest rates. Rising interest rates do not affect the GDP deflator.

Along with rising inflation, the period from 1987 to 1989 witnessed a large rise in the balance of payments deficit, shown in figure 13.4 and table 13.1. For most of the cycle the balance of payments was in surplus, due mainly to the UK becoming a net exporter of oil. From the mid-1980s, however, a deficit emerged, partly because of falling oil production, but also because of a deterioration in the non-oil balance — rapid growth was causing imports to grow faster than exports. By 1989 the deficit was over 4 per cent of GDP, an enormous figure, even compared with the deficit caused by the 1973-4 oil crisis, and constituted the main economic problem confronting the government.

13.2 MACROECONOMIC POLICY DURING THE 1980s

The initial deflation, 1979-1980

The first year of this cycle was one of rapidly rising inflation. There were a number of reasons for this. World oil prices rose following the Iranian revolution in 1979. There were also two policy decisions made by the incoming Conservative government which contributed to the inflation rate rising so dramatically. The government was committed to reducing income tax rates and reduced the basic rate of income tax from 33 per cent to 30 per cent, and the top rate from 83 per cent to 60 per cent. It financed this by raising VAT from 10-12 per cent (different rates were charged on different goods) to a uniform rate of 15 per cent. This provided a one-off boost to prices, but fed into wage demands, raising inflation over a longer period. In addition, the government had committed itself, during the election campaign, to implementing the recommendations of the Clegg Commission on public sector pay. When this recommended very large pay increases the government was committed to pay them. Even if there is no strong link from public sector pay settlements to those in the private sector, these pay increases made it clear that the previous incomes policy, which had begun to break down during 1979, had ended. Inflation thus reached 20 per cent per annum in 1980.

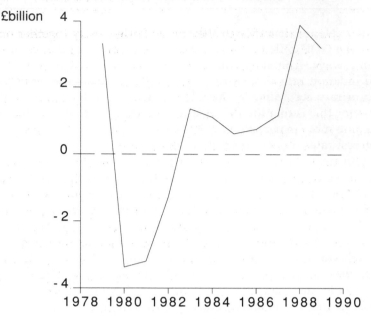

Figure 13.5 Investment in stocks, 1979-89

Source: Economic Trends.

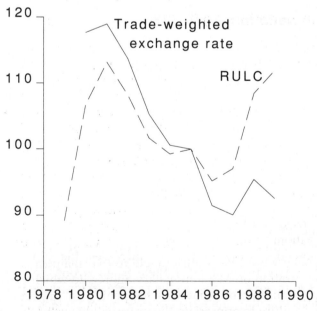

Figure 13.6 The exchange rate, 1979-89

Source: Economic Trends.

The new government immediately pursued a restrictive monetary policy, the Bank of England's minimum lending rate rising to 17 per cent by November 1979 (it had been as low as 12 per cent in April). One of the problems facing the authorities was that attention was focused on M3 which was growing rapidly, whereas other measures of the money supply (including both M0 and M5) were growing much more slowly. Because inflation was so high, the real value of many monetary aggregates fell very sharply indeed. Monetary policy was very restrictive. The way this affected the economy was through the exchange rate, sterling's real exchange rate (measured by relative unit labour costs) rising by over 50 per cent in two years from 1978 to 1980 (see figure 13.6). About half of this rise was due to UK prices rising relative to foreign prices, and the other half to an appreciation of the exchange rate. The causes of this massive appreciation probably include both tight monetary policy, together with any effects on expectations concerning future monetary policy (see box 11.2), and the effects of North Sea oil production (see chapter 9).

If we look at the components of aggregate demand we find that the fall in output can be accounted for by the fall in stockbuilding from £3,325 million in 1979 to *minus* £3,357 million in 1980, a fall of £6,682 million. GDP fell by £6,363 million. The explanation of this enormous fall in stockbuilding is that when exporters were faced with the rise in the exchange rate and a massive loss of competitiveness, they cut their profit margins and cut back on their inventories rather than reducing exports. This can be viewed in two ways. One is to see exporters as concerned to maintain their foreign markets, on the grounds that once lost these would be hard to regain. To maintain their exports they cut profit margins, and they reduced costs by cutting production, meeting export orders by depleting their stocks. Alternatively, we could argue that firms were forced, by the financial squeeze, to cut their stocks, and they did this by selling them abroad, accepting lower profit margins in order to be able to do so.

In conclusion, we can see this brief period as one in which government policy decisions contributed to both the rise in the inflation rate and the very severe recession which took place in 1980. The government's failure to realize quite how severe the effects of its monetary policy would be is attributable to two main causes. The first is their concentration on M3, a monetary aggregate which proved to be a misleading indicator of what was happening in the economy. The second was a failure to appreciate the potential effects of their policy in a world of floating exchange rates where the removal of regulations was making capital ever more mobile. It was the exchange rate movements, rather than the direct effect of high interest rates, that caused the recession to be as severe as it was.

The Medium Term Financial Strategy, 1980-1987

In March 1980 the government introduced its Medium Term Financial Strategy (MTFS). This set the series of targets for both PSBR and M3 (formerly sterling M3) as percentages of GDP. Both percentages were targeted to fall progressively over a five year period, as shown in table 13.3. The idea behind linking reductions in the growth rate of the money supply to reductions in PSBR was to permit tight monetary policy to go together with falling interest rates. This would result in both falling inflation and rising private sector demand. The intention was that these objectives would be achieved gradually.

Table 13.3 The Medium Term Financial Strategy, March 1980

Financial year	1979/80 (actual)	1980/1	1981/2	1982/3	1983/4
Growth of M3 (%)	13.2	7-11	6-10	5-9	4-8
PSBR/GDP(MP) (%)	4.8	3.85	3.0	2.25	1.5

Source: W. Buiter and M. Miller 'The Thatcher experiment: the first two years', *Brookings Papers on Economic Activity*, 1981 (2), p. 340.

The government's plans soon had to be modified. For a number of reasons, including increased unemployment benefits, public expenditure exceeded the target. Similarly, the target for M3 was abandoned as it became clear that it was a misleading indicator of monetary policy. In the summer of 1980 interest rates were cut, not increased as would have been required if the government was to achieve its money supply targets. The deficit in 1980-1 turned out to be 5.7 per cent of GDP, compared with a target of 3.75 per cent, and monetary growth was running at around 18 per cent, compared with a target of 7-11 per cent.

This was the background to the 1981 budget. The MTFS appeared to be in disarray, and the budget was aimed at restoring its credibility. Despite the economy being in what had become the most severe recession since the war the government raised taxes, setting a substantially lower target for PSBR, either than had been achieved in

Table 13.4 Successive targets for PSBR

	1979/80	1980/1	1981/2	1982/3	1983/4	1984/5	1985/6	1986/7	1987/8	1988/9
March 1980	4.75	3.75	3.0	2.25	1.5					
March 1981	5.0	6.0	4.25	3.25	2.0					
March 1982		5.7	4.25	3.5	2.75	2.0				
March 1983			3.5	2.75	2.75	2.5	2.0			
March 1984				3.3	3.25	2.25	2.0	2.0	1.75	1.75
March 1985					3.2	3.25	2.0	2.0	1.75	1.75
March 1986						3.1	2.0	1.75	1.75	1.5
March 1987							1.6	1.0	1.0	1.0
Actual	4.8	5.6	3.4	3.2	3.2	3.1	1.6	0.9		

Source: OECD Economic Surveys — United Kingdom, 1986-87, p.20.

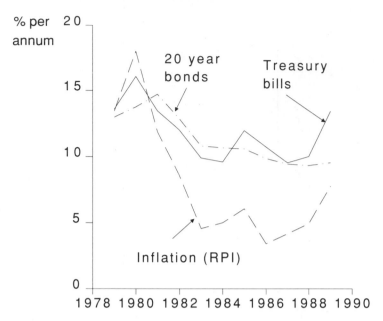

Figure 13.7 Interest rates, 1979-89

Source: International Financial Statistics and *Economic Trends*. Figures are averages throughout the year.

1980/1, or than was forecast to happen in 1981/2 if policies remained unchanged (see table 13.4). In the event, PSBR fell to 3.4 per cent of GDP in 1981/2. Bearing in mind that the economy was still moving into recession, it has been estimated that the cyclically adjusted deficit fell by 6 per cent of GDP. The intention behind such a tight fiscal policy, apart from being an attempt to restore the credibility of the MTFS, was to permit the government to lower interest rates and yet to achieve its monetary targets. Interest rates began to fall (see figure 13.7) but the government nonetheless came close to hitting its money supply target for 1981/2. At the same time sterling began to fall from the high level it had reached during 1980, this possibly being due as much to the outlook for oil prices as to government policy.

Over the following few years the government's strategy gradually changed. It moved away from M3 as its monetary target, dropping it altogether in 1987. M0 was introduced as an indicator of the stance of monetary policy, but the emphasis was increasingly on looking at a broad range of monetary aggregates rather than a single one, the behaviour of which could be unreliable. This broadened out still further into a policy of considering all the evidence available, including the

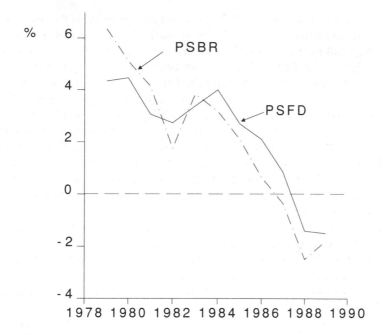

Figure 13.8 The government deficit as percentage of GDP, 1979-89

Source: Economic Trends.

exchange rate. Monetary targets were eventually abandoned. Policy gradually loosened up, despite the government's adherence to its fiscal targets, which were met very soon. By the end of the period the budget was in surplus. Instead of speaking of PSBR, the term PSDR (Public Sector Debt Repayment — the negative of PSBR) has increasingly been used instead. Part of the reason for this success, however, was the privatization programme, the revenues from which served to reduce PSBR (see chapter 4). The financial deficit was normally higher than PSBR (see figure 13.8).

Exchange rate policy, 1987-1989

The government gradually moved away from its original policy of setting a target for the money supply. After the experience of 1979-81 the idea of an exchange rate target was attractive. At the same time, as the European Monetary System developed, the UK was under increasing pressure to participate in its exchange rate mechanism. In 1987 the Chancellor of the Exchequer, Nigel Lawson, adopted a policy of tying sterling to the German mark, the major currency in the ECU, at a rate of approximately 2.9 DM to the pound. The background to this was the large fall in the price of oil which occurred in 1986. This caused sterling to fall to 2.7 DM at the start of 1987, after which it started to rise, perhaps because the markets decided that they had over-estimated the significance for sterling of the oil price fall. At the point when the Bank of England started to intervene, sterling was at a level that was low both relative to previous levels and relative to purchasing power parity. The result was that in order to maintain this parity, the Bank of England had to intervene on the foreign exchange markets, selling sterling on a massive scale in order to prevent it from rising. As a result the Bank of England's foreign exchange reserves grew substantially. Interest rates were kept low.

This policy was the cause of disagreement between the Prime Minister, who was opposed to the policy of setting an exchange rate target, and the Chancellor of the Exchequer, its architect. It was abandoned early in 1988, but controversy continued, focusing on the issue of whether or not sterling should be brought into the exchange rate mechanism of the EMS.

The major economic event during this period was the stock market crash, in October 1987. The big fear resulting from this was whether it would push the world economy into recession. It was against this background that the 1988 budget cut taxes, albeit fairly modestly. These two factors, namely the low exchange rate and tax cuts, contributed to raise consumer spending during 1988. The result was the consumer boom discussed in more detail in the following section. In retrospect, it is easy to see mistakes in policy making, notably the expansionary budget of 1988, introduced at a time when demand was already expanding rapidly. There are, however, several reasons why things were not as clear as this at the time. The first is that the stock market crash had created the fear of worldwide recession; or a repeat of what happened after the 1929 crash. Had the world's major economies undertaken deflationary policies in 1987-8 it is still not clear that this would not have happened. The second is that the strength of the consumer boom was not clear. Different measures of output growth were giving conflicting versions of how fast the economy was growing. There were also problems with the statistics on consumer spending.

The result was that in 1989 the government was forced to take measures to restrain consumer spending, and to reduce the emerging balance of payments deficit. Its main policy instrument was interest rates, which rose sharply during the year. In May 1988 the interest rate on treasury bills was 7.28 per cent. By the end of 1989 this had doubled, to 14.7 per cent. By raising interest rates it was attempting to do two things: to restrain domestic demand, and hence to reduce the balance of payments; and to prevent sterling from falling, for a fall in sterling would raise import costs and contribute to inflation.

13.3 THE LEGACY OF THE 1980s

The growth of demand

The main macroeconomic problems resulting from the 1979-89 cycle are the enormous balance of payments deficit and rising inflation. Both of these are the result of aggregate demand having risen too fast. Figure 13.9 makes it clear that the main reason for demand having grown too fast is rapid growth of consumption and investment. Government spending has grown very slowly, whilst exports have been growing at less than 5 per cent per annum since the mid-1980s. In contrast, the

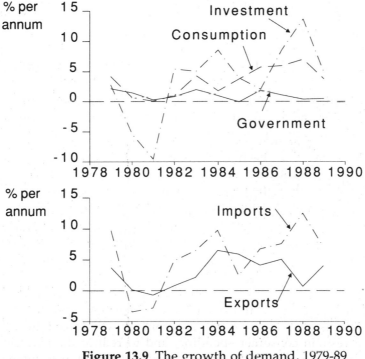

Figure 13.9 The growth of demand, 1979-89

Source: Economic Trends.

growth rate of consumption rose steadily to a peak of nearly 7 per cent in 1988. Investment grew very rapidly in 1987-8, but is less of a problem, for two reasons. The first is that investment serves to raise productive capacity, offsetting its effect on aggregate demand. The second is that investment responds to demand (the accelerator, discussed in chapter 3), which means that as soon as growth slows down, we would expect investment to fall. The substantial fall in the growth rate of investment in 1989 could be due to higher interest rates, or to firms' anticipating that demand is going to grow more slowly.

Consumers' spending and saving

Figure 13.10 shows the growth rates of consumers' expenditure and real personal disposable income, together with the savings ratio. It shows that the reason why consumption has grown so rapidly is that the savings ratio has declined, from 13 per cent in 1980 to under 5 per cent in 1988-9. To understand why demand has grown so rapidly during the late 1980s, therefore, it is necessary to understand why the savings ratio has declined, and how this is linked to the policies that have been undertaken during the period.

The causes of the decline in the savings ratio are still far from certain, but there are strong reasons to believe that it is connected with both the housing market and the deregulation of financial markets that took place during the 1980s. With deregulation, far fewer households find themselves subject to credit rationing: borrowing is now very easy, whereas at the beginning of the 1980s many borrowers, and potential borrowers, found that they were unable to borrow as much as they wished. There has thus been a large growth in borrowing by the personal sector. At the same time, and partly because of easier access to borrowing, the wealth of the personal sector has increased enormously, particularly as a result of rising house prices. Financial deregulation has made it easier for households to borrow against the wealth they hold as housing. In addition, greater wealth explains why consumers save less.

The role of housing and other forms of wealth in influencing consumption is also important because it is likely to be through this channel that interest rates affect consumption. Expenditure on durable goods clearly depends strongly on interest rates, but there is evidence that spending on non-durables, which accounts for around 90 per cent of spending, does not. Interest rates affect non-durable consumption through affecting wealth.

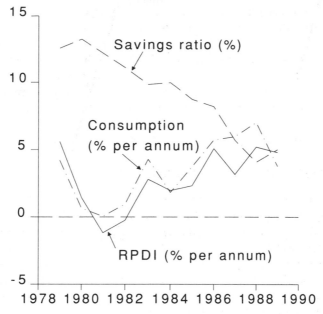

Figure 13.10 Consumption and income, 1979-89

Source: Economic Trends.

13.4 THE 1990s

The outlook in July 1990

This section, written in July 1990, is already out-of-date. It is still worth reading, however, because it is important to say something about the decisions policy-makers have to face, and the easiest way to do this is with an example. The situation facing the UK economy in the first half of 1990 should be seen as an example, or case study.

The outlook, from the early summer of 1990, is for a recession. Rising inflation and above all the massive balance of payments deficit mean that there must be a period of slower growth: a deficit of 4 per cent of GDP is probably not sustainable for a very long period. In addition, the required slowdown in the growth rate seems already to have started. The main questions are how severe the recession will be, and how long it will last. In the fashionable terminology, will the economy undergo a 'hard' or a 'soft' landing?

The obvious place to turn is to forecasting models. The forecasts produced by three of the main modelling groups are shown in figure

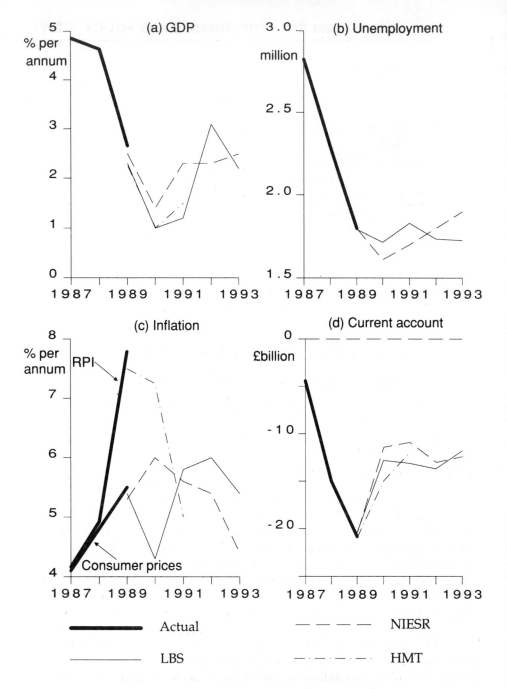

Figure 13.11 Forecasts made in February/March 1990

Source: Economic Trends, March 1990.

13.11. Before considering the forecasts in detail, two things need to be pointed out: the exact dates of the forecasts, and the different time-horizons over which forecasts are made.

❏ The forecasts were published in February (LBS and NIESR) and March (HMT) 1990 (see chapter 12 for further discussion of these models). By this date much of the information about 1989 was available, but not everything. In figure 13.11 the series labelled 'actual' give the Central Statistical Office's first estimates of what actually happened in 1989. The first point in each of the forecast series gives what the forecasters thought, in February or March 1990, had happened. For example, because GDP figures were available for the first three quarters, they were able to predict the growth rate very accurately. Any discrepancies concerning 1989 are due to surprises that happened right at the end of 1989. In particular, output was growing *very slightly* more strongly than the forecasters thought, though it is important to realize that small differences like this are *well* within the margins of error for the CSO's estimates of GDP.

❏ The Treasury produces forecasts for only the very short term. In March 1990 a forecast was published for 1990 and the first half of 1991. All the Treasury forecasts cited as being for 1991 are thus for the first half of 1991, though figures are all given as annual rates.

The forecasters all predict a substantial fall in the growth rate of GDP to a figure of 1-1.5 per cent per annum in 1990, with a recovery in 1991. The Treasury is more pessimistic, though this may be due in part to the fact that its forecast is just for the first half of 1991. For manufacturing alone there is wide disagreement, ranging from the LBS forecast of 2 per cent growth, to the NIESR forecast that output will fall by 2 per cent during 1990. The LBS expects unemployment to remain fairly static (perhaps because it has a fairly optimistic forecast for manufacturing, a major employer), whereas the NIESR expects unemployment, after falling during 1990, to rise towards 2 million by 1993.

The positive side of these forecasts is that the balance of payments is expected to stabilize at around £12 billion per annum, substantially below its current level of £21 billion. This is more optimistic than it might seem because inflation and growth in GDP mean that this represents a declining fraction of GDP. By 1993 both the LBS and the NIESR imply a deficit of about 2 per cent of GDP.

The Treasury's inflation forecasts are very different from those of the NIESR and the LBS because the Treasury's forecasts are of the RPI, whereas the others are of the consumers' expenditure deflator. Notice that in 1989 inflation as measured by the RPI rose to nearly 8 per cent, whereas measured by the consumers' expenditure deflator it rose only to 5.5 per cent. The difference is because of rising mortgage interest rates. This means that even if interest rates were to stay at their present levels, the RPI inflation rate would fall towards the end of 1990 as interest rate rises dropped out. If interest rates fall, the RPI inflation rate will be forced down still further. This explains why the Treasury is predicting such a sharp fall in inflation. The other two forecasting groups differ about what will happen to inflation, but they agree that it will remain between 4 and 6 per cent per annum. No surge in inflation is predicted.

This scenario, which has deliberately not been rewritten since July, was overtaken by events in the summer of 1990, when Iraq invaded Kuwait. By October the price of oil, which in July had generally been forecast at around $18 per barrel, had touched $40 per barrel. The oil market became very volatile with forecasters not being able to say much more than that it was likely to be in the range $20 to $40 per barrel. To discuss the outlook for the 1990s, therefore, it is necessary to consider in some detail how a rise in the price of oil affects the UK economy.

Oil prices and the UK economy

A rise in the price of oil has two main effects: raising costs and redistributing wealth from oil importers to oil exporters.

❑ A rise in oil prices raises costs, increasing the inflation rate directly. Rising costs also cause demand to be reduced, especially if governments respond by raising interest rates or cutting back on spending plans — which happened in many countries (including the UK) after the 1979 oil price rise.

❑ Redistributing wealth from oil importers to oil exporters is deflationary in the short term, because importers have to reduce their consumption very quickly, whereas it takes longer for oil exporters to start spending their increased wealth. In the longer term, however, the effect could go the other way: by transferring wealth from low-spending countries (such as Japan) to countries with a higher propensity to spend (such as Mexico) a price rise may raise demand.

In the UK, however, the situation is more complicated because of North Sea oil. The most noticeable effects of rising oil prices are the rise in tax revenues from the North Sea, and the increased value of oil exports. A rise in oil prices thus leads directly to an improvement in the balance of payments, which should strengthen sterling. This creates problems for the non-oil sectors of the economy, notably manufacturing, so that whilst it is correct to say that a rise in oil prices raises UK wealth, there are important losses that have to be set against increased oil wealth. There is the further problem that rising costs both raise inflation and reduce output.

The effects of these different factors can be analysed using the forecasting models discussed in chapter 12. The direct effects of a rise in oil prices are shown in figures 13.12, 13.13 and 13.14. Figure 13.12 shows the effects on the Treasury forecast of a rise in the price of oil from $18 to $24 per barrel, which is assumed to be maintained from 1990 to 1993. We can see that it predicts a fall in the growth rate of GDP for two years. These two years, 1990 and 1991, when growth is low, see a rise in unemployment. In addition, inflation is reduced.

The reason why the Treasury model predicts that a rise in oil prices will cause the inflation rate to fall is that the deflationary effects of lower GDP growth and rising unemployment outweigh the direct effects of oil prices on costs. In other models the effect via costs is much stronger than in the Treasury model. This is the reason why the NIESR model (see figure 13.13) predicts that rising oil prices will raise inflation, albeit only for one year, after which, after which the effects of lower demand dominate. The three models agree on the short-run effects of oil prices on GDP growth, unemployment and the current account balance, though they disagree about the size of these effects and about the long-term effects. For example, the Treasury and NIESR models (see figure 13.13) predict that the immediate effect on the current account will be about £1 billion, whereas the LBS model predicts an improvement of £3billion.

So far, we have assumed a rise in the price of oil of $6 per barrel in 1990, a rise which is thought to be compatible with the likely strength of the OPEC cartel over the next few years. It is possible, however, that oil prices will remain much higher than that, which is why the effects of a $20 per barrel price rise are shown in figure 13.14. Once again the price rise is assumed to be permanent (i.e. last until 1993). This time the

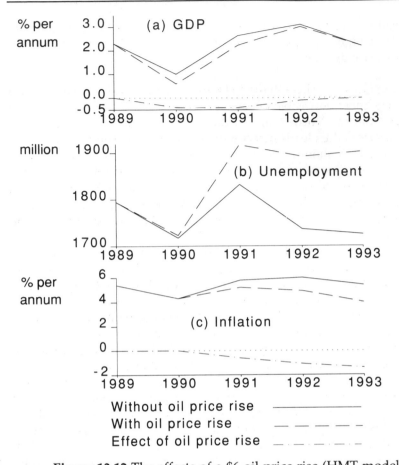

Figure 13.12 The effects of a $6 oil price rise (HMT model), I

Source: calculated using PC Ready Reckoner. Note that the base forecast is that of the LBS model, as the Treasury publishes only very short-term forecasts.

LBS model is used, and predictions for manufacturing output, wage inflation, the PSBR and the exchange rate are also shown. Figure 13.14 shows the growth rate of manufacturing output falling by more than the growth rate of GDP, and that the exchange rate will rise by 13.1 percentage points in 1990 — i.e. that the trade-weighted effective exchange rate (1985=100) will rise from 88 to 101.1. This is the mechanism whereby manufacturing output is reduced. In subsequent years the exchange rate falls and the growth rate of manufacturing output recovers.

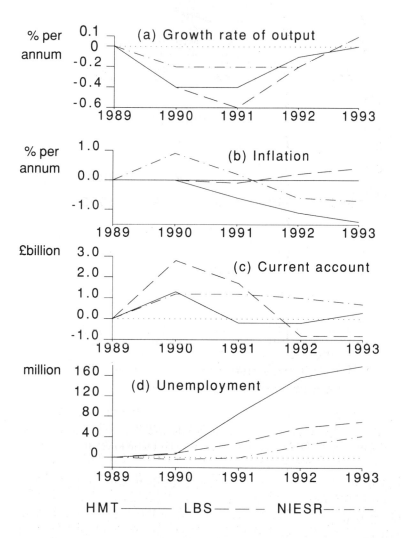

Figure 13.13 The effects of a $6 oil price rise (three models)

Source: calculated using PC Ready Reckoner.

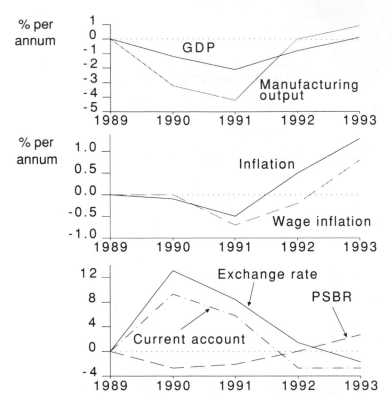

Figure 13.14 The effects of a $20 oil price rise (LBS model)
Source: calculated using PC Ready Reckoner.

These forecasts are concerned with only the direct effects of an oil price rise. Figure 13.15 shows the effects of a $6 per barrel price rise taking account of its likely impact on world trade and inflation. It is assumed that this price rise will reduce the growth rate of world trade by 0.4 percent per annum, and that it will raise world inflation by 0.8 per cent per annum. These have the expected effects. For example, the fall in world growth worsens the current account (through reducing demand for exports) whereas the rise in world inflation (through improving competitiveness) raises it.

Policy options

The policy options open to the government have been changed considerably by taking sterling into the exchange rate mechanism of the EMS. As long as sterling was outside the EMS it was possible for

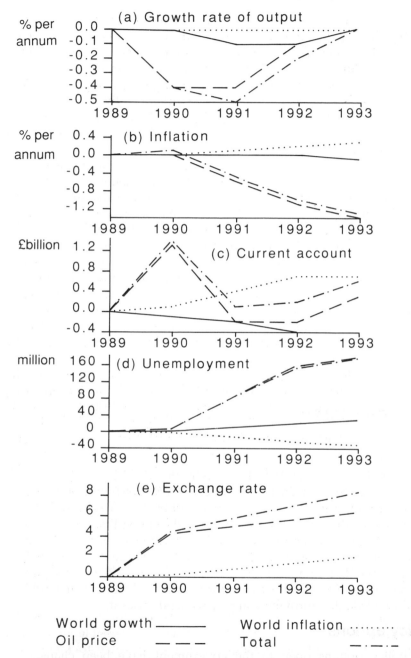

Figure 13.15 The effects of a $6 oil price rise (HMT model), II

Source: calculated using PC Ready Reckoner. See text for details of assumptions.

the government, if it wished, to prevent unemployment from rising too fast by allowing inflation to remain high. Competitiveness could be maintained by allowing sterling to depreciate. Entry into the exchange rate mechanism means that the option of letting sterling depreciate is no longer available. Even if a realignment of sterling within the EMS were allowed (the decision cannot be taken unilaterally by the UK) it is likely that any devaluation would be less than was necessary to maintain competitiveness. The EMS thus acts as a constraint on the choices available to the government.

On the other hand, joining the exchange rate mechanism may improve the situation in two ways. The first is that joining the exchange rate mechanism could, if it increases the credibility of the government's anti-inflation strategy, reduce the unemployment cost of keeping inflation down. The second is that if investors believe that joining the EMS has committed the government to maintaining the value of sterling relative to the other EMS countries (i.e. if they are convinced that there will be no realignment of sterling within the EMS), interest rates could be lowered without precipitating a depreciation. The reason is that UK interest rates are currently higher than in, say, Germany in order to compensate for any expected depreciation of sterling. This is why interest rates were lowered when sterling was taken into the exchange rate mechanism.

In the short term, the main objective of policy must be to reduce the balance of payments deficit and the inflation rate without precipitating an excessively severe depression. In the first half of 1990 the prospects for a favourable outcome, certainly compared with the last recession, in 1980-1, seemed fairly good, as shown by the forecasts discussed above. The main reason for this optimism was that the world economy was growing much more strongly than it was in the early 1980s. The LBS predicted that world trade in manufactures would grow by 3.6 per cent in 1990, 4.6 per cent in 1991 and 4.7 per cent in 1992, and the NIESR and the Treasury were predicting even higher growth rates: much higher than the rates of 2.5 per cent, -1.6 per cent and 2.9 per cent achieved in 1981, 1982 and 1983. In addition, many economists expect that the creation of the single European market in 1992 will stimulate growth in Europe. Higher growth in Europe will make it easier to reduce the balance of payments deficit.

The oil price rise has complicated this picture because of the uncertainty it has introduced. Not only is it impossible to forecast future oil prices with any confidence, it is impossible to know how governments will respond. Putting these problems aside, suppose that the outcome is, as some forecasters are predicting, an oil price of about

$25 per barrel. This should help the UK by improving the balance of payments and strengthening sterling though, as have seen, there is considerable uncertainty concerning both the strength and the timing of these effects (see figure 13.13). It will also depress demand and raise unemployment, partly because of its direct effects, but also because it will reduce the growth rate of world demand. On the other hand, whilst the oil price rise helps the government's anti inflation and balance of payments strategies, it increases the danger of a severe recession. If these effects could be accurately quantified the government could adjust policies accordingly. The problem is that this is not possible.

Government policy is to control demand through high interest rates, the rise in demand during 1989 being the reason for the rises in interest rates towards the end of the year. Though it is impossible to be certain of this, there are several reasons why this is likely to be sufficient.

❑ Consumer spending should eventually respond to higher real interest rates. Given that housing prices appear to play a crucial role in the mechanism linking interest rates and spending (see chapter 2) the collapse of the housing market and falling house prices should lead to a decline in consumption.

❑ The ratio of stocks to GDP has risen sharply relative to its long-term trend since the middle of 1988. At some stage this is likely to be reversed, leading to a large fall in stockbuilding. A sharp fall in stockbuilding could easily lead to a large fall in output.

❑ Industrial and commercial companies have moved from being in surplus in the mid-1970s to running a large deficit. Companies' saving has been falling at the same time as investment has been increasing, which is likely to lead to a fall in investment at some stage.

❑ The likely effects of a high oil price.

There are thus strong reasons for thinking that, even though consumer spending has so far continued to grow more strongly than desired, demand could fall quite sharply in the near future.

The other uncertainty concerns inflation. Wages are rising very rapidly during 1990 and as yet show no signs of slowing down. On the other hand, the evidence on wage equations discussed in chapter 8 suggests that wage inflation may slow down when the effects of falling house price inflation and company profits are felt. If this is the case, wage inflation may be reduced towards a more acceptable level without either further government action or a prolonged period of high unemployment. The outcome, however, is far from certain.

Overall, therefore, though a recession seems inevitable during 1990-1, there are still some grounds for optimism about the length and depth of the recession. As regards policy, there seems little room for manoeuvre: the balance of payments deficit and the inflation rate are the over-riding problems, and whilst there may be room for debate over exactly what policies are required, the need for a fairly tight policy to restrain demand seems clear. High interest rates may be unpopular, and the results may be inequitable, but recent evidence does suggest that the price of housing has played a crucial role in the boom, and that over the next few years house prices must fall relative to incomes. Insofar as many of the problems associated with high interest rates are really problems associated with falling house prices, they may be unavoidable.

13.5 CONCLUSIONS

In this chapter there has been extensive discussion of the immediate problems facing the UK economy in 1990. This will very soon get out of date. It does, however, make very clear some of the problems involved in policy-making. Even by the spring of 1990, economists did not know exactly how strong the boom had been during 1989. Neither did they know whether measures already taken had brought it under control. The Iraqi invasion of Kuwait and the resulting effects on the oil market were completely unexpected, and gave rise to further uncertainty. If the government had managed to get its policies right in the summer of 1990, they would have been pushed off course by the rise in oil prices. In addition to not knowing exactly what is happening in the economy there is the further problem that economists are not sure about the correct models for either wages or consumption, or of the precise channels through which interest rates affect the economy. Judgements have to be based on relatively new models, because the old ones are clearly inadequate, even though the new models have not been thorougly tested. Forecasting models are useful aids to policy-making, but they cannot replace more rough-and-ready methods altogether.

FURTHER READING

The early years of Mrs. Thatcher's government are discussed in detail in: W. Buiter and M. Miller 'The Thatcher experiment: the first two years', *Brookings Papers on Economic Activity*, 1981 (2), pp. 315-79; W. Buiter and M. Miller 'Changing the rules: economic consequences of the Thatcher regime', *Brookings Papers on Economic Activity* 1983 (2), pp. 305-65; A. K. Chrystal 'Dutch disease or monetarist medicine? The British economy under Mrs. Thatcher', *Federal Reserve Bank of St Louis Review*, May 1984, pp. 27-37; N. Healey 'The UK 1979-82 "monetarist experiment": why economists still disagree', *Banca Nazionale del Lavoro Quarterly Review*, December 1987. The first of the articles by Buiter and Miller provides detailed evidence for the claim that monetary policy was exceptionally tight in 1979-80, despite the rapid rise in M3. A good, more extended discussion of the first seven years is contained in Geoffrey Maynard *The Economy under Mrs. Thatcher* (Oxford and New York: Basil Blackwell, 1988). Other commentaries on her first two terms include: T. Burns 'The UK government's financial strategy', in W. A. Eltis and P. Sinclair (eds.) *Keynes and Economic Policy: The Relevance of the General Theory after Fifty Years* (London: Macmillan, 1988); K. Matthews and P. Minford 'Mrs. Thatcher's economic policies, 1979-87', *Economic Policy* 5, 1987, pp. 57-102. For an evaluation of policy by one of Mrs. Thatcher's economic advisers, read A. Walters *Britain's Economic Renaissance* (Oxford: Oxford University Press, 1986).

The tenth anniversary of Mrs. Thatcher's premiership was accompanied by a host of appraisals of her policies: C. Bean and J. Symons 'Ten years of Mrs. T.', *NBER Macroeconomics Annual*, 1989, pp. 13-61 (see also the comments by William D. Nordhaus and Walter Eltis, pp. 61-71); R. Layard and S. Nickell 'The Thatcher miracle?' *American Economic Review* 79 (2), Papers and Proceedings, 1989, pp. 215-20; R. Layard and S. Nickell 'The Thatcher miracle', LSE Centre for Labour Economics Discussion Paper No. 343, March 1989. See also chapter 6 for references concerning whether or not productivity growth has been higher under Mrs. Thatcher than before. Some provocative if controversial assessments of the state of the economy are provided in T. Congdon *et al. The State of the Economy: an Assessment of Britain's Economy by Leading Economists at the Start of the 1990s* (London: Institute of Economic Affairs, 1990).

For detailed discussion of macroeconomic policies as they looked at the time, see OECD *Economic Surveys: United Kingdom* (Paris: OECD, annual). The issue of appropriate exchange rate policies is covered in the reading list at the end of chapter 11.

Appendix: regression equations

Statistical details of equations used in the text are provided here. Please note that these are not provided to show that these equations provide a good statistical description of the data. Most of them fail to meet conventional criteria for goodness of fit. The criteria for choosing these equations included the following: that they are appropriately simple; that they use familiar and accessible data; and that they approximate (in a simplified form, and subject to the other criteria) published results. For example, the consumption and trade equations, though they fail many standard tests, have coefficients broadly similar to certain, more 'respectable' published equations. Their purpose is to help students who would otherwise ignore such work, to read and understand what is going on in more complicated studies. Except for chapter 6, discussed below, data sources are as described in the chapters concerned. SP denotes sample period, DW the Durbin Watson statistic and parentheses t ratios.

Page 26

$$C = 3.65 + 0.89Y$$
$$(1.16) \quad (53.6)$$

$R^2 = 0.988 \quad DW = 0.23$
$F = 2874.2 \quad SP = 1953\text{-}89$

Page 27

$$c = 0.19 + 0.95y$$
$$(2.46) \quad (64.1)$$

$R^2 = 0.991 \quad DW = 0.26$
$F = 411.2 \quad SP = 1953\text{-}89$

Page 28

$$c_t = 0.27 + 0.94y^p_t$$
$$(2.60) \quad (46.2)$$

$R^2 = 0.983 \quad DW = 0.36$
$F = 2138.8 \quad SP = 1953\text{-}89$

Page 29

$$c_t = 0.26y_t + 0.73c_{t-1} + 0.05$$
$$(1.76) \quad (4.63) \quad (0.78)$$

$R^2 = 0.995 \quad DW = 0.81$
$F = 3266.8 \quad SP = 1953\text{-}89$

Page 31

$$c_t = 1.006c_{t-1} + \varepsilon_t$$
$$(1525.1)$$

$R^2 = 0.994 \quad DW = 1.21$
$SP = 1953\text{-}89$

Page 33

$$\Delta c_t = -0.001 + 0.63\Delta y_t + 0.19s_{t-1} - 0.13\pi$$
$$(0.15) \quad (8.61) \quad (1.81) \quad (2.72)$$

$R^2 = 0.838 \quad DW = 1.59$
$F = 36.2 \quad SP = 1956\text{-}80$

Page 35

$$\Delta c_t = -0.009 + 0.73\Delta y_t + 0.19s_{t-1} - 0.09\pi + 0.018RHP - 0.51\sigma.$$
$$(1.10) \quad (6.20) \quad (2.14) \quad (1.29) \quad (2.14) \quad (1.74)$$

$R^2 = 0.833 \quad DW = 1.66$
$F = 28.1 \quad SP = 1956\text{-}89$

Page 48

$$\Delta GK_t = 0.30Y_{t-1} - 0.076GK_{t-1}$$
$$(21.5) \quad (17.0)$$

$R^2 = 0.906 \quad DW = 0.88$
$SP = 1961\text{-}88$

Page 48

$$\Delta S_t = 0.22Y_t - 0.36S_{t-1}$$
$$(5.48) \quad (5.61)$$

$R^2 = 0.536 \quad DW = 1.19$
$SP = 1961\text{-}88$

Page 50

$\Delta GK_t = 0.31 Y_{t-1} - 0.082 GK_{t-1}$.

    (8.33)   (6.14)

    $R^2 = 0.395$ DW $=0.76$

    SP $= 1961$-79

Page 89

$X = 0.052 X^w_{t-1} - 0.285 RULC_{t-1} + 40.2$

    (48.6)   (6.39)   (11.7)

    $R^2 = 0.993$ DW $=2.47$

    SP $= 1964$-88

Page 90

$M = 0.338 TFE_{t-1} + 0.392 RULC_{t-2} - 0.549 XSC_t - 78.7$

    (28.0)   (4.86)   (4.37)   (11.1)

    $R^2 = 0.982$ DW $=1.33$

    SP $= 1964$-88

Page 91

$M_t = 0.246 TFE_{t-1} + 0.00103 (TFE_{t-1} . RULC_{t-2}) - 0.568 XSC_t - 43.9$

    (11.8)   (5.59)   (4.90)   (11.5)

    $R^2 = 0.985$ DW $=1.51$

    SP $= 1964$-88

Chapter 6

The variables used are defined as follows: $t_0 = 0$ in 1960, rising by 1 each year thereafter; $t_1 = 0$ till 1973, rising by 1 each year thereafter; $t_0 = 0$ till 1979, rising by 1 each year thereafter; $t_0 = 0$ till 1980, rising by 1 each year thereafter. TFP $= \log(Y/L) - (1/3)\log(K/L)$. The sample period is 1961-89. Y/L are the index numbers (1980 = 100) of output per person employed. K/L is constructed as an index (1985 = 100) from gross capital stock and indices of the employed labour force.

Figure 6.1 — Whole economy

$\log(Y/L) = 4.02 + 0.0287t - 0.0162t_1 + 0.0098t_2$ $R^2 = 0.995$ DW $=1.65$

    (513.2) (31.2) (7.0) (3.8)

$\log TFP = 2.78 + 0.0163t - 0.0500t_1 + 1.0146t_2$ $R^2 = 0.981$ DW $=1.49$

    (330.1) (16.5) (6.0) (5.36)

Figure 6.1 — Manufacturing

$\log(Y/L) = 3.82 + 0.0376t - 0.0326t_1 + 0.0388t_2$ $R^2 = 0.990$ DW $=1.28$

    (255.0) (21.4) (7.36) (8.00)

$\log TFP = 2.67 + 0.0239t - 0.0356t_1 + 0.0429t_2$ $R^2 = 0.950$ DW $=0.99$

    (140.8) (10.7) (6.35) (7.00)

Figure 6.3 and Table 6.2

$\log(Y/L) = 3.83 + 0.0366t - 0.0234t_1 + 0.0508t_2 + 0.879t_3$ $R^2 = 0.995$ DW $=1.74$

    (351.4) (28.5) (6.3) (2.7) (4.9)

$\log TFP = 2.67 + 0.0225t - 0.0223t_1 - 0.0865t_2 + 0.126t_3$ $R^2 = 0.982$ DW $=1.85$

    (229.4) (16.3) (5.6) (4.36) (6.5)

Figure 6.4 (estimate c)

$TFP = 0.8492 + 0.0161t - 0.0143t_1 + 0.0132t_2$ $R^2 = 0.980$ DW $=1.57$

where TFP $= \log(Y) - (1/3)\log(K) - (2/3)\log(L)$, with Y being real GDP at factor cost (£billion); K being the gross capital stock (£billion) and L the employed labour force (million).

Index

Abbey National, 204, 207
Accelerator, 46-8
Alogosgoufis, G., 181
Alsopp, C., 93
van Ark, B., 119-20
Artis, M. J., 258
Baily, M. N., 119
Balance of payments, 13-15, 79-81, 92, 174, 224, 226, 247, 248, 280, 281, 300, 79-81; see also Oil
Bank of England, 211, 213, 216-17, 222, 224, 230, 283, 288; see also Forecasting models
Batstone, E., 120
Bean, C., 120, 181, 200, 303
Begg, D., 78
Berndt, E. R., 111, 116, 119
Blackaby, F. T., 20
Blanchard, O. J., 181
Boltho, A., 93
Bover, O., 180
Britton, A., 93
Brooks, S., 93
Brown, W., 120
Bruno, M., 137
Budd, A., 182
Budget, 1981, 284-7
Building Societies Act, 205
Buiter, W., 78, 93, 284, 303
Burda, M., 181
Burgess, S., 148, 153, 182
Burns, T., 303
Burtless, G., 181
Calmfors, L., 120, 181
Canada, 278
Capacity utilization, 90-1, 106, 115-16; see also Full-capacity output
Capital stock adjustment mechanism, 47
Capital stock, measurement of, 43-4, 53, 103
Capital-output ratio, 47, 49
Carlin, W., 181
Carroll, C., 40
Carruth, A. A., 158, 180
Caves, R. E., 20, 120
Chan-Lee, J. H., 52
Chrystal, A. K., 258, 303
Clements, M., 93

Coen, R. M., 138
Competition and Credit Control, 211, 222
Competitiveness, 83, 84-9, 243, 245-6, 247, 248, 250-1, 282, 300
Congdon, T., 303
Consumption, 25-36, 288-91, 301
Corset, 222
Cost of capital, 54
Counterparts to change in M4, 225-9
Crafts, N., 20
Cripps, F., 93
Cross, R., 181
Currie, D., 258
Daly, A., 120
Davidson, J., 40
Davis, E. P., 40
Dean, A., 40
Deindustrialization, see Oil
Denison, E. F., 119
Depreciation, 42-3, 53
Divergence indicators, 253-4, 255, 256
Dornbusch, R., 20, 78, 180, 200, 230, 258
Dow, J. C. R., 20, 230
Dowd, K., 258
Drèze, J., 181
Driffil, J., 181
Dutch disease, 195-9; see also Oil , North Sea
Eltis, W. A., 303
Employment, see Unemployment
Energy prices, 104
Energy prices, and productivity growth, 112-3
Englander, S., 119
Environment, 113-14
Ermisch, J., 60, 180
Error correction mechanisms, see Consumption
ECU, 253-4
EMCF, 256
EMS, 241, 252-8, 287, 288, 298, 300
Exchange controls, 248, 252

Exchange rate, 83, 86, 92, 104, 241, 246-53, 268, 282, 283, 287-9, 296
1967 devaluation, 15, 88, 248
1976 crisis, 18, 248
overshooting of, 250-1, 268
real, 243-4, 245-6, 267; see also Competitiveness
spot and forward, 238-9
ERM, see EMS
Expectations, 30-2, 47, 59-60, 164, 166-7, 168, 174, 211, 223-4, 250-1, 264, 265, 300,
Expenditure lag, 199
Exports, 82-4, 89-90, 192-4, 248
Fallon, P., 180
Family Expenditure Survey, 156
Feinstein, C., 20, 119
Financial markets, liberalization of, 215
Fiscal policy, stance of, 74, 78; see also Government deficit; Government spending
Fischer, S., 230
Fisher, P. G., 303
Flows of funds and money supply, 223-9
Forecasting models, 261-73
Bank of England, 261
HMT, 261, 265, 265-7, 269-70, 271, 292-4
LBS, 261, 264, 265, 265-7, 268-71, 270-1, 273, 292-4
Liverpool, 261, 264, 265
NIESR, 261, 264, 265, 265-7, 270-1, 272, 273, 292-4
and 1990s, 291-4
and oil price, 295-8
usefulness of, 272-3, 302
Forsyth, P. J., 192, 200
Forward premium, 237-41
France, 111, 130, 242, 245, 278, 279
Freeman, R. B., 181
Full-capacity output, 6-7, 107-11, 125, 135-6

Garcia, J., 182
Gavosto, A., 181
General Household Survey, 156
Germany, 111, 130, 242, 245, 278, 279
Giavazzi, F., 258
Giersch, H., 119
Giovannini, A., 258
Godley, W., 93
Gordon, R. A., 181
Government debt, 72-7
Government deficit, 65-6, 223-5, 227-9, 284-7
cyclical adjustment of, 67-8, 70-1
financing of, 223-5, 227-9
and fiscal stance, 66-7
inflation adjustment, 67-72
Government spending, 61-4; see also Multiplier
Governments, list of, 12
Hall, S., 200
Healey, N., 303
Hendry, D. F., 39, 40
Henry, S. G. B., 200
Hickman, B. G., 138
High-powered money, 211-13, 222
Hitchens, D., 120
House prices, 58-9, 162-3, 171, 302
and consumption, 290-1
and unemployment, 160-2
and wages, 171, 172, 173
Hysteresis, 172
Import prices, 159, 170
Imports, 82-4, 90-1, 192-4, 262
Income expenditure model, 262
Income tax, 281
Incomes policy, 15, 16, 18, 88, 132, 164-5, 170, 178, 248, 281
Inflation, 7-8, 10-11, 62-3, 229-30, 234-6, 252, 279-80, 281, 300-1; see also Government deficit
Interest payments, 72, 74
Interest rate, 231, 234-6, 268-70,
control, see Money supply
real, 71-2, 234-6
term structure of, 231-4

see also Interest rate parity; Money supply, theory of
Interest rate parity, 237-41, 268
Investment, 41-60, 62-3, 184-7, 188, 289-90; see also Stockbuilding
Italy, 242, 278
Jackman, R., 144, 145, 180, 182
Japan, 111, 278, 231-4
Job search, 150-1, 156-7
Johnson, C., 20, 40, 230
Kay, J. A., 192, 200
Keating, G., 303
Knight, K. G., 182
Krause, L. B., 120
Kuwait, Iraqi invasion of, 294, 302
Labour, demand for, 127-9, 173-4
Labour, shortages of, 146
Laidler, D., 230
Lawrence, R. Z., 181
Lawson, Nigel, 287, 288
Layard, R., 20, 78, 120, 146, 170, 172, 178, 179, 180, 181, 200, 258, 303
Levine, P., 182
Lindbeck, A., 119
Liquidity, 203-4
Long-term unemployment, see Unemployment, duration of
M0, see High-powered money
MacDonald, G. A., 265, 274
Malinvaud, E., 138
Manning, A., 181
Manufacturing, 97-9, 102, 106-7, 111, 132, 144, 189-94, 269, 275-6, 296
Marris, R., 181
Martin, J. P., 120
Matthews, K., 303
Matthews, R. C. O., 20, 119
Mayer, C., 60
Maynard, G., 303
Meen, G., 20, 111
Metcalfe, D., 181
Miller, M., 78, 258, 284, 303
Minford, P., 303
Mismatch, 143-7, 170-2, 178
Mittelstadt, A., 119
Modigliani, F., 120

Monetary base, see High-powered money
Monetary base control, see Money supply
Money, demand for, 211
Money multiplier, 212-15, 222, 229
Money supply, 78, 203-9, 213-15, 283, 284-7
control of, 216-17, 222-3
and inflation, 229-30
theory of, 204-7, 212, 218-21, 224-6
Morris, D., 119, 303
MTFS, 19, 252, 284-7
Muellbauer, J., 39, 40, 119, 180
Mueller, P., 78
Multiplier, 265-8
Murphy, A., 40, 180
NAIRU, 163-5, 167-8, 170, 173-80
Narendranathan, W., 157, 182
National debt, see Government debt
National Plan, 15
Newell, A., 181
Nickell, S., 146, 157, 158, 170, 172, 178, 179, 180, 181, 182, 303
NIESR, see Forecasting models
Nordhaus, W. D., 303
Odell, P., 200
Oil, North Sea, 83, 174, 178, 183-200, 252, 264, 270-1, 283
Oil price, 183-5, 248
1973-4 rise, 16, 112-13, 131, 140, 248
1979 rise, 132, 281
1986 fall, 288
1990 rise, 294, 300-1
effects of, 83, 186-9, 294-8
and terms of trade, 82
Oswald, A. J., 158, 180
Oulton, N., 120
Output gap, see Full-capacity output
Parity grid, 255-6
Peel, D. A., 303
Permanent income, see Consumption
Phillips curve, 163-7
Pissarides, C., 152, 182

Policy, politics and, 13-19
Portfolio balance theory, 218-21
Prais, S. J., 119, 120
Price, R., 78
Price setting, 174, 175-7
Privatization, 65, 66, 67
Product wage, see Wage, real
Productivity,
  cyclical behaviour of, 97-8
  growth of, 97-117, 130-2, 276, 277, 278
  measurement errors, 103-5
  slowdown of 1970s, 111-15
  total factor, 99-107, 113
Profitability, and competitiveness, 86
Profits, 162-3, 172-3, 187-8; see also Investment
PSBR, see Government deficit
PSDR, see Government deficit
PSFD, see Government deficit
PSL2, see Money supply
Purchasing power parity (PPP), 244-6
q, 51-3, 57
Rational expectations, see Expectations
Recession,
  1974-5, 3, 6, 45-6, 97-8, 99
  1980-1, 3, 6, 45, 50-1, 97-8, 99, 114, 115, 160, 210, 283
  1990-1, 291, 302
Replacement ratio, 154-5, 157, 158, 170, 171, 178
Reserve ratio, in theory, see Money supply, theory of
Resource movement effect, 195-6, 198
Return on capital, 54-5
RNDI, 83
Roper, S., 144, 145, 182
Rossi, V., 93
Roubini, N., 78
Sachs, J. D., 78, 130, 137, 138
Sargent, J. R., 20
Saville, I. D., 230
Saving,

by companies, 56, 301
by personal sector, 24-5, 27, 34, 36-9,
Savouri, S., 182
Schultze, C. L., 181
Scrapping, 42-3, 53, 104-5, 115-16
Share prices, 54-5
Sinclair, P. J. N., 303
Siven, C.-H., 138
Smith, A., 93
Smith, P., 182
Social contract, see Incomes policy
Soskice, D., 181
Spending effect, 195, 197-8
Srba, F., 40
Steedman, H., 120
Stern, J., 157, 182
Stock market crash, 1987, 288
Stock ratios, 46
Stockbuilding, 45-6, 49-50, 282, 283, 301
Stop-go, 13-14
Summers, L., 40
Summers, L. H., 181
Supplementary special deposits, 222
Surrey, M. J. C., 20, 303
Symons, J., 181, 303
Target real wage, 171
Taxation, and unemployment, 159
Terms of trade, 82, 83
Thatcher, Margaret 106, 288, 303
Thompson, J. L., 303
Torres, R., 120
Trade, and growth, 91-2
Trade balance, see Balance of payments
Tradeable goods, and oil, 195-8
Turner, D. S., 265, 274, 303
U-V curve, 141-2
Unemployment, 5-6, 140-1, 275, 279
  benefits, 114, 154-9, 178; see also Replacement ratio
  classical, 121, 122, 137, 124-6, 127-9, 132-3
  duration of, 148-9, 155-7, 163, 172, 173
  flows, 147-54

and inflation, 139-80
  Keynesian, 121, 124-6, 127-9, 137
  microeconomic evidence, 155-8
  regional, 143-4
  theory of, 127-9
  and vacancies, 140-7
Union power, 159-60, 170, 171, 178
Unit labour costs, 87
USA, 111, 130, 131, 132, 231, 237, 240-1, 242, 244, 278, 279
User cost of housing, 171
Vacancies, 279; see also Unemployment
Valuation ratio, see q
VAT, 281
Velocity, 209-11
Venables, A., 93
Verry, D., 180
Vinals, J., 78
Wadwhani, S., 119, 120
Wage equations, 170-3
Wage gap, 121, 124-6, 129, 131, 132, 137, 139
Wage setting, 175-7
Wage share, 125, 132-3
Wages, real, 122-3, 130, 131, 139, 199
  oil discovery and, 195-6, 198-9
  and Phillips curve, 168-9
  and productivity, 130-2
Wagner, K., 120
Wall, M., 119
Wallis, K. F., 60, 200, 303
Walters, A., 303
Whitley, J. D., 303
Wolter, F., 119
Wood, D. O., 111, 116, 119
Yeo, S., 40
Yield curve, 232-3
Zis, G., 258